Critical Health Psychology

Also by Michael Murray

Health Psychology: Theory, Research and Practice (co-authored with D. Marks, B. Evans and C. Willig)

Qualitative Health Psychology: Theories and Methods (co-edited with K. Chamberlain)

Critical Health Psychology

Edited by
Michael Murray

First published 2004 by
PALGRAVE MACMILLAN
Houndmills, Basingstoke, Hampshire RG21 6XS and
175 Fifth Avenue, New York, N.Y. 10010
Companies and representatives throughout the world

PALGRAVE MACMILLAN is the global academic imprint of the Palgrave
Macmillan division of St. Martin's Press, LLC and of Palgrave Macmillan Ltd.
Macmillan® is a registered trademark in the United States, United Kingdom
and other countries. Palgrave is a registered trademark in the European
Union and other countries.

ISBN 0–333–99033–1 hardback
ISBN 0–333–99034–X paperback

This book is printed on paper suitable for recycling and made from fully
managed and sustained forest sources.

A catalogue record for this book is available from the British Library.

A catalog record for this book is available from the Library of Congress.

10   9   8   7   6   5   4   3   2   1
13   12   11   10   09   08   07   06   05   04

Printed and bound in Great Britain by
Creative Print & Design (Wales), Ebbw Vale

Contents

List of Illustrations

Acknowledgements

This book has been a long time in the making. I would like to thank all of the contributors for persevering with the many delays. It has finally seen the light of day.

I would also like to thank my secretaries Christa McGrath and Jacquie Hansford for putting up with my many requests for assistance. In addition, I would like to thank the various editorial staff at Palgrave, including Andrew McAleer, Frances Arnold, Philippa Thomas, Magenta Lampson as well as Sowmya Balaraman of Integra for their continuing support and guidance with this project.

Finally, I would like to thank my wife Anne and my sons Matthew and Daniel for keeping me critical.

Notes on the Contributors

Mary Brydon-Miller is Associate Professor of Educational Foundations and Urban Educational Leadership in the College of Education, Criminal Justice, and Human Services at the University of Cincinnati. She has edited *From Subjects to Subjectivities: A Handbook of Interpretive and Participatory Methods* (New York University Press 2001, with D. Tolman), *Voices of Change: Participatory Research in the United States and Canada* (Bergin and Garvey 1993, with P. Park, B. Hall and T. Jackson), and most recently *Traveling Companions: Feminism, Teaching, and Action Research* (Greenwood Publishing 2004, with P. Maguire and A. McIntyre). She is also a member of the editorial boards of *Action Research* and *ASAP*.

Catherine Campbell is Reader in Social Psychology at the London School of Economics, and Adjunct Professor and Fellow of the Centre for HIV/AIDS Networking (HIVAN) at the University of Natal, Durban, South Africa. She works on the social psychology of health and community development for health, an interest she is currently pursuing in research into HIV-prevention and AIDS-care in southern Africa. She is the author of *Social Capital and Health* (Health Education Authority 1999) and *Letting Them Die: Why HIV Prevention Programmes Fail* (James Currey Publishers and Indiana University Press 2003). She is also co-editor of *Learning from HIV and AIDS* (Cambridge University Press 2003, with G. Ellison and M. Parker).

Kerry Chamberlain is Reader in Health Psychology at Massey University at Albany, Auckland, New Zealand. His research interests are centred in health psychology, and focus primarily on chronic illness and social disadvantage. He also has interests in research methodology and specifically in varieties of qualitative research. He has edited *Qualitative Health Psychology: Theories and Methods* (Sage 1999, with M. Murray) and *Existential Meaning: Optimizing Human Development across the Life Span* (Sage 1999, with G. Reker).

Robert Kugelmann is Professor of Psychology at the University of Dallas, Texas, USA. His particular research interest is in the discursive and cultural construction of health, illness and pain. He is also at work applying hermeneutical principles to study the effects of pain and suffering in social situations.

He is the author of *Stress: The Nature and History of Engineered Grief* (Praeger 1992) and *The Windows of Soul: Psychological Physiology of the Human Eye and Primary Glaucoma* (Bucknell University Press 1983).

Uwe Flick is Professor of Methods of Empirical Nursing Research at Alice Salomon University of Applied Sciences in Berlin and is Privatdozent in Psychology at the University of Technology in Berlin, Germany. He is also Adjunct Professor at Memorial University of Newfoundland, St John's, Canada and Visiting Professor at the Pontifica Universidad Católica de Chile in Santiago de Chile. His main research interests are qualitative methods, social representations in the fields of individual and public health, and technological change in everyday life. He is the author of *An Introduction to Qualitative Research* (Sage 1998, revised edition 2002), editor of *Psychology of the Social* (Cambridge University Press 1998) and *Innovation durch (through) New Public Health* (Hogrefe 2002), and co-editor of *Qualitative Forschung: Ein Handbuch* (Rowohlt 2002) and the English language edition entitled *Qualitative Research: A Handbook* (Sage 2003).

Malcolm MacLachlan is Professor of Psychology at Trinity College, Dublin, Ireland. His research is concerned with elucidating how individuals (patients and clinicians), health service organisations, local communities and societies are influenced by, and represent, cultural constructions of illness and health. He has authored or edited a number of books including *Culture and Health: Psychological Perspectives on Problems and Practice* (John Wiley & Sons 2003), *Image and Body Function* (Churchill Livingstone 2003, with P. Gallagher), *Cultivating Health: Cultural Perspectives on Promoting Health* (John Wiley & Sons 2000) and *Cultivating Pluralism: Cultural, Psychological and Social Perspectives on a Changing Ireland* (Oak Tree Press 2000, with M. O'Connell).

David F. Marks is Professor and Chair of the Department of Psychology at City University, London, UK. Previously he held positions at the University of Sheffield and Middlesex University, UK and at the University of Otago, New Zealand. He has authored or edited several books including *Theories of Image Formation* (Brandon House 1986), *The Quit for Life Programme: An Easier Way to Stop Smoking and not Start Again* (BPS Blackwell 1993), *Improving the Health of the Nation* (Middlesex University Press 1996, with C. Francome), *Dealing with Dementia: Recent European Research* (2000, with C.M. Sykes), *The Psychology of the Psychic* (Prometheus Books 2000), *Health Psychology: Theory, Research and Practice* (Sage 1999, with M. Murray, B. Evans and C. Willig), *The Health Psychology Reader* (2002) and *Research Methods for Clinical and Health Psychology* (Sage 2004, with L. Yardley). He was Chair of the Special Group in Health Psychology of the British Psychological Society and Convenor of the Task Force on Health Psychology of the European Federation of Professional Psychologists' Associations. He is editor of the *Journal of Health Psychology*.

Michael Murray is Associate Dean of Community Health and Professor of Social and Health Psychology at Memorial University of Newfoundland, St John's, Newfoundland, Canada. His research interests are narrative and social representation theory, qualitative research, community health action, literacy and occupational health. He is the author of *Health Psychology: Theory, Research and Practice* (Sage 1999, with D. Marks, B. Evans and C. Willig), and editor of *Qualitative Health Psychology: Theories and Methods* (Sage 1999, with K. Chamberlain). He is an associate editor of the *Journal of Health Psychology* and is currently Chair of the *International Society of Critical Health Psychology*.

Alan Radley is Professor of Social Psychology in the Department of Social Sciences at Loughborough University, UK. His research interests include the social context of health and illness and the field of charitable giving. His book publications include *Prospects of Heart Surgery: Psychological Adjustment to Coronary Bypass Grafting* (Springer 1988), *The Body and Social Psychology* (Springer 1991) and *Making Sense of Illness: The Social Psychology of Health and Disease* (Sage 1994). He also edited *Worlds of Illness: Biographical and Cultural Perspectives on Health and Disease* (Routledge 1993). He is editor of *Health: An Interdisciplinary Journal for the Social Study of Health, Illness and Medicine*.

Henderikus Stam is Professor in the Theory program, Department of Psychology at the University of Calgary, Alberta, Canada. His primary research interests concern the theoretical and historical foundations of psychology, especially early 20th-century psychology and 19th-century psychiatry. He is founding and current editor of the journal *Theory & Psychology* and has edited several book collections including *Recent Trends in Theoretical Psychology* (Springer Verlag 1993, with L. Mos, W. Thorngate and B. Kaplan), *Power/Gender: Social Relations in Theory and Practice* (Sage 1994, with H.L. Radtke), *The Body and Psychology* (Sage 1998) and *Theoretical Psychology: Critical Contributions* (Captus 2003, with N. Stephenson, H.L. Radtke and R. Jorna).

Sue Wilkinson is currently Ruth Wynn Woodward Endowed Professor in the Department of Women's Studies, Simon Fraser University, Vancouver, Canada. Her research interests are in feminist and critical approaches to health and illness, with a focus on breast cancer, lesbian health, sexual identity construction, and the analysis of health talk. She has published seven books, including *Women and Health* (Taylor and Francis 1994), *Feminism and Discourse* (Sage 1995), *Representing the Other* (Sage 1996) (all with C. Kitzinger) and *Feminist Social Psychologies: International Perspectives* (Open University Press 1996). She is the founding and current editor of the journal *Feminism & Psychology*.

Carla Willig is Senior Lecturer in Psychology at City University, London, UK. Previously she held positions at Plymouth and Middlesex Universities. Her research is primarily concerned with the relationship between discourse and practice, particularly in relation to risk taking. She has published journal articles and book chapters on the discursive construction of trust and sexual safety, and has contributed to theoretical and epistemological debates concerning social constructionist psychology. She has authored *Introducing Qualitative Research in Psychology: Adventures in Theory and Method* (Open University Press 2001) and edited *Applied Discourse Analysis: Social and Psychological Interventions* (Open University Press 1999). She is also an associate editor of the *Journal of Health Psychology.*

Introduction: Criticizing Health Psychology

Michael Murray

Introduction

The modern world is currently torn by many contradictions. On the one hand there is the land of excessive consumption where obesity is now considered to be the major health problem of the Western world whereas on the other hand thousands die of hunger and disease. On the one hand science holds out the promise of conquering disease and extending life through genetic engineering and on the other hand millions do not have any access to basic health care. On the one hand pharmaceutical companies promise relief from pain and suffering while on the other hand patients argue that health professionals do not understand their agony. What does health psychology have to say about these issues? It is the contention of this book that if health psychology is to begin to answer these challenges, it needs to step outside the traditional limits of the discipline and begin to engage with broader social theories and to reflect on the adequacy of traditional ways of conducting research and developing interventions. In this introductory chapter, I review the development of the sub-discipline and then consider in some more detail the structure and content of the book.

Disciplining Health Psychology

The advent of health psychology, less than 30 years ago, offered much promise. It was heralded as an opportunity for psychology to expand our understanding of the experience of health and illness and to contribute to the great task of improving the health of society. In the eager rush to establish its credentials this new sub-discipline largely adopted the theories, methods and disciplining techniques of its parent discipline. Now that we have reached this early stage of our growth, it is time to pause and to reflect on some of the broader questions.

Since its establishment, health psychology has grown rapidly forming its own national and international organizations, establishing journals, and designing its own training programs. In the United States, the Division of Health Psychology is one of the largest in the American Psychological Association (APA). Indeed, in terms of resources it has reserves of several hundred thousand dollars. Its journal called *Health Psychology* now has one of the largest number of subscribers of the dozens of journals published by the APA. In the United Kingdom, the Division of Health Psychology has also grown dramatically and is now one of the largest in the British Psychological Society. It too has its own journal called the *British Journal of Health Psychology*. In other European countries, health psychology societies have been established. The European Health Psychology Society attracts hundreds to its annual conferences and publishes the very successful journal entitled *Psychology & Health*. In addition, several independent journals have been established including the *Journal of Health Psychology*, and *Psychology, Health and Medicine*.

In North America, Europe and elsewhere hundreds of students receive advanced training every year in health psychology. Both the American Psychological Association and the British Psychological Society now lay down guidelines for trainees in health psychology. There are accreditation committees to ensure that trainees receive what is considered as appropriate training.

The sub-discipline has gained the recognition of many other health professions and government bodies who now call upon representatives to advise them in the development of particular programs. It has gained access to research funding and has now begun to establish the trappings of a profession. Yet despite these apparent successes there is less enthusiasm to reflect on the assumptions underlying the sub-discipline and its role in the broader society.

The rise of health psychology in the West in the late 1970s and early 1980s was prefaced on the one hand by the growing challenge to the basic biomedical model of health and illness and on the other hand by economic crisis facing the political system (see Chapter 1 for more detailed discussion). The introduction of the so-called biopsychosocial model of health and illness provided an opportunity for psychologists to venture into a domain that had previously been controlled by medicine (Engel 1977). The scientific approach of medicine was now going to be tamed by the more humanistic approach of psychology.

The economic crisis led to the introduction of government policies designed to reduce public expenditure on health and social services. The growth of these policies was coupled by the enthusiastic promotion of an individualistic ideology that urged self-responsibility. The influence of this ideology on health care was evidenced by the publication of documents encouraging people to take responsibility for their own health and the rise of a 'healthist' culture (Crawford 1980). Psychology was quickly co-opted into this endeavor to encourage people to look after themselves. As Matarazzo (1982: 12) concluded when issuing a call for the establishment of the new sub-discipline: 'we must aggressively investigate and deal effectively with the role of the individual's behaviour and lifestyle in health and dysfunction. Furthermore, representatives from many segments of our society are increasingly looking to the science and profession of psychology for help with this problem.'

Naturally since they had access to such valued knowledge it was not surprising that some psychologists took steps to regulate access to it. The professionalization of the sub-discipline was introduced with the idea of maintaining standards and protecting the public but it also held out the prospect of more closely policing the discipline. Nikolas Rose (1996) in his history of psychology has detailed how certain theories and methods have gained ascendancy. He claimed: 'truth ... is always enthroned by acts of violence. It entails a social process of exclusion in which arguments, evidence, theories, and beliefs are thrust to the margins, not allowed to enter "the true"' (p. 55). While this description may seem very dramatic, in practice it entails ensuring that critical ideas are excluded from debate. Indeed, a review of the main health psychology journals would confirm that a certain agreed approach to the subject has been established. This is one that limits itself to a limited range of psychological theories and methods, and which disdains any engagement with broader social critique.

Conflict and Change

However, the past ten years has seen the growth of various critical approaches within psychology as a whole (e.g. Fox and Prilleltensky 1997). This growth reflects an increasing disillusion with the whole enlightenment project of the discipline, an engagement with the critical debates within the broader social sciences, and a growing demand from the public that its voice be heard.

Health psychology could not hold itself immune from this re-evaluation of the dominant psychological theories and methods, and over the past five years there has been growing critical debate within the sub-discipline. Initially this debate focused on issues of methodology but then rapidly spread to consider issues of epistemology and underlying values (e.g. Marks 1996; Stainton Rogers 1996; Yardley 1997; Murray and Chamberlain 1998a,b 1999a,b). The intention of this book is not to resolve this debate but rather to introduce some of the issues.

The book grew out of the discussion at the *First International Conference on Critical and Qualitative Approaches to Health Psychology* that was held in St John's, Newfoundland in 1999. Some of the key papers at that conference had been initially published (Murray 2000a), but it was felt that a more organized collection would help extend the debate. This book is a somewhat delayed result. Times have rapidly moved on since the original conference, and it is exciting to see the enthusiasm with which the debate has grown in that short period (e.g. Crossley 2000; Marks 2002a; Prilleltensky and Prilleltensky 2003). In standard textbooks and in readers, there are now specific attempts to consider some of the major critical issues. This collection should be seen as a supplement to that work.

Although the book is an edited collection, there is an overall structure and the chapters are organized in a similar format. The book is broken up into four broad sections – theory, context, research and practice – although each interpenetrates the others. This organization is used to provide some coherence to the book and also to encourage readers to see the interplay of theory, context, research and practice. Each chapter has a short introduction, followed

by a review of key theoretical issues, certain applied issues or examples, a conclusion, some key points, sample questions, and key readings. To set the scene
it is useful to provide an overview of each of the chapters and to consider their
interconnections with each other and with the broader field of social and
health research.

Theory and Health Psychology

The first section of this book is designed to encourage health psychology to
deliberately adopt a more self-critical stance to the generation of theoretical
frameworks. It begins with a chapter by Hank Stam in which he pursues his
earlier plea (Stam 2000) for more sustained attention to theory. He draws our
attention to the often ignored truism that health psychologists frequently work
within a health care system that is dominated by the ideas of biomedicine. This
in turn shapes the very meaning of health and illness, the patient and the
character of patient care. The clear separation of mind and body that is characteristic of medicine is reflected in the everyday practice of many health
psychologists.

Admittedly, health psychologists have proudly acclaimed the biopsychosocial
model as a more advanced and integrative approach. However, as Stam clearly
demonstrates, this model is really a variant of the traditional functionalist
approach that treats the patient in terms of inputs and outputs. Stam argues
that the biopsychosocial model is neither a theory nor a model in the classic
sense. Indeed, he claims that it is more a rhetorical than a theoretical contribution in that it presents a supposed integrative theory that places health
psychology at the center while not threatening biomedical dominance.

Stam extends this argument by claiming that health psychology has generally
neglected the need for more theorization replacing it with simplified statistical
models. There is a need for health psychology to adopt a more critical approach
to biomedicine. In particular, Stam calls on health psychologists to adopt
a more reflexive stance and to consider the broader forces that shape our ways
of defining concepts. Health and illness are not simply the property of individual
patients but are socially and politically located. Stam concludes by emphasizing
the role of health psychology in adopting a more reflexive stance. In addition,
we need to be aware of the moral dimension of our sub-discipline in that as we
attempt on the one hand to grasp the voice of the patient, on the other we
should be aware of the need to challenge those broader social and political
forces that create opportunities for ill-health.

This is followed by a chapter by Alan Radley in which he argues that health
psychology needs to develop a theory to understand the experience of suffering.
People who are ill suffer. Despite this, health psychologists have generally
ignored the whole meaning of suffering. The large research program on pain
is limited and has tended to reduce the experience of pain to scores on

psychometric scales. Radley begins to develop a social theory of suffering that positions the experience in the relationship with the Other.

Radley also considers the fact that suffering cannot always be spoken. Indeed, this mute dimension could be considered one of the central characteristic of suffering. He argues that knowing suffering requires more than a verbal summary of feelings, it requires a particular act of imagination. While the study of illness narratives may provide insight into the pain of illness, there is the need, as it were, to live with the patient to understand their pain. Radley also raises the challenge of the role of the health psychologist as a researcher and the extent to which she can speak for the sufferer. These issues are taken up again in Chapter 7 in the discussion about reflexivity in the research process.

Robert Kugelmann rounds up this first section by developing a hermeneutical phenomenological approach to the study of health and illness in Chapter 3. This chapter complements that of Radley by developing further a relational approach to the study of health and illness. He begins by establishing the basic tenets of the hermeneutical phenomenological approach that the self and the situation belong together. Health and illness are basic modes of our existence that engage both the self and the situation. They are different ways of being in the world. Conversely biomedicine considers health and illness as physiological qualities of the individual.

Borrowing from the ideas of Gadamer (1978), Kugelmann argues that health and illness can be considered as dramas that we enact in relation with others. They do not exist as qualities in themselves. Health is living well in the world. It is not a condition in itself. In illness our living in the world is disrupted and this leads to reflection back on ourselves. Whereas in health there is full engagement and a forgetfulness of self, in illness we begin to remember ourselves. Here he is taking up some ideas similar to those discussed in the classic work on social representations of health and illness by Herzlich (1973) (see Chapter 11).

Kugelmann then contrasts this perspective on health and illness with what he describes as standardized health and disease. This is the process by which biomedicine defines health as the property of autonomous individuals who are responsible for its maintenance. Health care is thus designed to assist in the management of health so as to ensure the effective functioning of the individual for the supposed national interest. Disease is some biomedical dysfunction that is defined by medicine. While health psychologists may criticize this viewpoint it has attained widespread currency in the western world. These medical definitions have become part of how the layperson defines and indeed experiences health and illness. It is not just the health psychologist but also the patient who is shaped by the language and technology of biomedicine.

Kugelmann ends by emphasizing that biomedical discourse in turn does not exist in itself but is intimately tied to economic power. Thus our discussion of health and illness moves from understanding the experience of the individual in the world, through connection with medical discourse and the health care arena through to connections with broader social and political issues.

Context of Health Psychology

Kugelmann's closing comments provide an entrée to the next part of the book. He refers to the overlapping definitions of the term 'critical'. On the one hand is the concern with meanings while on the other are the issues of power and exploitation. It is this latter dimension that is explored in the second group of chapters that considers how health and illness are enmeshed in relations of class, gender and ethnicity. In Chapter 4, David Marks clearly outlines the endemic social inequalities in health that exist both within advanced industrialized countries but even more dramatically between rich and poor countries. His chapter provides detailed evidence on the character of what he describes as a death gradient and how this is closely tied to the political and economic arrangements in our world.

This chapter is an enthusiastic extension of previous work (see Marks 1996, 2002a) and indicates the urgent need for health psychologists to get involved in the larger political domain if we are concerned with improving the health of the world's masses. In particular, he highlights the importance of support for debt cancellation in those impoverished countries where social and political development and consequent health improvements are prevented by their mammoth national debts. But he continues that in itself this debt cancellation is insufficient unless it is accompanied by efforts to reduce income inequalities within these societies. He also challenges the solutions offered by the World Bank that concentrates on social and behavioral changes in developing countries while neglecting the economic and political bases of such processes.

Marks concludes by advocating for an agenda of social change based upon the principles of social justice and activism. This will require health psychologists to work as part of multidisciplinary teams participating in both sustained community development and advocating for more extended social and political change. One cannot be separated from the other (see also Murray and Campbell 2003). Health psychology cannot remain aloof from politics and economics. It must participate in the broader campaign for human rights and freedoms if it is to challenge the basic roots of illness and disease throughout the world.

In Chapter 5, Sue Wilkinson considers the varied contribution of feminist theory to understanding health and illness. Health is bounded not only by economic arrangements but also by relations of gender. From the early days, feminists have been involved in direct challenge to the oppressive role of traditional medical science. This struggle with medicine is far from over. Modern medicine still subjects women to unnecessary surgery and other forms of medical intervention. In her chapter, Wilkinson indicates how women have historically challenged medical dominance using various strategies of resistance. Contemporary feminism can be considered a form of resistance to mainstream medicine and also to mainstream health psychology.

Wilkinson distinguishes between three traditions of feminist research, each of which, she argues, contributes to the challenge to the dominant medical approach. She begins by arguing that what she terms feminist positivist empiricist research can be integrated into a critical health psychology by critiquing various biases such as inappropriate sampling and generalization within much mainstream research and so contribute to 'better' forms of traditional research.

She also considers feminist experiential approaches. These use a variety of qualitative methods to explore the experience of health and illness. The emphasis in these approaches is to give legitimacy to the voices and experiences of women and oppressed groups that have often been ignored by medical science. The third approach considered by Wilkinson is feminist discursive research. This itself is a broad field ranging from conversation analysis to the more radical Foucauldian discourse analysis (see also Chapter 9). Each of these approaches, argues Wilkinson, can provide different ways of challenging women's oppression and enhancing health and well-being.

Malcolm MacLachlan in Chapter 6 considers the relationship between culture and health. In order to clear away the conventional approaches that have largely been concerned with contrasts between 'us' and 'them', and to develop a more critical approach he proposes a sevenfold typology. The first three approaches are the more traditional mainstream ones. These range from concern about how 'they' differ from 'us' to strategies for managing the health needs of 'them' now that they are among 'us'.

MacLachlan then proceeds to consider a more critical approach to considering the connection between culture, health and illness. This begins with the growing critique of biomedicine and the increasing acceptance of alternative frameworks for understanding health and illness and practicing health care. It proceeds by emphasizing the need for an awareness that many of the health problems afflicting indigenous communities are the result of cultural annihilation of those communities. Thus, attempts to alleviate these health problems will fail without attention to the ongoing challenge to their traditional cultural norms and values. Sixthly, MacLachlan returns to the issues of globalization that were considered by Marks in Chapter 4. He emphasizes that globalization is destroying indigenous cultures and developing systems of exploitation in the interests of western corporate culture.

Finally, he emphasizes that culture is not something that we can confine to the other, nor is it something that is fixed, but rather that all of us are in many ways transitional beings moving from one culture to another. The very pace of this transition may contribute to vulnerability, uncertainty and the emergence of new health problems. MacLachlan concludes by re-emphasizing that a critical health psychology must recognize the importance of culture in our very sense of being. It is culture that gives every community and society a sense of meaning and a sense of purpose.

Research Methods and Health Psychology

The third part of the book is broadly concerned with a third meaning of the term 'critical' – the underlying assumptions and implications of our research methods. Critical health psychologists have enthusiastically adopted qualitative research as a methodology that seemed to offer a clean break from the sterile assumptions of quantitative research while at the same time being rooted in everyday experiences. But what about the assumptions underlying qualitative research?

In Chapter 7, Kerry Chamberlain argues that all forms of research are based upon certain epistemological assumptions. There is a need to reflect upon these and on the role of the researcher and the purpose of the research. This raises many questions with which critical health psychologists are just beginning to grapple. Chamberlain considers the issue under three broad headings: being reflexive, being ethical and being critical. Being reflexive means that we are aware not only of our role in the research process but also of the product of the research. Thus we should be aware of the epistemological and methodological assumptions in the design of our research and also how the product of the research is shaped by such factors as the conventions of scientific writing and implicit or explicit connections with other research findings.

Being ethical means considering the role of the research participant in both the research process and the research product. The researcher needs to consider not only such formal issues as consent and voluntariness but also such more challenging issues as what message is being conveyed in the final report, and whose voice is represented – that of the participant or that of the researcher? This leads directly to the issue of being critical. Chamberlain argues that health psychologists need to consider the broader social and moral worth of our research. Research findings are not things in themselves but are social products that can have an impact on the world. It is our responsibility to consider the character of that impact.

In Chapter 8, Uwe Flick returns to the issue of the purpose of research in considering the connection between qualitative methods and social transformation. He tackles this topic by contrasting different meanings of the term 'transformation'. On the one hand it can be something that is occurring and which the researcher is exploring. Flick contends that qualitative methods, and in particular narrative research (see also Chapter 10), and ethnography are especially appropriate methods in this context. Both of these approaches can describe changes over time rather than the snapshots that are more typical of quantitative research. However, the study of illness narratives often focuses on the patient as some sort of individual hero. There is a need to consider the broader social context within which the narrative is constructed. On the other hand transformation can be something that is not occurring naturally but that occurs as a result of the research and may or may not be fostered by the researcher. Thus in telling one's illness story the participant becomes more aware of the impact the illness is having on his or her life and may lead to them attempting to implement certain changes. In addition, the researcher being aware of such an impact may use the research process as an opportunity to promote certain changes at the individual or at the social level. Flick contends that this desire to implement change itself raises many ethical and moral issues that the critical health psychologist must consider.

Within qualitative research there are a variety of different stances. Discourse analysis is one approach that has gained substantial sympathy among some psychologists as offering a way to critique and to challenge the very language that is involved in constructing our everyday social reality. In Chapter 9, Carla Willig argues very clearly that there are different forms of DA – discursive psychology (DP) and Foucauldian discourse analysis (FDA). The former can provide insight into how everyday language is shaped by the rules of social interaction. It is concerned with how individuals make use of certain discursive resources and what is the effect of particular discursive strategies. In the case of health research, discursive psychology is concerned with how the participant, who may or may not be ill, uses certain discourse resources to construct a particular version of reality.

Foucauldian discourse analysis considers the availability of certain discourses within a culture and how access to these promotes certain ways-of-seeing and ways-of-being in the world. In the case of health psychology, FDA considers the relationship between certain discourses and how individuals think and feel about particular health-related issues. FDA also considers the material conditions within which potential practices may occur. Thus FDA extends the connection between available discourses and subjectivity to consider human practices and their social and political situatedness.

Willig argues that while discursive psychology can help us understand the dynamics of social interactions within a health care setting, FDA is particularly appropriate for understanding why people act in healthy and unhealthy ways and how they experience health and illness. In addition, Willig raises the challenging issue of the ethics of the different forms of discourse analysis. This issue revolves around the extent to which the research participants' accounts are social performances or self-expressions. This return to ethical and moral issues echoes the concerns identified in the previous two chapters.

Health Psychology Practice

The final part of the book considers the fourth meaning of the term 'critical' that meshes with the other three parts. It is concerned with how health psychology can more directly position itself as an agent for promoting health through varied methods of social rather than individual change. It begins with a chapter on narrative and social representation theory. Both of these theories provide an opportunity to begin to understand the broader dimensions of health and illness that are ignored by popular social cognition models. People tell stories about their experiences of health and illness. It is through these stories that people define and redefine themselves. In addition, communities and societies share collective stories about health, illness and health care. Some of these stories can attain mythic status and can be drawn upon to provide moral guidance and justification for social actions.

Social representation theory is concerned with those shared belief systems that develop in everyday social interaction within a community. It is argued that narratives can contribute to the development of social representations. At the same time, people draw on social representations in telling their stories. There is a growing research tradition exploring social representations of health and illness. Narrative theory provides a way of exploring further the character of these social representations.

Certain social representations provide a justification for the continuation of oppressive social relationships and consequent human suffering. The chapter briefly considers how challenges to oppressive social representations open up the prospect of enhancing community health. Such undertakings can be led by minority groups and can involve deliberate attempts to challenge accepted personal and community narratives.

In the section concerned with developments in method, one underlying issue was the need to work with the study participants rather than attempting to impose a particular framework. This orientation is developed further in the chapter by Mary Brydon-Miller on participatory action research. This approach breaks down the traditional distinction between research and action. It engages the researcher directly with the community in a collaborative change process. The research project is not something from which change or transformation is excluded but rather change is deliberately a task of the research. It is change aimed at enhancing and strengthening the resilience of a community, and research becomes a means to facilitate this change.

Research in this tradition has historically focused on work with deprived communities. There is a particularly rich tradition of this form of research in Latin America that is only now being recognized (Fals Borda 2001). A particular influential contribution has been the work of the Brazilian popular educator Paulo Freire (1970/1993). In this chapter Brydon-Miller traces other traditions and explores the various methods that this approach subsumes. Underlying the approach is the commitment to social justice and social change. This method of research can be time consuming and often frustrating but ultimately it offers a strategy for overcoming the scientistic distance that has traditionally defined much of health psychology and introduces the prospect of combining scholarship with social action.

This prospect is developed further in the final chapter that is concerned with how critical health psychologists can work with communities to promote health. Catherine Campbell begins this chapter by reviewing different approaches to health promotion. On the one hand there is the traditional information-provision approach that is associated with the individualistic victim-blaming model. The alternative approach is one that focuses on community development. However, there is still limited understanding of the processes underlying community mobilization.

Campbell considers three mechanisms underlying participatory community-based health campaigns: identity, empowerment and the development of health-enabling community contexts. Social identity is concerned with how

health practices are linked to collectively negotiated social identities. Empowerment is concerned with how communities can grow in confidence and strength
to change, through the development of a critical consciousness.

In terms of community context Campbell considers the current debate about
the nature of social capital. She refers to the role of political power in providing
the opportunity for or obstructing the development of local social capital.
While community development efforts can work at promoting health-enabling
communities they often have to compete against the broader political forces.
Campbell concludes that members of marginalized groups need to form links
with more powerful social groupings if they are to create opportunities for
local social change. So once again health psychology returns to the issue of
political power in shaping the prospects for health.

A Beginning

These chapters provide an outline of some of the important issues within
a revitalized health psychology: one that does not adopt a scientistic objectivist
attitude but one that is much more reflexive and socially engaged. As we move
into the 21st century, the very future of the discipline of psychology is contested.
Within health psychology we should be concerned not with the discipline as
an entity to be preserved but as something to be questioned and challenged.
It is not the intention of this book to define a new sub-discipline of 'critical
health psychology' but rather to raise questions about the nature of the whole
sub-discipline of health psychology. We live in a world of constant change in
which it would be naïve to assert access to a certain uncontested truth. We
should, however, realize that we are social and moral beings whose work is not
without a potential impact on the wider world. As such, it is all the more important that we deliberately take time to reflect on some of the broader questions
introduced in this book and review how we can best orient ourselves.

📖 Further Readings

Fox, D. and Prilleltensky, I. (1997) *Critical Psychology: An Introduction*, London: Sage.

This book has become a classic text for those interested in critical psychology in that it
provides a comprehensive overview of some of the key issues facing psychology today.
It provides a discussion of theoretical, methodological and applied issues.

Rose, N. (1996) *Inventing Ourselves: Psychology, Power and Personhood*, Cambridge:
Cambridge University Press.

This book provides an overview of the social and political forces that have shaped the
discipline of psychology.

PART 1

Theory and Health Psychology

A Sound Mind in a Sound Body: A Critical Historical Analysis of Health Psychology[1]

Henderikus J. Stam

Summary

This chapter examines the nature of the interdependency between psychologists and health care systems, especially with respect to the autonomy of psychology, the way in which psychological theorizing appropriates medical definitions for its understanding of health and illness, and the way in which some topics and concerns remain invisible to health psychology. It concludes that psychologists cannot escape the moral dimensions inherent in their subject matter.

Introduction

The great Roman poet and satirist Juvenal never quite said what his phrase has come to mean (*mens sana in copore sano* – a sound mind in a sound body). The implications that a healthy body leads to a healthy mind or that only in a healthy body one might find a healthy mind is a reading of the phrase that has come into being over the last several hundred years. Frequently carved in stone on school buildings as an exhortation to students, it acts as a reminder that one look after one's physical well-being as well as one's mental development. Indeed, the interpretation that we have come to accept is downright dualist, framing the body and mind as separate entities, although related. History clarifies for us how we came to read this into Juvenal for it was an interpretation that, once wedded to Christian morality, was turned into common sense in the same way that we might say 'an apple a day keeps the doctor away.'

It is this problematic relationship between what might constitute 'a sound mind' and 'a sound body' that health psychology takes as its starting point.

For it is not at all obvious just what those two phrases mean, however frequently they have been cited. It is indeed not just a problem of dualism – the problem of trying to determine what constitutes mental events and how these are physically realized – but also the problem of coming to grips with the body as more than a mere machine. René Descartes is important in this respect and not just for historical reasons. He is credited with beginning a way of thinking that led us, through the British empiricists such as John Locke and David Hume, through the 19th-century positivists such as John Mills, to a position wherein we came to understand the body as natural, physical or biological and the mind as, well, mental. Moreover, what 'mental' exactly meant was never quite worked out but it certainly came to stand in opposition to, or sometimes was overshadowed by, the powers of the body.

In this chapter, I want to create a problem more than I want to solve one: what we have considered bodily, physical, and natural is in some ways less clear than we might assume at first glance, especially when we inquire after health and illness. Health Psychology, by taking for granted a particular kind of relationship between mind and body or between the psychology of illness and the suffering of the body (or its prevention), has aligned itself largely with the aims and institutional priorities of biomedical science and practice. In this chapter, I want to examine the origins of that area of psychology now called Health Psychology and to pose some theoretical or foundational questions that might lead us to think differently about this sub-discipline of psychology.

The aim of this process is to have you evaluate the practices in which you might engage as a health psychologist by taking what is referred to as a 'reflexive stance.' Reflexive here means not automatic or unthinking but quite the opposite. It is used to refer to our self-conscious participation in practices as professionals or as professionals-in-training. This seemingly obvious stance is nevertheless ignored in traditional Health Psychology. Indeed, the methods of science are in place precisely to prevent us from personally inserting ourselves into research and practice – they encourage what we have come to see as objectivity. Being a professional typically means that you are someone who (a) is specially trained by others already in the profession, (b) has achieved your credentials on your own merit rather than receiving them merely for payment or through birthright, (c) belongs to a group that is self-governing and has been designated so by legal statute, and finally, in many professions, (d) is in the business of receiving, passing on and/or creating scientific knowledge.

These systems of professionalization seem to guarantee that one would not be self-consciously 'reflexive' precisely because that is what a profession urges one to keep at bay. One of the questions that I hope to answer for you in this chapter is why *critical* health psychologists ask you to be reflexive and practice in ways that are not traditionally professional but are responsible and ethical nonetheless. This reflexivity will refer to our appreciation of the way in which our human practices with other human beings are based on an understanding of shared linguistic and cultural customs.

History and Theory in Health Psychology

The brief overview of health psychology that follows is not meant to be a complete history. As far as I know, a complete history of the field has not yet been written, largely because it is such a new sub-specialty of psychology dating largely from the 1970s and 1980s. This need not detain us from detailing a number of key issues that come out of its brief history.

Any history is going to reflect the enthusiasm and disappointments of those who write it. Disciplinary histories are deeply committed to telling the stories of those who contributed to and developed their discipline, a problem that has been widely discussed in the history of psychology (e.g., Danziger 1994). It is not enough to be able to say, for example, that in 1911 there was a panel at the American Psychological Association (APA) meeting to consider how psychology could contribute to medical education and practice and that this was 'the first semi-official action of organized psychology...regarding the health system' (Rodin and Stone 1987: 18). Health psychology as a separate professional designation in the discipline of psychology is one associated with contemporary disputes concerning licensing and regulation, competence, the increase in chronic as opposed to acute illnesses, and so on. The appropriation of history to that professional designation will always be 'celebratory' meaning that it is meant to celebrate the accomplishments of those who have established the sub-discipline and are its promoters.

It is important then to recognize that a critical institutional history of health psychology can tell us a different tale from those histories written in this celebratory vein (such as those of Stone 1980 or Rodin and Stone 1987). When psychologists first sought to promote their newly minted discipline (referred to as the 'new psychology' to distinguish it from the old, philosophical psychology) in the late 19th century, they had to convince skeptical governing boards of universities that they had something of value to offer. One way to do this was to promise a discipline that could solve real social problems by finding the scientific foundations of the human mind and behavior (e.g., Leary 1987).

Likewise, when health psychologists began to write the history of health psychology at about the same time as the sub-discipline came into being, it was meant to buttress the very idea of such a sub-specialty. Of course, psychologists had been engaged in research related to health for many years; and of course, psychologists could easily configure an understanding of health into contemporary clinical and cognitive psychology. However, the idea of a specialty of health psychology that supported a new professional designation with its own research agenda, journals, organizations, conferences, and university training programs was uniquely related to the following developments in the 1960s and 1970s (noting of course that here we mean largely North America and what was then Western Europe): (1) the increasing prevalence of chronic illnesses such as cancer and heart disease that previously killed outright and were now more likely to be long-term illnesses with acute phases, (2) the demise of neo-behaviorism as the core theory or central theoretical dogma of psychology and its gradual dispersal into multiple sub-disciplines, (3) after the expansion of universities in the 1950s and 1960s, a shortage of employment opportunities for clinically and academically trained psychologists along with an increase in the number of people trained, and (4) the professionalization of related groups of practitioners (e.g. nurses, family physicians, physiotherapists) who sought to make psychological aspects of health care their domain of practice and expertise and, thus, led to the sensitization of psychologists to a domain of health care that could legitimately be called their own.

The American Psychological Association division of Health Psychology was founded in 1978. Shortly thereafter at least half a dozen new journals devoted to health psychology appeared (including the Division's own *Health Psychology*). At about the same time, *Behavioral Medicine*, a seeming competitor sub-field, was launched in 1977 at a Yale conference. In 1978, the Academy of Behavioral Medicine Research and the Society for Behavioral Medicine were both founded. By that year almost 2500 psychologists (or 5 percent of the membership of APA) were on the faculties of US medical schools (Matarazzo 1980).

Those who advocated the founding of these organizations were nothing but enthusiastic. Taylor (1986: 3) argued that 'our current state of knowledge has virtually demanded the development of the field of health psychology.' Others claimed that health psychologists were like explorers landing on new continents, that psychology could be a pillar of modern medicine and so on. What was obvious to anyone who dug beyond the rhetorical features of such enthusiastic founders was that there was in fact very little by way of research or practice that actually made up these fields. Like the 'new psychologists' of the late 19th century, those responsible for founding health psychology and related fields were indeed promoting the possibility of a science in the absence of real accomplishments. The fact that two major organizations with two different names could lay claim to the same area of expertise within a year of each other was itself an indication that there were professional turf wars at play. In addition, various other designations, both old and new, were added to the fray (e.g. psychological medicine, psychosomatic medicine, comprehensive medicine, clinical health psychology, and so on). Psychiatry, family medicine, psychology, and other health specialists were all vying for similar terrain: psychological aspects of health and illness.

Theory in Health Psychology: The Biopsychosocial Model

Given the need to develop health psychology in the 1970s, where did psychologists turn for foundations and what consequences did this have for the field? What I want to describe here is a model and then indicate how this model, in practice, is simply a variant of the functionalism that characterizes contemporary psychology. Indeed, although health psychologists claim to rely on several models, including systems theory, biopsychosocial theory, and self-regulatory theories among others, these are all variants of functionalism. For example, systems theory has been espoused as providing a foundation for understanding adaptive mechanisms (e.g. Stone 1980; Taylor 1999). However, systems theory, especially the version that circulates in health psychology, adheres in practice to the three necessary conditions for a functionalist model (Evans-Pritchard 1951): First, systems are natural phenomena with inter-dependent levels that serve to maintain the system, second, within systems theory social events are reduced to empirical relationships that are predictable, and third, systems theory is ahistorical about the make-up of systems. In this sense, systems theory is neutral about the nature of biomedical systems (McLean 1986). Within the context of health and health care, such a functional view espouses a concept of persons as well-tuned machines (rather than sentient beings) whose actions are intelligible in larger control systems. Self-regulatory models are likewise driven by functional considerations; the 'self' or person, however conceived, is entirely absent in these formulations.

The 'biopsychosocial' position and related concepts have a unique place in health psychology and are used not only by health psychologists but also by those proffering a critical health psychology. Engel's original publication in *Science* in 1977, where the term originated, was primarily a critique of biomedicine. Only the latter half of his paper concerned itself with the biopsychosocial model proper and most of this was by way of example rather than the development of a model, theory, or position. In fact, he does not even define the term but argues that the 'model must...take into account the patient, the social context in which he [or she] lives, and the complimentary system devised by society to deal with the disruptive effects of illness, that is, the physician's role and health care system' (p. 132). Furthermore, argues Engel, the dichotomy between 'disease' and certain 'problems of living' is clear neither for patient nor physician. As an example, he describes the case of grief. It exemplifies a phenomenon in which psychological factors are primary yet it constitutes a discrete syndrome with a relatively predictable symptomatology, which includes bodily and psychological disturbances. A biopsychosocial model would merely take all of these factors into account, and Engel alludes in his conclusion to the relationship between the biopsychosocial model and systems theories.

It is an interesting phenomenon in its own right that such a loose formulation has become the rhetorical mainstay of theory in health psychology (see Stam 2000) but the term 'biopsychosocial' is now thoroughly embedded in the discipline. Indeed, it appeared almost obligatory to mention the model although very few contemporary textbooks cite papers beyond the original formulations by Engel (1977) or the revision published by Schwartz in 1982. The 'model' has simply been taken for granted and, remarkably, there is absolutely no discussion of what this term could mean other than the 'interplay' or 'interaction' of biological, psychological and social factors. Taylor (1999) is even less committed by noting that these three factors are merely 'involved' in the model. No author notes that this is neither a theory nor a model, at least not in the sense of a model that we understand in the philosophy of science. Here a model refers to a partial simulation derived from a theory and hence a limited test of a more advanced and developed theoretical formulation (Suppe 1989). Nonetheless, it is the case that in the social sciences the term 'model' is often used loosely to describe a guiding formulation that is not related to a particular theory but is associated instead with functional properties. It is only in this sense that the 'biopsychosocial model' can be considered a model at all.

We can conclude then that the term 'biopsychosocial' has a certain rhetorical function that is more important than its purported theoretical contribution to the discipline (see also Armstrong 1987). As a neologism it makes it possible to argue that health psychologists are committed to studying the social and psychological as well as the biomedical. On the other hand, the absence of theory and the vagueness of the model can be construed as a useful ploy because anything can be covered by it, anything remotely relevant counts as a topic under 'health.' As Taylor (1999: 489) pronounces in the last sentence of her textbook on health psychology, 'the opportunities for the fledgling health psychologist are boundless.' Opportunities indeed, so long as they do not interfere with institutional privileges. In short, the functionalist prescriptiveness and lofty inclusiveness of the biopsychosocial 'model' make it a useful theoretical device for the appropriation of a set of topics in health and illness into psychological practice and research. It also has the advantage of not challenging the biomedical dominance of definitions of 'health' and 'illness' and ensures that psychological research will take biomedicine for granted as a background rather than foregrounding it in the very conceptualization of health and illness.

This perspective on health psychology comes to us from asking about the nature of professionalization. This is what Turner (1986) and other social scientists refer to as 'social closure.' It happens when a profession's knowledge base serves as a strategy of market regulation. Why would health psychology be concerned with something as unrelated as market regulation? Precisely because it is continually in competition with neighboring disciplines for the same territory. Family medicine, community medicine, nursing, social work, epidemiology, sociology of health, and other health-related disciplines have marked as their domain certain problems and topics in health care that are also part of the practice and research repertoire of health psychologists. These include topics such as family, living with chronic illness, prevention of diseases, and so on. In that sense, part of health psychology's success is derived from its capacity to innovate and to secure new markets, clients and rewards.

We know from an endless stream of media reports that health care is a deeply contested political and social topic in contemporary North Atlantic societies. One of the major expenses of governments, individuals and families is health and health care. These societies are dominated by mixed models of physicians as private entrepreneurs/public servants who work within both private and public medical facilities. Health care has been (in the post-World War II period) in a constant state of crisis and restructuring. The biomedical model has been challenged on many fronts and a steady growth and proliferation in health professions and specialties (within medicine but also in dentistry, pharmacy, and so on) and complementary occupations (nursing, physiotherapy, laboratory specialists) have transformed the health labor force. As other groups have joined this labor force through a strategy of professionalization (among others, psychologists, chiropractors, nurses), and administrative and support services have proliferated, the medical domain has become a contested and fragmented one (see Aries and Kennedy 1990; Burke and Stevenson 1993). Health psychology has been largely silent on these structural issues. Consequently, psychologists tend not to be able to articulate how these events impact their own research and practices, their conceptions of health and illness, and the importance of these considerations for their intended end-users, the research participants, and the ill. This is also a function of the individualism that characterizes psychology; its focus is on the self-contained individual who is the subject of psychological research and theory.

A second important feature of psychological research and theory that contributes to this isolation is its focus on the research as functional, something I have already alluded to above. What functionalist theory allows is the discursive construction of health and illness as a set of *variables* whose identification is obvious and whose analysis requires no more than the use of aggregate statistics that allow one to make simple yes/no judgments. I wish to say a few words about this, which I hope will clarify my understanding of theory when I return to the question of theory as a moral project.

How Methodology Constrains Theory

Like theory in psychology generally, what passes for theory in health psychology is loosely related to a version of positivism (modeled on the philosophical version of logical positivism) that has dominated psychology since the mid-20th century. According to the philosophical version of logical positivism, a theory is no more than an axiomatized collection of sentences that has a specified relationship to a set of observables. This relationship (dependent on a theory of verification) was much in dispute for the life of logical positivism. Psychology generally bypassed this view (and the concomitant debate). Instead, it has relied on the 19th-century positivism of Ernst Mach that was gradually modified and introduced into psychological research through behaviorism with an explicit emphasis on observation as the key element of scientific research (Danziger 1990; O'Neil 1995; Mills 1998). On this view, observations were separate from theory, and gradually came to rely on models, such as Clark Hull's, which were 'deductive-nomonological' in nature. Theories in this context came to mean statements that had a specific relationship to the events to be explained, a deductive-nomonological relationship. In the ideal case, the theory was a universal law that could act as a 'covering law' that explains the events under consideration.

For all its elegance, the model can be seen in very little research after that of Clark Hull. Practically, the development of inferential statistics and the demise of behaviorism as an all-encompassing theory for psychology led to a much more liberal approach in understanding theoretical claims. Although the emphases on observation and quantification persisted and were strengthened by post-World War II generations of psychologists, inferential statistics encouraged the wider use of theoretical models or 'hypotheses' in psychology and discouraged formal theorization (with the exception of some areas such as mathematical psychology). It has only been the advent of cognitivism in the last 40 years that has gradually re-introduced theory in a more formal manner by way of (cognitive) functional analyses, analyses that have come to rely on and require the kind of statistical averaging used in tests of statistical inference.

My argument here then is that the use of a particular form of statistical technique and the development of theorization around these techniques of hypothesis testing encouraged the 'thin' theorizing that characterizes most contemporary psychology, including health psychology (Gigerenzer 1993; Stam and Pasay 1998). Danziger (1990) gives an account of how, in response to the demand for an applied form of knowledge in the early 20th century, research in psychology came to be conducted on groups that were constituted so that they could be contrasted on an abstract variable. For example, research in intelligence demanded some conception of normative levels for the development of intelligence tests. Individual scores came to be reported in the aggregate and deviations were construed as 'error.' Aggregate scores however make it difficult to develop concepts about intra-individual processes and these were the most important to the development of the discipline. The introduction of inferential statistics solved this problem for psychologists, namely, it allowed the identification of functional psychological properties with the hypothetical distributions of statistical analyses. In other words, individual scores no longer mattered but rather the distribution of scores came to represent the theoretical processes at hand. For example, such processes as memory or intelligence could be captured not by studying individual acts of remembering but by comparing how different groups (created by setting up 'experimental conditions') of individuals performed some restricted tasks such as learning and recalling a list of nonsense syllables. The resulting, functional theoretical notion was one that no longer referred to any single participant in the experiment but instead to an abstract property of 'memory.' It was described by the mean performance of each group and does not refer back to the individuals who make up that group.

Methodological prescriptions, including the requirement of confirmation through observations analyzed using statistical inference techniques, severely constricted the possibilities of theory development. However sophisticated one's psychological notions, the indiscriminate use of tests of statistical inference led to a mechanical and routine use of the technique that by its very nature foreclosed rather than advanced theory (Gigerenzer 1993). Psychological theory, therefore, remains relatively simple because the techniques of adjudication between theories require uncomplicated, elementary and simplified models and hypotheses.

For health psychologists the problem is no different. In less official publications, health psychologists sometimes even acknowledge this problem. Using his presidential column in the APA Division 38 newsletter, Howard Leventhal (1996: 1) remarked that 'many of our theories are little more than broad themes that guide but do not constrain our thinking; they are frames of reference rather than theories.' Unfortunately, Leventhal had no solution to this problem.

Given this situation, we can now see more clearly how the restriction of theory in health psychology allows the practices of psychologists to coincide with those of biomedicine. Note that this does not necessarily have to be intentional; institutional prerogatives and agendas rarely are in any case. With its focus on prevention, adjustment, and coping, health psychology considers 'healthy' the patient who has regained the ability to perform. Health in this sense is a functional entity, not one negotiated in a shifting discourse of health and illness encompassing the activities of falling ill or becoming well (see also Spicer and Chamberlain's 1996, notion of 'flowcharting'). It is also individualistic in the sense that there is never a conception of the collective responsibilities for health beyond that of individuals in the aggregate. I would argue instead that any substantial theorization of the psychology of health and illness must begin by taking a critical distance from the discourse of biomedicine. This distancing is almost impossible to do in mainstream health psychology. Discursively and methodologically, it is tied to a single simplified model, the very maintenance of which is also a strategic discursive act even as it masquerades as scientifically pure.

There are obviously occasions and questions associated with health that demand an empirical descriptive strategy. For example, we might want to know the motives for condom use among young adults (e.g. Cooper *et al.* 1999), or the relations among ethnicity, wealth, and health (e.g. Ostrove *et al.* 1999). Note however that many such questions are broadly epidemiological or social and not just psychological. That is, they concern social and community health questions, precisely the kinds of questions for which one wants to have descriptive data so that policy and practice issues can be brought to the fore. They do not even begin to address what is psychological about such issues. What remains as theorizing in health psychology hides the professional and authorial source of knowledge, makes reciprocity between the source and the production of knowledge impossible, and treats the producers of that knowledge as professionals carrying out a job in the name of science. It is unreflexive about its knowledge production, namely that of constituent players engaged in the construction of health and illness. Behind its universalism lies an individualism that characterizes much of psychology; what the scientific knower knows is independent of who the knower happens to be, the knower's social position, and the use to which such knowledge is put.

There are many alternatives to this form of knowledge production that have been prescribed over the last four decades by theorists and methodologists in the name of various emancipatory or post-positivist projects, many of which will be described in this book. Feminism, critical theory, postmodernisms of various kinds as well as the wide prevalence of qualitative methods have sought to reclaim territory from the wider fields of health sciences just as these have pervaded other domains of psychology (e.g. Stainton Rogers 1996). Nevertheless, qualitative research does not, in itself, guarantee an escape from more traditional mainstream forms of knowledge production. It is an easy step to reformulate qualitative research so that it is yet another neutral method of inquiry that captures better, and implicitly, more faithful and true characterizations of health and illness.

Responsible Health Professionals

What multiple critical perspectives have foregrounded, however, is the place *from* which we do research or *from* which we practice. Feminist philosopher, Kathryn Addelson (1994: 18) has argued that as professionals, 'being morally responsible requires foresight in acting from *one's place*, foresight on the outcomes of collective activity in which one takes part.' This means that we devise 'theories and practices that can make explicit what the collective activity is' and what the outcomes of that activity might be (p. 18). In other words, our interventions in health do not arise *de novo* from rational objective theories but always first and foremost from a discursive position within such seemingly objective theories that have as their ends the production of certain 'goods' be they function, adaptation, understanding, insight, and so on.

In addition, what the new epistemologies have taken from us is the possibility of a fixed, certain or rational standpoint from which to engage in professional activities. Instead, our activities are always politically engaged because of our positions as professionals in the social order. Reflexivity then means recognizing not only the inevitability of being so positioned but also deciding what moral goods we will pursue in our activities.

The institutions that employ us grant our cognitive authority as professionals to us. Indeed, Addelson argues that all professions, and this certainly includes the service professions, are obliged to have knowledge makers providing that 'difficult body of knowledge' that legitimates their professional status. In addition, it is this body of knowledge that distinguishes professionals, such as health psychologists, from workers in other occupations. As health psychologists, we use this knowledge to define more clearly the need that we in turn service. Hence, there is an intimate relationship between our knowledge base and our practical endeavors. If we define needs in terms of abstract functional variables such as coping and adjustment, or in terms of the Diagnostic and Statistical Manual of Mental Disorders (DSM)[2] criteria, our research priorities will reflect the objective and abstract definitions of those needs. That makes the service and research context simpler and more manageable. If, on the other hand, we negotiate these needs in the terms that the ill give us, in terms of their own life histories and in terms of their needs to negotiate a complex health system, then we also create more responsible but less comfortable service positions for ourselves.

However, it is not only needs and practices that we establish, we also have a hand in defining outcomes. When these are to be constituted as empirically verifiable constructs such as adjustment, 'quality of life' objectively defined, or compliance with a medical regime, we deny that we are collectively, as a profession, defining a set of outcomes for others. The process of objectification denies the historical constitution of those outcomes. Historical constitution here means simply that outcomes always take place in collectives whether these range from the conversation between two people to the discussions that take place in a conference on health psychology (cf. Addelson 1994). Professional accounts of outcomes are special kinds of outcomes, produced in the context of and supporting existing social, political, and economic orders.

To return for a moment to Kathryn Addelson's work, I would like to pursue her general proposal that 'truth' is always enacted in collective action. Our claims as professionals, even as critical or qualitative researchers, make sense so long as others recognize the talk. As collectives (such as at a conference or writing for, and reading, specialized journals) we then elaborate on, seek out further clarification of, and redefine our professional talk. However, in our interactions with the ill or with other health care professionals we also come prepared and sensitized to the setting. Working on a defined terrain, we know *how*, from within our professional activities. Addelson argues that we are socially embodied actors who not only do professional work but in doing so, we are also significant moral and political actors. We are taken to be 'trustworthy instruments of governance' (p. 208).

Illustration and Conclusion

My argument has thus far been largely abstract and somewhat removed from the practices of the health psychologist. In this context, I would like to provide several examples of how theoretical development can alter the way in which we examine key health problems. These two cases involve very different settings but are both concerned with important health issues, one is a discussion of the experience of cancer and the other a case study of the difficulties of addressing HIV/AIDS prevention.

Cancer Narratives

Several years ago, Cynthia Mathieson and I conducted a number of studies on the nature of identity and cancer (Mathieson and Stam 1995). For many of us this is not an experience with which we are unfamiliar. As I write this, two close family members have cancer, one in old age and the other in mid-life. Our concern with the research setting and the questions we would pose to the patients who spoke to us was to try, on the one hand, to allow those with cancer to tell their own stories and, on the other hand, to theorize those aspects of the stories that would allow us to reflexively feed back into the experience of having cancer some semblance of the commonality of those experiences. People with cancer must negotiate their way through regimens of treatment, changing bodies and disrupted lives and hence the telling of one's story takes on a renewed urgency. In the end, they are not just 'stories' but the vehicle for making sense of not only an illness but also a life. The conversations that we had with those who shared their lives with us take on a narrative quality that reflects the ongoing struggle to maintain an identity in the face of conditions that often make it difficult to maintain a coherent sense of self.

Rather than problematize the lives of cancer patients and represent their illness for them – as is so often done in health psychology and psychosocial oncology literatures (often under the guise of personality, clinical or attitude scales) – we treated the interviews of patients as ongoing narratives of illness. Of the multiple features we eventually settled on as a relevant analytic tool to grasp the experience of illness, one of the most important was the notion of 'biographical work.' Indeed, we all engage in something like biographical work over the life span as a requirement of having and maintaining an identity. The diagnosis of cancer however challenges older self-narratives and motivates the search for newer narratives that incorporate the experience and meaning of illness. Persons with cancer often express this as a distinction of an 'old self' and a 'new self' with cancer. As one woman with breast cancer said, 'I think what cancer does is . . . it makes you look at yourself; it makes you look at your life . . . . Your perception changes. It *has* to.' Biographical work is that effort required to guide the revision of self-narratives. It acknowledges that the illness has disrupted the older narratives and it foregrounds the illness into a revised narrative.

Prevention and HIV/AIDS

The study I have just described is but one example of psychological research with those who are already ill. This book contains many others. Much community and public health research, however, is actually carried out on the problems of primary and secondary prevention. Primary prevention is aimed at intervening before a pathogenic process has begun when individuals may be susceptible to disease but have not yet contracted it. This form of prevention attempts to separate the agent from contact with the host or to drastically reduce the susceptibility of the host. This is generally accomplished through health promotion (which may include not only physical factors such as hygiene but also obvious psychological ones such as education or anti-smoking programs) or through protection against specific diseases through immunization programs or the treatment of water. We now take this form of prevention largely for granted, but after 1900 it resulted in the dramatic reduction in death from infectious diseases such as diphtheria, influenza and so on.

Secondary prevention refers to those attempts to detect and treat disease early. It is focused on presymptomatic diseases such as those found through screening. Numerous screening tests for communicable and inherited diseases are now available. HIV infections and death from AIDS continue to be a major world health problem. A recent study projecting causes of death to 2020 indicates that while HIV infections were ranked 30th on a rank order of all causes of death in 1990, it will likely be ranked 9th by 2020 (Murray and Lopez 1996). It will rank 7th on the list of 'projected years of life lost' by 2020 (from 20th in 1990). Therefore, it would seem that one important role for psychology is to work on the prevention of HIV infections, indeed many health psychologists devote their research efforts to such topics as the use of condoms by at-risk-groups, and other, related preventive measures.

To appreciate how this requires the participation of multiple social actors and is not captured by functional theory, I would like to describe briefly the work of Ian Lubek, Mee Lain Wong, and their colleagues (e.g. Lubek and Wong 2002, 2003). In the area surrounding Angkor Wat, the ancient temples in Northern Cambodia, the influx of tourists in the 1990s at the end of years of conflict led to an HIV/AIDS pandemic. Almost a quarter of these tourists are 'sexual tourists.' Using a model of participant action research (see Chapter 11), these investigators began by seeking ways to prevent the high rates of HIV infection in this area. This included founding a local grass-roots citizens' action committee and targeting the groups most likely to be affected. These groups included the so-called 'beer girls' and the married women whose husbands also visited the beer restaurants and local brothels (Lubek and Wong 2003). The 'beer girls' try to meet quotas of selling about two-dozen beers per evening. They work for and promote such companies as Labatts, Fosters, Budweiser, Stella Artois, Heineken, and so on. The beer companies, who pay about $2 per day, take no responsibility for their employees who wear the logos of the company and often offer sex for money to clients when both are inebriated. Lubek and Wong report that the local HIV sero-positive rates may be between 19 and 55 percent and local men are now transmitting the virus to their wives and subsequently to their newborn children.

Lubek and colleagues, and the local grass-roots community have discussed various forms of intervening in the local context (see Lubek and Wong 2002 for further details). What makes this an important lesson in the vagaries of disease, prevention, politics and community action is that the external interventions must be made in such a way that they come to be owned by the local community, interventions must be modifiable, and the collective community voice 'now organizes the scientific activities of the action researcher' (Lubek and Wong 2003). Furthermore, an important link from this local case is its entrenchment in the processes of globalization through the recalcitrance of the beer companies to take responsibility for the activities they support and whose logos the 'beer girls' wear. In addition, Cambodia is still recovering from years of foreign-sponsored civil war including the genocide of the Pol Pot regime. Many men argue Lubek and Wong have lost not only years of their lives but also many family members in the fighting and dislocation. Hence, they are very willing to take risks. Lubek and Wong (2003) note that their research and intervention into this context is a complex inter-relationship among theory, research, and practice (see also Chapter 12).

Conclusion

Perhaps the most obvious conclusion to be drawn from this chapter is that the multifarious nature of health and illness, its embeddedness in the social and political communities in which we live, and the complex natural processes of pathogenesis make any singular attempt to classify a psychology of health and illness nigh impossible. However, that would be the wrong take-home message. Complexity does not mean anarchy just as psychology's single functional model can explain neither the socio-political nature nor the personal experience of health and illness. Indeed, the complexity of the nature of health and illness demands that we pay close attention to the local and the personal. By this, I mean paying attention to the worlds of people who carry the burden of particular illnesses, refusing to let biomedicine speak for them or reduce their voice to singular and univocal instances of 'adaptation' and 'coping.' At the same time, we also need to monitor global processes that biomedicine sets in motion or fails to set in motion (for example, in the failure to provide relief for the HIV/AIDS pandemic in Africa). These global processes are intimately connected to other forces of globalization and corporatization.

Does this not seem like we have traveled a long way from the questions of theory? I do not believe we have, for it is in committing ourselves to theorize the local that we can understand the larger issues confronting us. Individuals who are ill and communities in need of preventive practices are real consumers of knowledge and care but also crucibles of wisdom and knowledge. If the health psychologist is going to mobilize that knowledge it will not be along the lines of some universal, functional model that is the outcome of processes far removed from the experiences of those for whom the professional seeks to speak.

To force the singular model/variables into a psychology of health and illness is wishful thinking. Juvenal would have had some understanding of this. His oft-quoted line from Satire 10, *orandum est ut sit mens sana in corpore sano*, was an exhortation to his fellow citizens not to pose foolish requests to the gods but, instead, to pray for a healthy mind in a healthy body. Juvenal understood that health was a great gift after all, much greater than the venial and pernicious requests otherwise made to the gods. Our contemporary world makes plain that understanding health and illness is also of great value. It is not to be grasped by forcing it onto a Procrustean bed for professional gain.

Key Points

- Psychologists work within larger contexts not of their own making when they address health topics. Institutional and social forces create ready-made definitions and understandings of everyday events.
- Psychological theorizing is never done in a vacuum but reflects the interests of those so engaged, and in health psychology is often deeply entwined with the interests of biomedicine.
- Methods are ways of understanding that are never totally separate from the theoretical context in which they are created. Functional definitions of the sort that are favored by psychologists are easily studied using aggregate statistics and null hypothesis testing. They are frequently theoretically 'light.'
- Being a professional psychologist in an institutional setting such as a health care setting means that you are also a moral and political actor.

Assignment Questions

1. Provide an example of a serious health concern that you have either experienced or that you have watched someone you know experience. Can you provide a psychological analysis of the situation? What was important to the person involved? How was this reflected or not reflected in the medical treatment? Generate a theoretical understanding of this situation that remains true to the experience.
2. Discuss the question of reflexivity. Why is it so difficult to acknowledge that we are also moral and political actors in professional settings? Does this matter if we are dealing with the objectives of providing health care?

Notes

1. Some of the material in this chapter is derived from an earlier article (Stam 2000).
2. This is the official manual of psychiatric diagnoses, now in its fourth edition, developed by the American Psychiatric Association and is widely used around the world.

📖 Further Readings

Addelson, K.P. (1994) *Moral Passages: Toward a Collectivist Moral Theory*, New York: Routledge.

This book provides a clear introduction to the need for professionals to consider the moral dimensions of their roles.

Danziger, K. (1990) *Constructing the Subject: Historical Origins of Psychological Research*, New York: Cambridge University Press.

This book provides an excellent critical introduction to the development of psychology as we generally know it.

Engel, G.L. (1977) 'The need for a new medical model: a challenge for biomedicine', *Science*, 196, 129–136.

This is the paper that outlined the basic biopsychosocial model that has been used as the cornerstone of health psychology since.

CHAPTER 2

Suffering

Alan Radley

Summary

This chapter examines the concept of suffering as a key experience of serious illness. Criticism is made of the assumption that, by encouraging people to communicate their suffering, this allows people to manage their pain in an acceptable way. Instead, I argue: (a) that *suffering is mute* because it often cannot be spoken, and (b) that *suffering is social* because it can only be acknowledged through compassion. The chapter proposes that it is *compassion that gives shape to suffering*. Thus, while people's feelings might be impossible to explain, these feelings can yet be acknowledged by others. This idea is considered in the context of the clinical setting where *health psychologists engage suffering*, using either traditional techniques of pain management or narrative-based methods. Even in the case of the latter, it is important to see the limitation of confusing talk about suffering with suffering as experienced. This approach to suffering recognises that for health psychologists to always insist that it be communicated (objectified) means the person's suffering risks being mistaken.

Introduction

In his account of the psychological study of pain, Kugelmann (1998) traced its history from the idea that pain is just a physiological phenomenon to the conception that it is an experience that the patient can control. The possibility that patients might participate in the management of their pain allowed psychologists to make the claim that they can, in some way, be made responsible for it. Through the activities of the pain clinic, health psychology takes on the job of attempting to reduce suffering by using such things as self-management techniques to alter the way that pain is experienced, and to defuse its power by helping the patient to re-frame it.

Kugelmann (1998: 197) criticises this endeavour by pointing out the consequence of moving away from the idea of pain as something located in the patient's body. Instead, 'Ironically, because pain is defined as essentially subjective, it is more rigorously objectified'. This aim (of objectification) does not follow

31

from the need to remove pain, for that is accepted as impossible when it is deemed 'intractable'. Instead, it follows from trying to manipulate its timing and forms of appearance so that it causes least disruption. The replacement of 'pain behaviours' by 'well behaviours' is guided by beliefs about what is personally and socially desirable. To achieve this end requires that therapist and patient work together, either to silence pain or else to give it acceptable forms of expression. This is a choice that Kugelmann sees as rendering pain either meaningless or as meaningful only when it is not socially disruptive. As a consequence, the objectification of pain implicit in this therapeutic practice fails to comprehend the conditions that produce suffering and, equally important, the consequences of silencing the patient's voice. From the perspective of the pain clinic, what remains to be understood is what is there to be changed, or can be considered changeable. All else is without meaning.

In this chapter I shall take up this issue of the 'meaningfulness' of suffering, with respect to pain and other matters. The reason for doing this is to question the ways that health psychologists, among others, make suffering meaningful. One might go further and say that the question ought to be posed as to whether suffering ought to be 'made meaningful' at all, if by that we mean it rendered generally understandable for others. Immediately, a further question can be asked about the conditions under which suffering is to be made meaningful – when, where, for whom and, most important perhaps, for what purpose? Somewhere between the idea that suffering is without meaning and the idea that it should be communicated lies a ground that provokes questions about how this is achieved, and where it is allowed to fail. For the possibility must also be considered that we do not always wish to know about suffering, or at least that we acknowledge it by means of keeping it in the shadows, so to speak.

This question of meaning making where suffering is concerned invites consideration of how this is achieved in the pain clinic, for example. Kugelmann (1998) goes on to note that the recruitment of the patient as person in the control of pain experience requires that she be open in the reporting of her experiences. The visibility of the patient in this scheme of things mirrors her visibility under the scrutiny of medicine, which has, with the emergence of the chronically ill, widened its surveillance to include both feelings and lifestyle (Armstrong 1984). The openness of the patient is a requirement in any medical endeavour (that includes health psychology) whose therapeutic aims develop in relation to new ideas such as 'quality of life'. That is, the meaning that can be made of suffering is inseparable from the practices in which medicine engages, and hence from the therapeutic relationships in which patients and medical professionals are joined together.

One consequence of this for the present chapter is that we shall need to address the issue of how evidence about suffering is elicited, by whom and for what purposes. Having determined a problem in the context of the objectification of pain, we are then obliged to follow up this point in the context of the wider issue of suffering. The assumption that suffering is, simply, an important topic that health psychologists ought to study is then made part of a larger question. This is realised by describing the interpersonal contexts in which suffering is or is not acknowledged and, following that, is understood in terms of the response that it calls out in others.

If, in this chapter, we are to examine the implications of these points for a critical understanding of suffering, we need to analyse some of the practical relationships in which it is encountered in the sick. By practical relationships I do not mean the technology of the clinic, but the social and psychological features that either encourage or discourage the acknowledgement of suffering and, with that, the actions that follow from these different possibilities.

Communicating Suffering

The methods of the pain clinic critiqued above are premised upon a recognition that suffering and pain are not the same things. While severe and long-lasting pain produces suffering, so does the belief that one's pain cannot be controlled, or that it may become worse to the point that it will become unbearable. As Cassell (1991) has pointed out, once patients gain the knowledge that their pain can be controlled, then their suffering is often diminished. This is not merely an informational advance, but a reduction in the threat to their sense of themselves as persons. Suffering can then be recognised as not the pain itself, nor the perceived consequences of pain but the apprehension of being overwhelmed by it. This is why suffering can be relieved even as pain continues, and thence why – to some degree – the methods of the pain clinic share in this insight. Cassell goes on to draw the important conclusion that if it is the antici-patory element of being out of control, of being overwhelmed, that is crucial to suffering, then suffering has a crucial temporal dimension. This is not merely a matter of predicting specifiable events that might happen (for example, 'When in pain I might not be able to be with people') but is an orientation towards the future, an anticipatory way of being in which the person senses total engulfment. As part of this, it is important to note that, 'at the moment the individual is saying, "If the pain continues like this, I will be overwhelmed" he or she is *not* overwhelmed' (Cassell 1991: 36, emphasis in original). This indicates that the state of 'being in suffering' is not the same as either its antici-pation, or the reporting of it as an experience from one's past. Of course, one may suffer in apprehension (this is Cassell's point) just as well as one might do in the course of remembering the time when one was overwhelmed. However, there is a distinction here within the 'times of suffering', that points not only to differences in the way it might be apprehended by other people (including health psychologists) but also to the ontological status of suffering itself.

We can obtain a further purchase on this issue by examining reports of suffering in people's stories about their illness. Charmaz (1999) describes the varied forms in which suffering is revealed in people's accounts of illness, especially relating to chronic disease. From her interviews, she notes that people rarely use the word suffering (though she acknowledges that it might not be a favoured North American form of expression). Instead, they mention the various problems, pains and difficulties that are part of their illness situation or have arisen from it. As she says, 'Talking about events that indicate past suffering is one thing; identifying self as continually suffering is quite another' (1999: 366). This indicates, once more, that suffering is not to be equated either with bodily feeling or with events in the outside world. And, yet, its articulation will often be in terms of these matters, precisely because, as a state of being, it is intangible, inexpressible in its elusiveness as a specifiable object. That is why it might be only some time after a person has undergone extremely testing experiences that these are recalled in the context of a story. Charmaz makes the point that some silent or ignored suffering can only be reclaimed when the person feels it is safe to do so.

What is clear from this, coupled with the points made by Cassell, is that suffering as understood is inseparable from its communicability to other people. When undergoing suffering, people may find it impossible to convey that which engulfs them. What is communicable to other people is the apprehension of, or the memory of, changes to self and world that suffering induces. It is quite possible, then, that others identify these expressions of pain and loss as being suffering itself. Out of this it is possible to consider the person 'as sufferer' in the light of having coped with the events that attach to his or her illness situation. Social judgements can then be made concerning the degree to which the person coped well with difficulties, so that suffering itself becomes a means by which the person can lay claim to a higher moral status. Once communicated in this way, suffering gains a social form, or rather the person's experience is made available as a concrete instance to which ideologies of coping can be applied. It is in this way that individual suffering enters the social arena, which it must do if the person is to be helped or treated by medicine, or by any other agency. It would appear that suffering cannot remain mute if it is to be answered.

The requirement for suffering to be communicated provides for a therapeutic response. Equally, from the perspective of medical power, the need for professionals to provide therapy necessitates that the patients speak 'in their own interests' (Armstrong 1984). And because that response is social, it is always value laden and hedged by its own practical possibilities. That is why medical practitioners who must deal with suffering so often have difficulties understanding it in medical terms. Medical knowledge is concerned with the physical body, which means that what is treatable is what is specifiable within the terms of physiology. Inevitably, then, the relief of suffering by medicine is always the product of work done on the physical body. This is precisely the aim of both patient and doctor (would anyone in severe pain have it otherwise?). However, it means that the comprehension of suffering is inevitably subverted by the need to treat. This matters very much when it comes to circumstances where medicine cannot relieve pain, for example, and where it cannot effect a cure, for another.

What this means is that the communicability of suffering arises precisely alongside the prospect (the danger) of suffering remaining mute. This question of muteness becomes a possibility that can be entertained only when we consider suffering in the context of the motivations and practices of sufferer and Other. Once communicated, the richness and the layered experiences that the term summarily labels – through the vegetative, appetitive and conative aspects of being (van Hooft 2000) – become the varieties of experience that researchers know as 'suffering'. And yet there remains the issue of the role that the researcher plays in the invitation for people to express or to describe their suffering. In addition, there are questions as to the consequences for patients of communicating these experiences to others, and of the response to their expressions that comes in return. As mentioned above, there is a moral dimension to being a sufferer, so there is perhaps a moral dimension to the act of inquiring into suffering. What is told, what can be told and what are the possible responses to expressions of suffering all bear upon the question of what suffering 'is'.

From these remarks it should be clear that we have put in question the idea that suffering is a kind of experience only. It clearly is that, but it is also both more and less. It is more in the sense that it involves other people in their response to the sufferer, and it is less in the sense that it resists being transformed by social schemes of understanding. I shall address both of these issues in the sections to follow.

Acknowledging Compassion: Suffering, Other and Self

In this section, I want to consider the idea that to understand suffering we need to acknowledge its counterpart – compassion. The idea of compassion presupposes that one person may know another's suffering and make an appropriate response. Indeed, the coupling of these terms makes for a complete praxis that implies a proper and balanced response of (observing) Other to (suffering) person. And, yet, this cannot be the only possibility, for the social response will depend upon the positioning of the Other within society – their prior experience of suffering and their participation in the workings of society that channel responses to need. Depending upon one's social positioning with regard to these matters, there follows very different ideas about what should be done for which groups in need (Radley 1999a). However, the idea of compassion as a legitimate feature of health research depends upon the acceptance of the notion of frailty as a guiding concept in understanding social relationships. This acceptance in turn depends upon seeing compassion as a continuing and extensive potential in social life, rather than a pre-modern response to be surpassed by the skills deployed by medical technology.

This means that the link between suffering and compassion is by no means a foregone conclusion, if we mean by this that every instance of suffering will produce a compassionate response in the Other. Events from around the world throughout the 20th century have shown that this is not the case. There is no guarantee that suffering will be appropriately responded to, and there is some haziness about what an appropriate response would be. Both of these difficulties are implicit in the need to resolve the issues concerning the communicability of suffering and the proper response to make to it. The fact that, in the health care context, these two terms directly imply each other is actually a barrier to our analysis of suffering, not an aid to understanding. We still have to say under what conditions suffering is likely to be apprehended and what kinds of response are possible. Only then will we be in a position to examine the question raised at the outset of this chapter, concerning the problem of what can be learned from *desisting* to ask patients to reveal their suffering. The question here is not how to find out more about suffering, but to turn this on its head and say, 'What are the proper responses to make so that suffering is understood, even where it cannot be explained?' This approach might go some way towards a critical appreciation of the therapeutic role of health psychologists in a context where their contribution has traditionally been to make things explicit in order to bring them under control.

Levinas (1988) put forward the idea that suffering is a vulnerability, so that it is more than mere receptivity or things just happening to you. It is a passivity, which is a 'pure undergoing'. From this point Levinas proposes that, intrinsically, suffering is 'for nothing', it is useless. He says this to counter the historic theodicy that has seen suffering as having its point in the struggles that people make when in the throes of illness. This idea has its modern counterpart in the moral demands that are made upon the sick to bear up in the face of illness (Charmaz 1999), to fight or otherwise counter the oppressive onslaughts of diseases like cancer (Sontag 1978). A human morality of goodness is coupled with an ideology of fitness to espouse the ways that the sick should bear their troubles. This enables their suffering to be justified through the ways that they have coped with them. In this, says Levinas, there emerges the 'scandal' that follows from my justifying my neighbour's suffering.

His counter to this is, first, the acceptance of the uselessness of suffering for the sufferer. This occurs for all who suffer, but can be more easily comprehended if one thinks of the suffering of those who are unable to conceptualise their situation. Some who are severely mentally disabled might fall in this category. But their suffering – like that of very young children – is precisely that which calls out a response in many healthy people. Their innocence and their inability to help themselves are the conditions for their suffering to be apprehended as pure, as unsullied by the politics of presentation or group. No matter what limitation the sufferer might have with respect to a comprehension of their agonies, Levinas points to the fact that their suffering is exposed *to me*, so that it takes its shape in the relationship between us. From this perspective, he says, 'a radical difference develops between *suffering in the Other*, which for me is unpardonable and solicits me and calls me and suffering *in me*...whose congenital uselessness can take on a meaning...in becoming a suffering for the suffering – be it inexorable – of someone else' (1988: 159). This suggestion poses together the issues of muteness and sociality in relation to this topic. First, that the Other's suffering has no intrinsic form, that it will not be further revealed through inquiry and explanation. Second, that the Other's suffering recognised in my own experience is that which provides not an explanation but a demand for a response, that in its immediacy is termed compassionate. And it is this demand that Levinas (1988: 158) sees as issuing in the medical response, which offers analgesia, 'more pressing, more urgent in the groan than a demand for consolation or a postponement of death'. That is to say, the medical response is premised upon the recognition of suffering which is at the root of all therapeutic endeavour. To discuss suffering is not to explore a derivative of health care delivery but to address its basis in human relations.

In addition, the recognition of suffering in the Other is seen here as less an explanation (of suffering) than as being the condition for, what we might term, its legitimated presence. By this is meant the failure to acknowledge the 'uselessness' of total suffering – and with that, the inability to provide relief or make it sensible – is actually to banish it further by 'speaking over it'. Whatever might be understood about suffering is therefore contingent upon acknowledging that, in evoking compassion in me, its potential lies in the acceptance of its 'uselessness'. This has implications for the psychological study of suffering of any degree, and for attempts to alleviate it in the clinical context. It also raises questions about the contingencies under which compassion might or might not arise, as well as the social mechanisms there might be for responding to another person's pain. We need to examine both of these things first before returning to questions about the way that suffering might be addressed within health psychology.

From what has been said already, it is clear that to know suffering requires more than the verbal summary of feelings or the analysis of discourse. Merely to summarise another's agony, to locate and bound it, is actually to diminish it and ultimately to dismiss it. It is to fall short in respect of engaging with the Other's way of being, so that their feelings are apprehended as surface objects to which a technical or generalised response is appropriate. On the other hand, to be so suffused with the other person's agony as to be rendered immobile by it is to pass beyond its acknowledgement to a state where one lives more fully in one's own suffering than in theirs. Both of these responses fall short of what is required of a compassionate response, which must issue in the giving of aid to the Other. For, it is in the Other's knowing that their suffering is acknowledged *by you* that its muteness is overcome; not by explanation, but in the course of it being recognised for what it is.

It has been argued that compassion – the recognition of suffering – requires a particular act of imagination on our part (Piper 1991). This raises the question of how easy it is for us to do this, in cases where we do not have first hand experience of severe pain or of serious illness. Why, for example, should we expect any health psychologist to be able to make this empathic connection? It is certainly wrong to demand that it be achieved successfully, but it is not out of the way to expect that it be attempted – as it so often must be. From the position of a commentary on practice, the issue is first to articulate the necessity, the desirability and the legitimacy of making such empathic connections.

My argument is that this is necessary in a context of care where the need to specify methods and technologies of response to suffering is overwhelming. A further part of this argument is that, for health psychologists especially, a critical appreciation of suffering as a basic feature of human relations is surely a *sine qua non* of their professional education.

But what of the potential for imaginatively grasping another person's suffering? If it cannot be specified, how do we know that we have grasped the essentials? If one has never experienced suffering of that kind, how can one grasp it in another? This is not too far from saying that no man can understand what it is like for a woman to be raped, or that no member of a racial majority can understand the pains of racial harassment. Piper (1991) makes the point that this position is all too often a way to shift the burden of having to make the attempt at any understanding at all. Instead, we need to recognise that while we might not know precisely the feelings of the Other, the conditions of suffering, as with other feelings, of pleasure, of sublimity, of horror, are of this kind too. I think the word precisely is important here, for it connotes 'exactly', 'directly'. In fact, we do know about other's feelings, even when they are not physically present to us. This happens through the ways that they are shown forth in, or made apparent in being performed within such things as music, painting, drama, narrative and painting. But this way of knowing is not through denoting, isolating, or describing feelings. Instead, understanding is achieved through grasping meaning by mimetically endorsing the Other's act – by 'living along with' the music/the story/the painting as it illustrates matters that cannot be specified, but which can only be set forth (p. 1). The symbolic form of this presentation (expressed in a word, a line or a tone) *is the shape of suffering*, and the witnessing of it when issuing in action is the structure of that act of imagination visibly enacted (Scarry 1985).

The problem with invoking art as expressive of feeling in this context is that such performances are not about the artist's personal emotions. They do not convey what the artist felt at the time, and as such are not 'outerings' of bodily passion, even though this is often the popular view. But suffering – of the moment – is precisely about the conveyance of what is unutterably felt at the time. It is elusive in the time-space it creates because it disables the sufferer, thus preventing any aesthetic expression that could show 'what it is like' to another. This in turn creates – in the groan, the physical state of dis-ease – the sign of its presence in the Other that simultaneously nullifies the adequacy of any adequate communicative bridge for those present. And at this point, there is no certainty that those present can do other than sense that suffering is there, and with that their own helplessness to do anything about it.

Compassion Gives Shape to Suffering

While compassionate responses may be considered appropriate, they cannot be guaranteed, nor their absence always a matter for condemnation. To illustrate this point, let me give an example from my own research experience. As part of a current project about recovery from surgery, I recently sought the consent for interview of a woman patient who was to be operated upon the next day in the course of treatment for cancer. It happened that her husband (a physician) was also present and he explained to me that her involvement in the project was probably dependent upon the outcome of her operation. As she was someone with a history of serious disease, the next day's surgery was to determine if any further treatment was possible, or whether medical interventions had reached their limit, with all the implications that would mean. I felt profoundly the difficulty of their situation, waiting to know what would happen over the next twenty-four hours, and aware that my request for her participation in the research was, at best, a minor irritation for them.

On leaving the hospital, I met my wife, as arranged, at a nearby supermarket where we were to buy some food for the day. Travelling up and down the aisles of the shop, picking up and putting down this or that possible foodstuff, the full force of the couple's situation was brought home to me. Suddenly, in the act of reaching for some trivial item, our seemingly limitless scope of action made their suffering tangible for me for the first time, in a way it had not been when I spoke to them in the hospital. I reflected on our relative situations; to be able to move about the shop (*versus* not to be trapped in a side room on a hospital ward), to be able to plan one's own eating for the evening (not to be denied food in preparation for surgery), for my wife and I to plan together the next twenty-four hours (not to have that time sense, perhaps ever again). And all of these things seemed to surface at once in the act of that reaching for a packet, so that I knew the couple's suffering through its implied absence (as an active emptiness) in the fullness of the presence of the world enjoyed by me and my wife at that time.

There is nothing so special here that could not be matched, I am sure, by any number of examples from people working in a range of health care capacities. The point I want to make, however, is that suffering is mute but need not be silent, and that compassionate responses (even if they do not issue in action) involve acts of imagination that depend upon being able to empathise in ways that are not always under rational control. The guilt of those who witness suffering without being able to alleviate it comes, in part, from the mistaken belief that because compassion is morally desirable it must be accessible, choosable, directable. This is far from the case and is complicated by the presence of so many technical frameworks through which the healthy can respond to the sick. It must be remembered that, in a technological world, compassion is not always the appropriate or indeed the professional response to make (Hafferty 1991).

All that I have said so far concerns compassion, which has been argued to be more than a response to suffering, but its condition of recognition. However, suffering does not always make its appearance locally, so that one could even attempt to alleviate it. There is the suffering of refugees that we see on TV, the suffering of those in hospices for the dying, of whom we might only hear, the suffering of children who are maltreated by parents or guardians. And the list could go on. In these cases of 'distant suffering' (Boltanski 1999) there has emerged political mechanisms to deal with cases that are deserving, so that the response is not to the suffering of any individual about which *I* could do anything, but the suffering of many, to which I might make a response. This response is *pity*, as compared to compassion, the former being premised upon a social distance manifested in the techniques and structures that society has put in place. Where compassion issues in an immediate response to the sufferer, by comparison pity is mediated by techniques and structures. It is to the general condition that pity answers, and its political form makes possible changes in the situation of those so afflicted. Charitable organisations and medicine engage suffering on this level, setting up durable institutions to respond to need. A politics of pity demands a 'kind of procession or imaginary *demonstration* of unfortunates' (Boltanski 1999: 12, emphasis in the original), brought together on the basis of both their individual suffering and other features that they have in common. In this way, it is not just *that patient there* who calls out a response in us, but also *any patient in that situation* who could have done the same.

Within medicine, therefore, we find scope for pity as well as for compassion. It is beyond the scope of this chapter to consider the various contingencies that give rise to one or other, or both. It is enough that we recognise that making a medical intervention (or a health psychological one) depends upon the deployment of techniques that have a distancing effect upon the practitioner's sensibilities. This is not a criticism of practitioners in any way, but a recognition that health psychologists, like doctors (less so nurses), operate with techniques that are conceived to treat general classes of disease or suffering. The organisation of medicine into nosological groups, and the way that this is so often followed in health psychology, produces a response to the general class of patient, to the sick. This does not mean that pity is necessarily the response of practitioner to patient, particularly where this interferes with medical practice: the use of medical techniques aims precisely at removing the causes of disease in order to alleviate suffering. This is the aim and, where it succeeds, the triumph of allopathic medicine. However, it is the extension of this approach to an understanding of the patient's troubles, in the widest sense, that produces a health psychology that aims to counter suffering by control, to relieve by minimising, and where possible excluding the very aspects of suffering that call out for acknowledgement.

To understand this we need to look more closely at how this is done and at its implications. The context for this inquiry is not the pain clinic, but some of the newer approaches to the understanding of the sick within health psychology.

Suffering: The Inappropriateness of Explanation

We are now in a position to return to the question of what it means for health psychology to research suffering. While I began with some critical comments about the methods of the pain clinic, we also saw that these same criticisms might be levied at attempts to explain suffering in the wider sense. The question then arises: Is suffering just another topic for health psychology, so that we should aim to have explanations of it and techniques for diverting it?

From what has been said so far in this chapter, suffering is not an emotion that belongs with the patient, but is inseparable from its recognition by the witness. The acknowledgement of suffering – of its uselessness – has been suggested as key to the recognition that it is only to be understood through practical engagements. In some of these, perhaps where extremes of suffering are involved, that agony must remain mute and unavailable to the psychologist *as researcher*. This does not mean that it is unavailable to the psychologist *as person*, although (as with my trip to the supermarket) it might have to involve other aspects of their lives to give some shape to their apprehension of the ailing person's experience.

If this is the case, then the question arises as to whether attempts to provide suffering with a form – to denote it directly – might be inappropriate. From the standpoint of seeing the researcher as someone who aims merely to ascribe feeling, to categorise experience, this is certainly the case. Such surface interpretations – albeit in the name of method – do nothing but transgress the requirement that the muteness of suffering be respected. We saw earlier on that we can learn much about suffering from people's stories of their illness (Charmaz 1999). Clearly, careful attention to the stories of sufferers is a primary road to an understanding of the pains that accompany ill health. And, yet, there are questions as to whether the analysis of illness narratives alone – taken as texts read by a third party – might void the conditions for acknowledging suffering that were set out above. I am thinking here particularly of cases where the researcher's analysis centres upon what is given in the text. If we know that suffering is mute, we should not only recognise it when it is given voice.

This issue was first raised for me by DiGiacomo (1992), in a paper where she took issue with critics of Sontag's book *Illness as Metaphor* (1978). These critics had upbraided Sontag for her insistence that the proper response to cancer was to face it as a biological entity, stripped of all social metaphor. There is a legitimate argument to be made here, because much about illness experience can be understood through metaphor (not just the stigmatising metaphors that Sontag criticised). However, DiGiacomo's argument was that to make the text primary, to make discourse central, is to reduce living and dying to footnotes. By portraying illness experience as a story that counters the social milieu from which disease is engendered, or as a narrative that restores the dignity of patients who have been objectified by medicine, one runs the risk of 'recruiting suffering into the service of an ideological agenda' (1992: 126). It is interesting that Arthur Frank, someone who has written extensively about his own and other people's experience of illness, should have questioned recently whether qualitative research enhances recognition of suffering without qualification (Frank 1991, 2001). The qualification here refers to the fact that sociological (and by the same token, psychological) texts are extra-local, employing discourses that subjugate the experience of persons to the powers that are inherent in those discourses. Breaking up narratives, categorising experiences, moving away from context, the health psychologist using the new critical methods might not be so far from the health psychologists of the pain clinic. By this, I mean that suffering is once again *made to appear*, forced out into the open, this time on different grounds and in different ways, but still on the terms of the researcher, not the sufferer.

What can the analysis made in this chapter contribute to this debate? Probably, it is the suggestion that we see suffering not as a topic, nor as a facet of the experience of ill persons. Just as suffering has been shown to be more than pain, so I have argued that suffering is more than conscious experience, more than can be said in words or even should be said in words. This 'more than' extends to the fact that suffering is mute and social, that it is inseparable in its appearance from compassion (for to fail to acknowledge fully another's suffering is to be without compassion). Compassion, as compared with pity, is direct and unmediated. It is there in the hand stretched out, the cover pulled over; it is by definition local. We can, of course, talk about it, just as long as we do not confuse our talk about suffering with suffering itself. This seems almost too naive a statement to be making today, except that the advice to ourselves to remember the elusory nature of such things as suffering and compassion need to be made over and over again. This is lest we continually fall back into a reification of those matters we hold most important to understand.

Key Points

- People who are ill suffer. One of the key roles of health psychologists is to understand the experience of suffering.
- A challenge to health psychology is that in many ways suffering is mute. While the descriptive study of illness narratives can provide some insight into the experience of suffering it also requires an act of the imagination.
- Suffering is a social experience. To understand suffering one has to acknowledge its counterpart – compassion. It is compassion that gives shape to suffering.

Assignment Questions

1. Discuss the differences between 'pain' and 'suffering' as problems for the health psychologist. What do these differences imply about the role of the health psychologist in the clinic?
2. Survey attempts to study suffering through patients' stories and accounts relating to their illness experiences. What can health psychologists learn about suffering from such stories, and what are their limitations?
3. Consider some examples of suffering that might arise from different circumstances. To what extent do these different contexts contribute to the way that suffering might be borne?

Note

1. For an extended discussion of this topic in relation to illness, especially concerning illness narratives, see Radley (1999b).

📖 Further Readings

Cassell, E.J. (1991) *The Nature of Suffering: And the Goals of Medicine*, New York: Oxford University Press.

This has been an influential book in the field because it provides a comprehensive examination of suffering within the clinical setting. It also makes a critical analysis of what modern medicine can and should aim to achieve in the context of recognising suffering as key to patient care.

Charmaz, K. (1999) 'Stories of suffering: subjective tales and research narratives', *Qualitative Health Research*, 9, 362–382.

This is a very useful paper that examines how suffering enters the sphere of research through narrative. It is a good introduction to how suffering is communicated through patients' stories and the ways in which this experience might be subjected to qualitative analysis.

Frank, A. (1995) *The Wounded Storyteller: Body, Illness and Ethics*, Chicago: University of Chicago Press.

Arthur Frank's work on people's stories of illness experience is central to developments in medical sociology. Frank writes as a survivor of cancer and its treatment and is concerned with the ethics of care and the witnessing of suffering. Using numerous examples, his book explores the diverse ways in which people recount their experiences of being ill, and how in the course of talking about these experiences they are able to place their suffering in a new light.

Scarry, E. (1985) *The Body in Pain: The Making and Unmaking of the World*, New York: Oxford University Press.

Elaine Scarry's book is essential reading for anyone wanting to understand suffering as that which can be communicated and yet also inflicted. Drawing on work in the humanities, as well as philosophy and phenomenology, this book provides a theoretical framework for the student wishing to put suffering in a wider context.

Sontag, S. (1978) *Illness as Metaphor*, New York: Farrar, Straus and Giroux.

This is now a minor classic in the field of health and illness. Sontag explores the way that metaphors about disease and illness have created burdens for the sick. The tenor of the book is that metaphor constructs how people see the sick and recognise (and often turn away from) their suffering. But the thesis unfolded at the end is that only biomedicine can provide relief and hope for cancer sufferers. Written at a time when she was diagnosed with breast cancer, this seeming paradox in Sontag's book points up the questionable value of talking about other people's suffering when you cannot provide them with any relief.

CHAPTER 3

Health and Illness: A Hermeneutical Phenomenological Approach

Robert Kugelmann

Summary

A hermeneutical phenomenological or relational approach looks at health and illness as ways of being-in-the-world. It looks at being healthy and being ill as experiences. An experience takes *place*, that is, it occurs in a concrete situation involving me and others living within a historical, cultural, social setting. Health and illness are types of dramas or games, metaphors chosen to emphasize the situational character of health and illness. On this basis, some useful distinctions help us understand how to accomplish a critical health psychology: We distinguish being healthy and being ill as dramas of human existence. Disease and standardized health are medically defined abstractions that usurp our understandings of being healthy and ill, and they are contemporary forms of being well and ill. These abstractions help to preserve the privacy and autonomy of the individual. The chapter ends with a call for a truly critical health psychology, one that keeps alive a philosophical questioning.

Introduction

> Or must sickness and death in general – even from a medical point of view – be primarily conceived as existential phenomena? (Heidegger 1962: 291)

A hermeneutical phenomenological approach starts with events, with what takes place in human existence. We start with events taken existentially, that is, with how they mean *me* or *you* or *us*. The basic idea behind this approach is that self and situation belong together as one structure. I exist within situations and they are a part of me. Things, places, and others matter to me. I cannot conceive of anything in my life that does not *take place* somewhere. This humble truth underlies a hermeneutical phenomenological approach in health psychology. For this reason, I call this a relational approach.

The term "hermeneutical phenomenology" derives from Heidegger (1962) and Gadamer (1978), and in psychology it means that we begin with *exist-ence*: with the ways a person finds himself or herself in situations with others (Van Kaam 1963). Health and illness are ways that we find ourselves. As such, health and illness are modes of our existing, our living. A hermeneutical phenomenological approach views health and illness as structures of existence, that is, as webs of meanings. In psychology there are approaches related to a hermeneutical phenomenological one, such as social constructionism, Gestalt psychology, narrative psychology and psychodynamic psychology. These approaches also emphasize the situatedness of human behavior and experience, and they stress the activity of the subject in making and finding meaning in the situation.

This approach differs from the biomedical approach to health and disease. Biomedicine specifies a disease as an effect of a physiologically defined malfunction. In seeking the causes of disease, it looks to the body as defined anatomically. Even where psychological and social factors influence the disease process, physiological mediators must form a link between them and the disease process. In contrast, a hermeneutical phenomenological analysis looks at sickness and health as ways that a person is. Being sick and being well are ways that I am, just as I am loving, envious, honest, dying. Another way to indicate the different starting points is to say that biomedicine begins with diseased physiological processes, and that hermeneutical phenomenology begins with the *experience* of *being*-ill and *being*-healthy.

Health and Illness as Experience and as Games

The term *experience* has two distinct but related meanings. First, it means that an event I live through has a relationship with my life. "In my experience, people are trustworthy" and "Now, I've really experienced love" are examples of this meaning, which emphasizes how I appropriate something that is personal. Second, it means an undergoing, a living through something that teaches me something about myself and the world. "Job applicants must have experience," is an instance of this meaning. In the course of such experience one undergoes a reversal: something happens contrary to what one had expected. Illness and suffering may be the "original" of experience in this regard. In serious illness, reversals or negations of expectations, indeed, of living, take place. Crossley (2000) describes the "shattered assumptions" about time, one's body, and others that pain and illness entail. Gadamer (1978: 357), more generally, writes that "experience is experience of human finitude." An illness entails a crisis – even if only as a disruption of my daily routine – and makes of it an experience. An experience in this second sense may alter one's understanding of one's self and world.

An experience *puts into play* the one who suffers a reversal. Gadamer (1978) uses play as a paradigm of all experience. I extend his analysis for an understanding of health and illness. Let me put it by way of metaphor: Health is a game. Illness is a game. Metaphors are not identities, so that I do not mean that health and illness are trivial. When the poet said, "My love is a red, red rose," he did not mean that she was a flower. To make the point clearer, let me put it this way: Health is a game of football: Not when considered outside the stadium by someone who has no interest in football, but by the players on the field, by the coaches with their clipboards, by the spectators who love the home team and have wagers riding on the game. The game organizes what these people do and say and experience: A football player cannot pick up a baseball bat and hit the ball or another player; a coach cannot kick the ball away from an opponent; and the spectators cannot enter the field. If any of these things happen – and they do, of course – the play breaks down, "all hell breaks loose," something else must then happen. Such are the experiences of health and illness.

I mean more than that for in health we play social roles, we do not take up the sick role, social expectations govern what we say and do. Health is a game means that it is a structure of existence. As a structure, it entails a situation, within which I and others find ourselves. This situation is not limited to the physical or the socioeconomic aspects of the situation. It includes the cultural and epistemic contours of the situation. To say it another way, health has a symbolic structure. The symbolic order provides important rules of the games of health and illness, within which we find ourselves. They are, of course, changeable.

An Example of a Relational Approach to Illness

A young man is in a room in his grandfather's house. In the next room, with the door closed, his father is helping his grandfather get out of a wheelchair and into bed. His grandfather is screaming in pain and confusion. He allows no one but his son to help him into bed. The young man finds the room oppressive, filled with tension. His sister is with him, crying, because her grandfather, once so strong is now so weak. The young man feels helpless too, and he tries to console his sister and himself. His younger brother walks into the room, annoyed at the "scene" grandfather is creating, and the young man sees this annoyance and becomes enraged with his brother. No one goes into the room where his grandfather is, out of respect for their grandfather's wishes. Eventually, the old man is settled in bed and he quiets down. The young man's father opens the door, comes out visibly shaken, and closes the door behind him.

The old man is sick, crippled with arthritis and pain and mental confusion. But where – and this is the relational question – is the illness? As this narrative recounts, it filled the room where his grandfather was absent, both physically and temporally, since they knew him in happier times, when he was in the fullness of health. The narrator describes the atmosphere of the room as "red," and in this word he evokes the presence of his grandfather's suffering as it pervaded the room and the family. Grandfather was hurting, and the pain was irrevocably *his*, to be sure. But the pain was also the grandson's, inalienably *his* as well. His sister's anguish, that the young man shared and sought to console, was *hers*. This was an event of the agony of illness, *their* agony, *their* illness. The anguish and the pain and the loss of grandfather's health, his decline and perhaps dying, were centrally located in this narrative – around the door. The closed door, the door that no one dared open, the door that had not been locked but was shut more tightly than if it had been. This closed door embodied this tormenting illness. Behind it someone was hurting, and no one could do anything. If we should understand this illness that the grandson experiences, we need to understand that door. As Lang (1984: 144) writes: "Though the door is the icon of intersubjectivity, it also speaks of a basic rift in our dialogue with others." The illness took place around that door.

A Relational Approach

What takes place has form. This form is spatial, temporal, social, historical, and personal. In the example above, I primarily address the "lived space" (Bollnow 1961) of the illness. The illness takes place in a particular physical, familial, and cultural place. There were family dynamics going on that we can only speculate about. The construction of the house, with rooms separated by doors is not inevitable. The family and the house reflect the symbolic and imaginary orders (Lacan 1978) in an ongoing drama. The layout of the rooms embodies gender and kinship relations, as well as the privacy characteristic of the modern age (Sennett 1977; Perrot 1990). For mainstream health psychology, in deference to medicine, the disease is located in the body, where biomedical procedures can find it and treat it. The relational approach does not dispute the corporeal location of sickness. But the place of sickness entails more than the physiological body. Its place is the situation.

What takes place has a temporal form characterized by the primacy of the future (Heidegger 1962: 386), by a present moment that endures, embracing what has been and what is coming, and by historicity. In the example above, the futurity of the event was in dread and anguish: Will this screaming stop? Is he dying? Its present was lived as endless. A glance at a clock might have surprised the young man at the small span of time the transfer of grandfather to bed lasted. Finally, the illness had a historical dimension in the lives of this young man and his family. Its historicity showed in the possibilities for action, in the materiality of the situation (the wheelchair, the diagnosis, and so on), in the understanding of what constitutes illness, old age, and care.

What takes place has a ground in the lived body (Straus 1980; Csordas 1994). The body, symbolized in various ways, including anatomy and traditional

Chinese medicine, is the navel of any situation, its primary place. The self or "I" is situated through embodiment. The lived body knows the world in a sensorimotor way, in intentionalities below and prior to explicit cognition, in gestural display (Toombs 1992). In illness, the "I am able" (Merleau-Ponty 1945/1962) of the lived body yields to an "I cannot." In the story above, the closed door made palpable the family's helplessness, its "we cannot."

An experience has boundaries, and beyond them, has an exteriority of what cannot be assimilated or symbolized. Death is the primary exteriority. The grandfather's anguish, indeed, all the participants' anguish, indicated something outside. For each of them, there was a closed door. Freud (1923/1961) spoke of a "stimulus barrier" that protects us from being overwhelmed by events; when breached, there is pain and possibly trauma. The intrusion of pain, suffering and death occurs in the screams from behind the closed door.

What takes place is a movement (an action, a change, or an undergoing). These movements are not the transpositions of a thing from one point to another, but ways of existing, that is, ways whereby one makes and makes manifest who one is. The movement of the narrative above was one of illness. Each of the family members suffered being-ill in different ways. The illness was playing through them all.

What takes place has the structure of a game. The game metaphor, though, sounds heartless in the context of suffering, so let us use another metaphor, drama. A drama includes not only plot and narrative – discourse – but also action and a place, the stage, where the action of the drama unfolds. A drama includes also the spectators. In the context of illness and health, the spectators are not only family members attending to the ill person, but also the doctors and researchers who are *dramatis personae*. One characteristic of drama is that there is no central or privileged point of view that trumps all others. The subjectivities involved are all decentered, including that of the ill person, in the drama of illness. In contrast to more idiographic approaches (Moustakas 1990; Smith *et al.* 1999), a relational approach does not privilege the speaker's meaning. The "I" is decentered, in the situation itself, with a limited view of it. Being healthy and being ill name two types of drama that "I" not only participate in but that "I" *am*.

Health and illness take place as dramas: They have spatial, temporal, social, embodied form. They exist as the total situation wherein we find ourselves.

Being Healthy and Being Ill

Health and illness are games or dramas. That means that they are ways that we are, more than they are qualities that we have. They are never "qualities" in the sense that things have qualities, such as color or size. Health and illness are ways that we dwell or live and, as such, they are possibilities of existing.

They occur as dispositions or attunements toward the world, as ways that we move toward death. Heidegger's analysis of death can serve as a starting point. Dasein, *who* (not *what*) I am, the individual human being in Heidegger's terminology, exists toward death. Dying is not an accidental trait or an imperfection. It is definitive, in more ways than one. A complete relational approach begins with what is non-relational, death, and the ways that we move toward it.

It is vital for health psychology to theorize health and illness. If we do not, we will take over uncritically biomedically and economically oriented constructions of them. It is here that good intentions can do the most harm. Health and illness are first of all ethical and cultural issues, and within these contexts they are medical and psychological issues.

Some Useful Distinctions

It is helpful to distinguish *disease*, *illness* and *sickness*. A disease is a biomedical entity, a physiological dysfunction. Essential hypertension and asthma are diseases. An illness is the experience of being sick. An illness can be a disease, as in the throat pain of a strep infection. Disease may be diagnosable in the absence of illness (as in hypertension), and illness may be present in the absence of disease (no diagnosis has been yet made, the illness is a "culture-bound" illness, or the person does not seek or want medical treatment). Sickness "refers to a particular status or role *in society* and is justified by reference either to the presence of disease or to the experience of illness" (Radley 1994: 3). For a relational approach, illness has a privileged status, since it is the basis for diseases and sickness: If no one had ever felt and acted ill, medicine would never have developed. The dramas of illness are the ground from which specialized knowledge emerges and to which it must return. Illness, then, is a way in which we *are*, a way in which we *find ourselves*.

To complement these distinctions, I propose that for health there is a similar set of terms. To disease corresponds *standardized health*, biomedically determined absence of dysfunctioning. To illness corresponds *being healthy*, the usually subsidiary sense of being able to engage the world. To sickness corresponds the *health role* as the absence of excuses for not assuming responsibilities. Because health is the background, existentially speaking, for illness, we consider being healthy first.

Being Healthy as a Mode of Existing

Being healthy as a mode of existing is well-being, "this condition of... being unhindered, of being ready for and open to everything" (Gadamer 1996: 73). It is a negative state, unmarked (Radley 1994: 6), noticeable primarily in its absence, though it has degrees. We typically have a subsidiary awareness of the body in health, although it can announce itself with exhilaration. An analogy to strength may help: If I have physical strength, then lifting or pulling or running comes as it were done effortlessly. I do not have the experience of duality, of body and soul.

Illich (1985) describes health in terms of subsistence, that is, in terms of the ability to be and to do outside of economic relations. Health in this sense means "aliveness," and Illich writes: "health will be high when survival in a society depends principally upon subsistence activities. Health will be low when subsistence activities have been largely replaced by the production and consumption of commodities" (p. 50). This way of looking at health emphasizes two things. First, it ties it to an idea of what human living means, specifically, to culturally defined understandings of the good life. Second, it ties health to the actuality of living in all its dimensions.

When I am healthy, I am "one," I have no parts, neither of soul nor body, my members geared into my tasks and pleasures. In a fundamental way, health is unity, wholeness. Health actualizes itself in our aliveness – to use Illich's term – by "making our own living" in multiple senses of that phrase. Existence is being-in-the-world with others, engaged in the activities of subsisting. Health does not qualify a world in some abstract way, but in terms of human dwelling and working. The situations of health are those that do not impede human dwelling and working – subsisting.

Health is living well, even in illness. Morris (1998) and Justice (1998) point out that health and illness are not opposites, that people can be healthy even when suffering from a chronic ailment or disability. Health is never complete. If health is "being able," this is always relative ability. To be human is to be disabled in various ways. Not only am I not optimally able; from day to day, from year to year, I have any number of limitations. As Hoinacki (1992) states the case, the fact of being healthy does not abrogate the human condition: "I suffer pain; I am afflicted with certain impairments; I will certainly die." We are tops, health our spin, getting sick and well the wobbles, spinning always until we fall.

Health has its own measure, specific to every individual. Health is a *that* we can recognize, not a *what* we can grasp. It is known precisely by being subsidiary, background. Health is discovered through reflection, especially when we feel sick. Then, we notice that something is wrong, that something is off or missing. The pleasures of recuperation are those of feeling healthy again, a moment we may seek to prolong but never manage to do. There is the enjoyment of well-being, a rudimentary presence to self that we experience when healthy. We are not only engaged with things and others when healthy, we enjoy them and feel the enjoyment. Levinas (1969: 113) writes: "Enjoyment is not a psychological state among others, the affective tonality of empiricist psychology, but the very pulsation of the I." Suffering is "a failing of happiness," (p. 115) a disturbance of the hidden harmony that underlies the self.

Being Ill as a Mode of Existing

Whereas health is recessive, illness stands out, stands over against us as that which resists us. Illness strikes us as other, even when it becomes familiar. Health is well-being, a condition of not being resisted. In health there is openness, lack of obstruction. In illness, we feel "the oppressive weight of things" (Gadamer 1996: 75), the suffocating sense of what Levinas (1978) calls the burden of existence, oppressing in insomnia and fatigue. One's own existence is a weight that cannot be discarded. Everything becomes a chore. If health is engagement in living, forgetful of oneself, in illness we come back to remember ourselves. Forgetfulness (Gadamer 1996: 138) is the means by which the harmony of health is concealed. Forgetfulness is not repression or denial: It is the lightness of being alive. Forgetfulness of self is the condition of being able to enjoy life. The inability to forget one's self reaches a peak in anxiety, and shows itself in ruminations and obsessions in illness, in irritability with disturbances that otherwise would be inconsequential.

Toombs (1992: 33) observes that illness first presents itself prereflectively in "some alien bodily sensation...the sensed experience of a change in function...[or in an awareness of] an alteration in the normal appearance of one's body." This prereflective sensory awareness is in the first instance noticed as a change in the way things and others appear: noises are louder, people are annoying, work is more tedious, sleep is so inviting. Or illness announces itself in a violent "attack" or "spell." We confront here an alteration in "attunement," with how we find ourselves being-*in* a situation. Attunement does not disclose merely one's subjective state, for according to Heidegger, attunement discloses the world and how it matters to us. The existential psychologist Gendlin (1978–1979) concretized this notion of attunement as "felt bodily sensing." It is admittedly difficult to capture easily the basic understanding of this aspect of being ill, for what I am aiming at is an account not of what we *have* but of how and who we *are* in this instance and how our place changes. It is typically the latter, the changing face of our situation, that begins our journey into illness.

The attunement of illness is not only to a specific condition; it is also a sense of simply being ill. Heidegger (1962: 174) writes that for the most part a finding of oneself in attunement "arises not so much from a direct seeking as rather from a fleeing." This is what we do, typically, and to do otherwise is seen by common sense as foolish: We flee illness in attempts toward healing. Surely this is not futile or foolish! The point, though, is that it is a fleeing of what is being revealed, of what is revealed of self and world. In those illnesses that allow no escape in a medical sense, still for the most part we look awry. At the same time, all illnesses are not the same and one's sense of self and world is not the same in all illnesses. For example, back pain following an automobile accident can disclose something about modern transportation that those who have not been injured may not sense, and stomach cramps and diarrhea may disclose yet other aspects of automotive transportation.

The felt bodily sense becomes a symptom when it is interpreted as such, an interpretation that need not be explicitly made; it can occur in a sense of uneasiness, of something being amiss. A symptom may be "an alien body sensation" (Toombs 1992: 33), but to sense something *as* alien is already to interpret it. As Radley (1994: 71) indicates, "symptoms do not necessarily precede sickness; instead, being deemed to be sick is an important element in appearing symptomatic." It may happen that this first interpretation is not made by the soon-to-be feeling ill person, but rather by another person who says, "You don't look well today. What's wrong?" The sensing *as* alien may arise from anywhere within the emerging drama.

It is impossible in a general way to say what will be lived as illness: Much depends on culture, language, gender, social status and other factors, all of which are relevant. There is a decentering from the lived body of health, where it "dis-appears" (Leder 1990) into the background of the event. Now it reappears as an "it." This initial interpretation, made prereflectively, is followed by another interpretation of it as an illness. The interpretation is made in many terms, some of which are biographical, that is, in terms of into which future and from which past the person moves. In addition, the illness is "influenced by the theoretical understandings that are embedded in his or her particular lifeworld" and "according to special significances within the distinctive lifeworlds shaped by class, ethnicity, age and gender" (Toombs 1992: 37).

How one makes these interpretations has much to do with the kinds of "arts of suffering" (Illich 1976) of the culture and time. "Any illness which does not include any possibilities is not a real illness" (Luijpen and Koren 1969: 108), meaning that in any illness, there is still a being-toward some future, however brief. Even in our own day, the illness may or may not become a medical event, that is, involve the health care system. That does not mean that the interpretative framework of the person is non-medical. For many in the world today, no sooner is an illness felt, than it is translated into a disease, on the basis of education and media exposure.

Standardized Health and Disease

> We live . . . in an environment which has been increasingly transformed by science and which we scarcely dare to term 'nature' any more, and . . . in a society which has itself been wholly shaped by the scientific culture of modernity. *Here we must learn to find our way.* (Gadamer 1996: 104, emphasis added)

Being-healthy is not the whole story. It is the phenomenological basis for further considerations of health. Even my being healthy "is a profoundly political issue" (Navarro 1986: 228), because health is a drama. As such, it is alienable, definable by others, often requiring medical determination. So while health has no measure other than the individual or community, it can be subjected to common measures and norms. In the modern world, these common measures occur as biopower, the bringing of the body of the individual and the collective into political and economic spheres (Foucault 1978: 143). Health within the framework of biopower I call "standardized health." Standardized health occurs when norms and risk factors, applicable in principle to everyone, are determined by biomedicine. It takes form at the intersection of two vectors operating in contemporary societies: Biomedical (and increasingly, the biopsychosocial) conceptions of normative functioning intersect the economic definition of well-being as the ability to produce and consume at age-appropriate levels with a minimum of health-care costs. Standardized health is a notion stripped of the historical, cultural and political aspects of health. Health care in this light is an input to improve or restore resources to optimum functioning in the national interest. Standardized health exists as the private property of autonomous individuals, and as health care becomes explicitly an economic thing, that is, a scarce resource, individuals are required to become responsible for this property (Arney and Bergen 1983). It is in this context that we must understand the World Health Organization's utopian definition of health, "Health is a state of complete physical, mental, and social well-being and not merely the absence of disease or infirmity." While the uses of this vague statement are legion, it primarily refers to not subsisting but to capital improvements of individuals and communities so that they are available for economic development.

Disease corresponds to standardized health, as biomedically discerned dysfunction. Strictly speaking, the naming of disease belongs to medicine, although non-professionals appropriate medical discourse and practices in various ways that complicate the picture. Disease and its treatment have privileged positions in contemporary society, for a variety of reasons. From a relational approach, the point is not whether we accept or reject biomedicine, not even whether or not it objectifies human beings, or that it is rooted in a mind-body dualism. Something else is required if we are to "find our way" in the contemporary world.

The overwhelming sense is that people today *believe in* standardized health and disease, see in them indicators of what will determine their well-being, prolong their lives, and cure their ailments. This belief in biomedicine is primary for a relational approach. James (1890: 311) observed that things that "give us sensations, especially interesting ones, or incite our motor impulses, or arouse our hate, desire, or fear, are real enough for us." Biomedical procedures, their effects and side effects "give us sensations" and so are real. They incite belief. Biomedicine has become so much a part of the lifeworld, that even a diagnosis, the mere assertion of the existence of disease, eases pain and distress. Keefe concluded that those who have received a diagnosis "seem to suffer much less than the people who are told, 'We're not really sure what's going on with your pain'" (in "Perspectives on pain and suffering," 1998: 168). Because medical treatments can kill as well as cure, this belief is not groundless. Medicine touches on exteriority.

Standardized health and disease are two of the things that matter to us, and because they matter, they integrate themselves into defining who we are. In a technologized society, being healthy is a drama of standardized health, and being ill of disease. These dramas can include scenes in physicians' offices and in hospitals, and even if they do not, the script for articulating what is going on includes biomedical discourse. The medical drama is one into which we are "thrown," to use Heidegger's term for that which we inescapably are. There is a danger here, as critics of the concept of disease have noted: In defining ill-ess as disease, there is an objectification of illness and of the person. That critique has served its purpose and it is time to listen again to the discourse of medicine as it plays throughout the dramas of our lives.

Heidegger observes that we are beings who tend to understand ourselves in terms of how we understand the things around us (Heidegger 1962: 36–37). In more mundane terms, people who live in industrial societies describe themselves in terms of the machinery that occupies much of their time: as information processors (computer metaphor), as blowing off steam (steam engine metaphor), as running out of gas, even as being under stress (an engineering metaphor) (Kugelmann 1992). In former days, agricultural and seasonal metaphors were more common, for example, in understanding illness in terms of the four humors. This grasp of ourselves in terms of our surrounding world is not so much a mistake as moving astray: Such "worldly" characterizations grasp only an aspect, not the whole of who we are. For a relational perspective, this moving astray becomes a mistake only when the part is taken for whole: human beings are nothing but their physiology or expressions of their ethnic place. The reductionism of biomedicine is such a taking of a part for the whole.

Being healthy and being ill: modes of existence.
Standardized health and disease: (1) biomedically defined conditions; (2) the manner in which being healthy and being ill are experienced in modern societies.

Standardized Health and Disease as Preservers of Autonomy

There is, however, another consideration, one I learned from a eulogy for an old man. The man who died was about 80 years old. The eulogist had visited the old man shortly before his death. The old man was quite ill, looking pale and weakened. He had been ill for many years with a form of leukemia, and he had participated heroically in experimental treatments. The speaker said that the old man was ready to discuss his medical condition but held in reserve, initially, any talk about his suffering. So first they spoke of leukemia. The listener realized that much was being said in what was not being said. Not in what was said, but in the saying of what was said shone some of the significance of his life and sufferings. In using biomedical discourse as a part for the whole (a synecdoche, in rhetorical terms) of his living, the old man gave his listener a glimpse of the depth of his life. That depth came through a discourse on white blood cells, which at the same time concealed what needed to remain veiled at first. The turn from discourse on the disease to direct conversation about suffering came only after the listener, who listened well, saw the joy that the old man radiated. He was ill, he was dying, but there was an attunement of joy and serenity in that discourse on leukemia. Biomedical discourse became, as it were, the poetry of joy and suffering in living and in dying.

That reserve, that sense of limit of what should be said on a given occasion, is a possibility of the dramas of standardized health and disease. It is especially a possibility of the merely negative definition of health so reviled by advocates of holistic approaches: Health as the absence of disease. Disease, as physiological dysfunction, allows the same limits and reserve. If I have an X-ray of my chest, my heart of hearts is never disclosed. Only that which can cast a particular kind of shadow shows up on the film. The medical exam touches the body-in-the-image-of-the-corpse, but does not touch other aspects of my being. The patient gives his or her anatomized body over for the exam, and the physician receives only that. This, an ethical dimension of biomedicine, is mundane and taken for granted in its practice. Biomedical discourse has the merit of severing the connection of disease from sin and moral weakness (Caton 1985). Crossley (2000) discusses the resistance some patients have to psychological interpretations of their illnesses, precisely on moral grounds. Today, we see a tendency to remoralize illness in the demand that the sufferer take responsibility for disease and standardized health. Psychological and other humane accounts of illness tend to remoralize, making that old man's reserve more difficult. The remoralization approaches shamelessness.

Implications for a Critical Health Psychology

The term "critical" has more than one meaning, and only one of them has been intended by the above analysis of health and illness. In this sense, to be critical asks about the conditions of possibility for something to be. A relational approach is critical in that it seeks to articulate the structures of human existence that manifest themselves in health and illness and that necessitate the distinctions made between being healthy and standardized health, and between illness and disease. In another sense, though, the above discussion has not been critical, because it has neglected questions of power and exploitation that also belong to the critical tradition in philosophy and in the human sciences. It is inadequate to say that biomedical discourse implicitly preserves the integrity of the human being, because it limits what it can speak about. Biomedical discourse represents the dominant form of medical discourse, one that is tied intimately with economic power, and it represents a medical industry embodying a technological domination of nature (Ellul 1965; Illich 1992).

Standardized health can be measured by income level on both national and individual levels. The economic underpinning of biomedicine makes of health care a scarce commodity with built-in inequities. Its hegemony by virtue of its scientific mantle silences non-biomedical forms of medical discourse or it assimilates them into its sphere of control. This brief sketch of this second meaning of "critical" is crudely drawn, but the point should be clear: There is a need for a relational health psychology to be in this second sense, a critical health psychology. A relational health psychology must be aware of not only how we "find ourselves" but also of how we are "put in our place" by the dramas and games of health and illness. We psychologists do not find ourselves outside the structures of inequality and lack of liberty. We have dirty hands.

One proposal, however, underlies this entire chapter. It is that a critical health psychology needs an adequate philosophical anthropology. By that I mean rigorous reflection on the question in both the abstract and the concrete sense: Who am I? What kind of being is a human being? Such a rigorous reflection is not practical in the short run and does not facilitate the aspiring psychologists with getting the proper credentials and licensure. But it is precisely an exclusive focus on what are called practical considerations that foreclose the possibility of health psychology becoming a critical health psychology.

Specifically, this proposal means that critical health psychology stay attentive to the dramas of health and illness in which it plays a part. We are in *it*, rather than outside observers. The *it* that we are in is what shows itself in the drama. "What the play is all about?" is the kind of approach that attends to the meaning or the "for the sake of which" illness and health matter to us. They matter to us as mortals, bound for death, living all the while.

Key Points

- Health and illness are experiences: dramas that take place in our social worlds. As the one healthy or ill, the self is within the drama.
- Health and illness have spatial temporal, social, and embodied form.
- Disease and standardized health are biomedical objectifications of these existential dramas.
- Biomedical accounts preserve the autonomy of the individual in its dualistic structure.
- A critical health psychology must be a philosophical discipline as well as an empirical and applied one.

Assignment Questions

1. The distinction between disease and illness is well established in the literature. Discuss the analogous distinction between being healthy and standardized health.

2. Consider an occasion when you have been with someone who is ill. Describe the drama that unfolded, in terms of this chapter.
3. How does biomedicine objectify the human condition? How does it tend to preserve individual autonomy?

📖 Further Reading

Bollnow, O.F. (1961) "Lived-space", *Philosophy Today*, 5, 31–39.

This brief essay spells out structures of spatiality from a phenomenological perspective. It is important reading to help one see past the bias that we tend to have that place can be best understood in terms of Cartesian coordinates.

Gadamer, H.-G. (1996) *The Enigma of Health*, Stanford: Stanford University Press.

An important set of essays by the philosopher who formulated contemporary philosophical hermeneutics. The readings explore health, death, anxiety, and the implications of technology for the practice of the healing arts.

Leder, D. (1990) *The Absent Body*, Chicago: University of Chicago Press.

A good discussion of the modes of appearances of the lived body in the tradition of Merleau-Ponty.

Toombs, S.K. (1992) *The Meaning of Illness: A Phenomenological Account of the Different Perspectives of Physician and Patient*, Dordrecht: Kluwer Academic Publishers.

A phenomenological philosopher who suffers from a debilitating illness reflects on the meanings of illness and on the physician–patient relationship.

van den Berg, J.H. (1972) *A Different Existence: Principles of Phenomenological Psychopathology*, Pittsburgh: Duquesne University Press.

A short and clear introduction to the existential analysis of psychopathology, this book serves health psychologists well by showing through anecdote and commentary how illness is embodied in our relations with our surroundings, with others, with our bodies, and with time. His discussion of the differences between the body that I have and the body that I am is a "must" for health psychology.

PART II

Context of Health Psychology

CHAPTER 4

Rights to Health, Freedom from Illness: A Life and Death Matter

David F. Marks

All animals are equal but some animals are more equal than others. (George Orwell 1945)

All human beings are born free and equal in dignity and rights. They are endowed with reason and conscience and should act towards one another in a spirit of brotherhood. (Universal Declaration of Human Rights 1948)

As in earlier times, advances in the 21st century will be won by human struggle against divisive values – and against the opposition of entrenched economic and political interests. (Human Development Report 2000)

Summary

All human beings have a right to an equal share of chances and opportunities. Yet in practice, as we all know, there are vast inequalities between individual people, communities, regions and countries. The human rights defined by the Universal Declaration are nowhere near being realized in practice. It is manifestly the case that all are not born free, nor are they born equal in dignity and rights. Poverty, powerlessness and inequality are, in every place and every time, the very fabric of life and death, peace and war. The Universal Declaration of Human Rights offers the hope that reason, conscience and "a spirit of brotherhood" may, some day, overcome the inequities that abound. The United Nations High Commissioner for Human Rights, Mary Robinson, re-asserted the universality and indivisibility of the declaration in 2000: "Universality is, in fact, the essence of human rights: all people are entitled to them, all governments are bound to observe them, all state and civil actors should defend them. The goal is nothing less than all human rights for all" (Human Development Report 2000: 113). If by cataclysmic revolution, or by dint of gradual reform, inequalities between people are ever removed, this will be a political and economic transformation of utopian proportions. In the meantime, the daunting task of working towards the reduction of inequalities must become a genuine priority for social policy and health care.

In this chapter, I argue that social justice in the form of equal rights and freedoms is a principle that has been sorely absent from human society, social policy and health care. In human societies, it is *in*equality that is the accepted norm, equality being the rare exception. Factors influencing unequal health, nutrition and population outcomes include neo-liberal economic policies, the consequential impoverishment of households and communities, and the organization of health care systems that are inaccessible to marginalized groups. Debt cancellation is of vital concern in ameliorating poverty. Strategies and theoretical frameworks for interventions to reduce health inequalities are outlined, together with their implications for policy and practice in health care. The aim of realizing equality in theory and practice should be a foundation for a revitalized health care.

Health Inequalities: Developed and Developing

Human history is the history of inequality. In many ways, the social and human sciences are the *sciences of inequality*. The inequalities that always were, and are today, so remarkable are replicated throughout human populations everywhere. Policies for their reduction are based on progressive social theories concerning the health, nutrition and well-being of the global human population.

Bullock and Lott (2001) call for a research agenda focused on classism and poverty and for advocacy of social justice. Examples of recent efforts toward such an agenda include the American Psychological Association's adoption on 6 August 2000 of its "Resolution on Poverty and Socioeconomic Status" (American Psychological Association 2000). Psychological research must be used to advocate for economic justice, *not only in the post-industrialised world, but in the developing world too*.

The effects of living and working conditions on health in post-industrial nations have been well recorded at least since Victorian times (Booth 1889: 1902a,b; Engels 1892). Manchester, in South-east Lancashire, became the first modern industrial city. Friedrick Engels' father was a German manufacturer and Engels worked as his agent in his father's Manchester factory. As a result, Engels combined real experience of the city with a strong social conscience. This resulted in his *The Condition of the Working-Class in England* in 1844. Engels described the separation of working people that was correlated with a severe degradation of the physical environment by industrial and domestic waste:

> I may mention just here that the mills almost all adjoin the rivers or the different canals that ramify throughout the city, before I proceed at once to describe the labouring quarters. First of all, there is the old town of Manchester, which lies between the northern boundary of the commercial district and the Irk [a river] ... In

dry weather, a long string of the most disgusting, blackish-green, slime pools are left standing on this bank, from the depths of which bubbles of miasmatic gas constantly arise and give forth a stench unendurable even on the bridge forty or fifty feet above the surface of the stream. But besides this, the stream itself is checked every few paces by high weirs, behind which slime and refuse accumulate and rot in thick masses. Above the bridge are tanneries, bone mills, and gasworks, from which all drains and refuse find their way into the Irk, which receives further the contents of all the neighbouring sewers and privies. It may be easily imagined, therefore, what sort of residue the stream deposits. Below the bridge you look upon the piles of debris, the refuse, filth, and offal from the courts on the steep left bank; here each house is packed close behind its neighbour and a piece of each is visible, all black, smoky, crumbling, ancient, with broken panes and window frames.

The unclean air and water was degraded further by the close intermingling of humans and pigs:

Here, as in most of the working-men's quarters of Manchester, the pork-raisers rent the courts and build pig-pens in them. In almost every court one or even several such pens may be found, into which the inhabitants of the court throw all refuse and offal, whence the swine grow fat; and the atmosphere, confined on all four sides, is utterly corrupted by putrefying animal and vegetable substances .... (Engels 1892).

A similar situation existed in many other industrial cities and towns in Europe in the nineteenth century, including London, where the sanitation arrangements had not changed since the sixteenth century, with cesspools lying beneath 270 000 houses at the time of the 1841 census. In the poorest houses the effluent would be forced up through the floorboards. The Metropolitan Commission of Sewers in 1847 ruled that all refuse was to be discharged directly into sewers and from there into the River Thames, which also provided the domestic water supply for many Londoners. Cholera outbreaks occurred in the poorer districts of London in 1831, 1848–1849, 1854 and 1866. During the third epidemic, Dr John Snow observed that the worst districts, Southwark and Vauxhall, obtained their water from a part of the Thames contaminated by sewage discharged from ships. Cesspits went out of use in the 1850s but the water was described as having a "brownish" colour (Ackroyd 2000). In the long, hot summer of 1858, the River Thames had become the "Great Stink". Joseph Bazalgette was commissioned to divert the sewage from the Thames to outfalls downriver at Barking and Crossness using 1100 miles of sewage pipes in Portland cement (Weinreb and Hibbert 1993). While the Thames is certainly cleaner today than in the 1850s, it is interesting that the maps of the distribution of housing and social classes across the districts of London drawn by Booth remain almost as accurate today as in the nineteenth century (Dorling *et al.* 2000).

The principles of improving public health were enacted in the 1848 Public Health Act of Sir Edwin Chadwick. This act emphasized the role of the state in improving the health of the people and the organization of public health at all levels. The 1848 act identified most of the major public health issues of the time and established a structure for dealing with them. Public health was seen to be the responsibility of local people, facilitated by the policies and resources of central government.

The purpose of the act was to promote the public's health and to ensure "more effective provision...for improving sanitary conditions of towns and populous places in England and Wales". The act was influenced by a piece of research on mortality and morbidity rates across the country that demonstrated clear inequalities in health and recognised that the fundamental issue of poverty had to be addressed.

The 1848 act included poverty, housing, water, sewerage, the environment, safety, and food, although not air, and not tobacco which was becoming popular and deemed safe. The act set out those accountable and the penalties involved. It emphasised the involvement of local communities. Two public health physicians in England recently had this to say in their imaginary Millennium Report to Sir Edwin Chadwick:

> Dear Sir Edwin, We live in a world which you would have envied. You played a dominant role in laying the foundations of this world. A clean and secure water supply for the population at large, coupled with the separate disposal of their sewage and waste, were the central planks of your crusade to protect public health in your day. However, Sir Edwin, we enter a caution here. The harmonious world referred to is, in essence, the "first world." The insanitary conditions which you were determined to eradicate still persist over large parts of the globe...(Sram and Ashton 1998: 592).

The "insanitary conditions", referred to by Sram and Ashton, and also the income inequalities, which exist over a significant part of the globe, are the main subjects of this chapter. The chapter will draw upon principally five sources of information: (i) the literature on the history of public health; (ii) the Human Development Report (HDR 2000) of the United Nations Development Programme (UNDP); (iii) the World Development Report 2000/2001 "Attacking Poverty"; (iv) the Demographic and Health Surveys (DHS) carried out by the World Bank; and (v) relevant literature in psychology.

The HDR is a useful source of information on human development and inequality on a global scale. Poverty and development are perceived differently today than ten years ago when they were perceived largely in terms of income and GNP. Development has been redefined as a process of expanding the resources for *the fulfilment of human potential* on a broad front, including health and education, rather than simply the increasing of national income: "Human development is the process of enlarging people's choices, by expanding human functionings and capabilities" (HDR 2000: 17). This change has been strongly influenced by the writings of Amartya Sen (2001). Improvements in health are no longer seen purely as the end product of medical care. Medicine

---

Box 4.1   Poverty – past, present and future – slow progress is being made

Poverty levels have fallen over the last 15–20 years: 23 per cent in 1998, of the world's population living on less than US$1 a day, only 5 per cent lower than in 1987 (Watkins 2001). However, 2.8 billion people – almost half of the global population – live on less than US$2 a day.

Malnutrition   Between 1980 and 1999 malnutrition was reduced with the proportion of underweight children in developing countries falling from 37 to 27 per cent and that of stunted children from 47 to 33 per cent.

Education   The record on universal primary education is not encouraging. On current estimates, at least 75 million primary-school children will still be out of school in 2015. Yet one of the international development goals is universal primary education by 2015.

Population growth   The world population will grow from 6 to 8 billion by 2025, with 97 per cent of the increase in developing countries.

---

has a role but this role is often overshadowed by many other powerful influences including politics, economics and education. Of key importance to human development in the twenty-first century are freedom from poverty and human rights. Poverty is the key issue (Box 4.1). The HDRs have evidenced the case that the rich/poor gaps in health outcomes can be reduced by changing *at global and national levels the distribution of assets, incomes and opportunities.*

Watkins (2001) argues that extreme inequality slows the pace of poverty reduction and is bad for growth. Global redistribution of resources through aid, debt relief and trade reforms, and also national redistribution will enable the health and developmental consequences of poverty to be ameliorated. In the next section, evidence on health and the Rich–Poor divide is described.

The Rich–Poor Divide

Since the public health reforms of nineteenth-century England, the epidemiological approach has been a strong element in the inequalities debate. The Black Report (1980) and the UK government reports that followed (for example, Acheson 1998) have highlighted the dogged persistence of inequalities across the population of England. The Black Report presented striking figures showing the health outcomes measured in standardized mortality rates against social status based on the Registrar General's coding system based on occupation of the head of the household. The persistent gradient that varies across the continuum of socio-economic status is referred to as a "health gradient". When mortality is the measure, a more apposite term would be "death gradient". The "death gradient" of the Black Report has been observed in all human societies in both developed (Kunst and Mackenbach 1994) and undeveloped countries (see below). On a global scale, the Rich–Poor Divide is geographically a North–South Divide.

Gradients are normally continuous throughout the entire range of economic variation. If the gradient were stepped, or flat at one end of the range and steep at the other, it could be inferred that the causative mechanism(s) had a threshold value before any of the "ill-effects" could appear. However there is no evidence of any such thresholds. On the contrary, for the vast majority of data, the gradient is a continuous one. The causative mechanisms that have been identified to date include the factors identified by Chadwick. These are: poverty, housing, water, sewerage, the environment, safety and food. In addition, there are illiteracy, tobacco, AIDS/HIV, and lack of access to immunization, medication and health care. For Victorian Britons, life in the industrial cities was less healthy than life in the country. For the people of the developing world, however, rural conditions are generally harder than urban conditions.

The universality of gradients across human societies is evidenced by information from the Demographic and Health Surveys (DHS) programme of the World Bank (2002). The DHS collect data on a large number of health, nutrition, population and health service utilization measures, as well as on the respondents' demographic, social and economic characteristics. The DHS are large-scale household sample surveys carried out at periodic intervals in 44 countries to date across Asia, Africa, the Middle East, Latin America and the former Soviet Union. The DHS use a standard set of questionnaires to collect individual, household and community level data. Socio-economic status is evaluated in terms of data concerning assets gathered through the DHS questionnaire that is typically answered by the head of each household. The asset score is generated from the household's ownership of a number of consumer items ranging from fan to television and car; dwelling characteristics such as flooring material; type of drinking-water source and toilet facilities used; and other characteristics that are related to wealth status.

Each household asset is assigned a weight or factor score generated through principal components analysis. The resulting asset scores are standardized and then used to define wealth quintiles. Each household is assigned a standardized score for each asset, where the score differed depending on whether or not the household owned that asset (or, in the case of sleeping arrangements, the number of people per room). These scores are summed for each household, and individuals are ranked according to the total score of the household in which they reside. The sample is then divided into population asset wealth quintiles – five groups with the same number of individuals in each.

The under-5 mortality rates (U5MRs) for the five asset quintiles for nine countries in Latin America and the Caribbean are shown in Figure 4.1. This indicator is defined as the number of deaths to children under five years of age per 1000 live births. Figures used are based on births in the ten years preceding

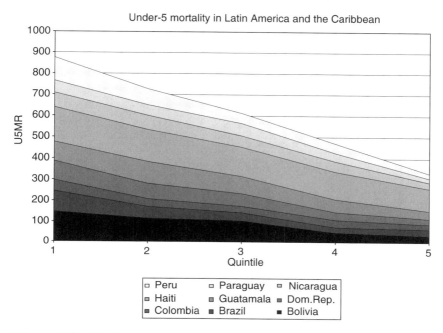

Figure 4.1 Under-5 mortality rates U5MR for Latin America and the Caribbean plotted against asset quintile (the areas under each line represent the individual country rates). Quintile 1 has least assets, quintile 5 the most

the survey. Data for 22 countries in Sub-Saharan Africa are shown in Figure 4.2. Both figures show death gradients in all countries in these two regions. A wide gap in health outcomes exists between the rich and the poor. Similar gradients exist throughout the 44 countries included in the DHS.

I have calculated the following correlations using the data from the DHS. U5MR in the 44 countries in the DHS are correlated positively with female illiteracy $(0.69, p < .0001)$ and with the proportion of households using bush, field or traditional pit latrines $(0.60, p < .0001)$ and negatively with the proportion of households having piped domestic water $(-0.65, p < .0001)$, with national health service expenditure $(-0.33, p < .01)$, the number of doctors per $100,000$ people $(-0.51, p < .0001)$, the number of nurses per $100\,000$ people $(-0.35, p < .01)$, and immunization rates $(-0.27, p < .05)$.

These findings indicate that the higher death rates among the poor are strongly associated with a multitude of factors including illiteracy of mothers, poor access to fresh water, lack of sanitation, and basic health services such as immunization. For example, the DHS in Benin found that 74 per cent of children from the richest families were likely to be fully immunized, while only 38 per cent of children from the poorest families were. Soucat and

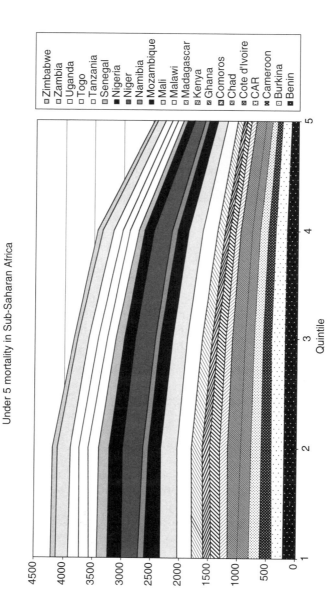

Figure 4.2   Under-5 mortality rates for Sub-Saharan Africa plotted against asset quintile (the area under each line represents the individual country rates). Quintile 1 has least assets, quintile 5 the most

Yazbeck (2002) suggest that poverty and ill-health are in a vicious circle (see Box 4.2). The question is, how can that circle be broken?

Another obvious consequence of inequality is conflict, including full-scale war and terrorism. Different social groups are divided by geography, class, culture and/or religion. When the exercise of political and economic power by one group over another becomes intolerable, the offended group may seek redress through violent means and civil war may break out (Cohen 1974). Stewart (2002a) describes four causes of within-state wars: group motivation, private motivation, failure of the social contract and environmental, or green, war. The first concerns the motives, resentments, and ambitions of different groups in open competition for resources of various kinds (Horowitz 1985; Gurr 1993; Stewart 2002b). Horizontal inequality between groups is a reliable feature of civil unrest with consistent evidence of sharp horizontal inequalities of power and influence of various kinds between warring groups (Nafziger *et al.* 2000).

Stewart (2002) concludes: "Reducing large horizontal inequalities is essential to eliminate a major source of conflict. Policies that diminish private incentives to fight, especially once conflict is under way, are also needed.

Box 4.2   Ill-health and poverty are in a vicious circle

Poverty leads to ill-health
Seventy percentage of the variance in infant mortality can be attributed to across and within country differences in income.

- Half the burden of communicable diseases is concentrated in the poorest 20 per cent
- Globally the poorest 20 per cent experience three and a half times the mortality and four times the number of DALYs'*loss of the richest 20 per cent, an equivalent of to excess mortality of nearly 10 million deaths a year.
- Communicable diseases are responsible for 60 per cent of both deaths and DALYs' loss in the poorest groups

Ill-health leads to poverty

- Africa's income growth per capita is being reduced by about 0.7 per cent per year because of HIV/AIDS
- A 20 per cent loss of GNP in Sub-Saharan Africa may be attributed to malaria
- Studies in East Africa show that 50 per cent of financial crises in poor families are triggered by illnesses such as TB, HIV, and severe malaria

Source: Soucat and Yazbeck (2002). *Disability Adjusted Life Year

Above all, there is a need to secure inclusive government from political, economic, and social perspectives and a flourishing economy so that all major groups and most individuals gain from participation in the normal economy." Stewart suggests that the same argument applies validly to the international situation including the sharp economic and social differences that exist between rich Western and poor Muslim societies.

In the future, the incidence of infectious diseases and shortages of food and water may be exacerbated by global warming. Gastrointestinal infections by a range of organisms, including bacteria that cause typhoid and cholera, are more common in hotter weather. Many infectious diseases are caused by parasites or viruses transmitted by carriers, for example, insects transmit conditions such as malaria, dengue, and yellow fever. Many of these vectors are heat and humidity sensitive, so an increase in one or both will put a larger proportion of the population at risk. Computer models predict the proportion of the world's population potentially at risk from malaria will increase from 45 to 60 per cent later this century (Hartog 2001). The impact on countries that could not afford countermeasures could be devastating as currently some 300–500 million people are infected with malaria from which two million (mainly young children) die each year (Martens *et al.* 1995).

Climate change is predicted to increase food production at high- and mid-latitudes but decrease it at lower latitudes. Food production will be reduced in the arid and subhumid tropics, where there are regions that are currently barely able to feed their populations due to high temperature, pests, and lack of water. One climate change scenario in Africa has predicted that there will be an additional 55 to 65 million people at risk of hunger by the 2080s (Parry and Rosenzweig 1999). The number of people affected by water shortages, currently about 1.7 billion, is also expected to rise sharply (Martens *et al.* 1995).

The World Bank (2002) has set ambitious goals for the 25-year period, 1990–2015:

> Infant deaths are most often the result of unhealthy conditions around the time of birth. Pneumonia, diarrhea, malaria, or measles frequently kill young children, especially those suffering from chronic malnutrition ...
>
> We know what needs to be done to reduce infant and child deaths. Malnutrition, unsafe water, war and civil conflict, and the spread of HIV/AIDS all contribute to the annual toll. And immunization, disease prevention, and campaigns to teach treatment of diarrhea can all help to reduce deaths ...
>
> There are large and persistent differences in mortality rates between regions and progress has been too slow to achieve a two-thirds reduction by 2015. Mortality rates in Africa, which had been falling, are now higher on average than in 1990.

Sadly, these targets will not be met simply because the richest countries do not have the heart and the political will to make them happen. We will discuss this issue in the remainder of the chapter.

Debt Relief, Cancellation and the Jubilee 2000 Movement

In repaying foreign debts, poor countries are forced to direct government resources away from health care, education, and other services. For instance, Zambia has been spending US$200 million annually on debt servicing, and is facing over US$600 million annual debt servicing bills after the year 2000. The result has been to deny many children the chance to go to school, women the access to pre-natal care, HIV-infected persons the access to counselling and treatment, and small farmers access to credit and technical assistance.

The Heavily Indebted Poor Countries (HIPC) initiative of the World Bank and the IMF is designed to assist poor countries with their debts. It was launched by the World Bank and IMF in 1996. The project was expanded in 1999. The Bank and IMF led a consultative review with NGOs, churches and civil society. The review led to three enhancements:

1. *Greater debt relief*: External debt servicing will be cut by approximately US$50 billion, more than twice the relief provided under the original framework. When completed in combination with traditional debt relief, the initiative will cut by more than two-third the outstanding debt to more than 30 countries. The World Bank itself will reduce its debt claims by nearly US$11 billion, the IMF by approximately US$4 billion;
2. *Faster debt relief*: Most participating creditors, including IMF, World Bank, and Paris Club, to provide debt relief beginning immediately or soon after at the decision point;
3. *Stronger link between debt relief and poverty reduction*: Freed-up resources will be used to support poverty reduction strategies.

To date, 24 countries (Benin, Bolivia, Burkina Faso, Cameroon, Chad, Ethiopia, The Gambia, Guinea, Guinea-Bissau, Guyana, Honduras, Madagascar, Malawi, Mali, Mauritania, Mozambique, Nicaragua, Niger, Rwanda, São Tomé and Príncipe, Senegal, Tanzania, Uganda, Zambia) have reached their decision point under the enhanced HIPC Initiative and four countries (Bolivia, Mozambique, Tanzania and Uganda) reached its completion point under the original HIPC Initiative. These 24 countries are now receiving relief which will amount to some US$36 billion over time. Unfortunately the number of countries receiving help and the amount of help being offered is insufficient to eradicate severe poverty and debt.

The World Bank claims that for the 24 countries that have reached their decision point, the enhanced HIPC Initiative will reduce total debt stock by nearly 50 per cent and cut the ratio of debt-to-GDP from under 60 per cent to under 30 per cent. Social expenditure in the decision point countries are projected to increase by an average of US$1.7 billion per year during 2001–2002, equaling about 1.2 per cent of GDP. Increases in education and health spending are expected to absorb about two-thirds of the total relief. Other priority sectors include HIV/AIDS, where almost every HIPC is creating or strengthening education and treatment programmes, rural development and water supply, governance and institution building, and road construction. About 36 countries could qualify for HIPC assistance. However, about a dozen are conflict affected or suffer from governance problems, which has prevented the possibility of effective debt relief.

Critics of the World Bank have rejected the HIPC Initiative as too little, too late. The focus of the criticism has been the Jubilee 2000 campaign. The "Jubilee" is a biblical mandate (Leviticus 25, Deuteronomy 15) intended to restore the bonds of community broken through injustice, unfair distribution of resources, and debt. Every 50 years, lands were redistributed, slaves were freed and debt was cancelled. During the jubilee year of 2000, religious and civic leaders, and two Irish activist-musicians Bob Geldof and Bono, called for the cancellation of the debt of the poor countries. In spite of all the rhetoric and publicity, to date the impact of the HIPC Initiative has been slow to deliver and much less than its full potential. Some have even spoken of hypocrisy (Denny 2003).

In dealing with debt, there are issues of social justice to consider. First, there is the justice of how the debt was acquired: how fairly was it negotiated; who participated in the decision-making; and who benefited from the loans? Unpayable debt and austerity that accompany new loans can inflame social conflicts that can lead to civil wars and even genocidal campaigns, as in Rwanda. Second, there is the justice of repaying the debt: how fair are the interest rates; where does the money come from for servicing the debt; and how does this affect the social conditions of the people? A large debt burden motivates poor countries to lower labour standards leading to lower wages and growing poverty. Countries with major debt burdens have unacceptable credit ratings for further investment. Debt encourages rainforest destruction and pollution, as poor countries use cheap but environmentally destructive ways to earn export revenue. Third, there is the justice of reducing vs cancelling the debt: whose voice is heard loudest in the negotiations – the poor or the rich; where will the resources go that are freed up through debt reduction/cancellation; and how accountable and participative is the process of reduction/cancellation?

The Heavily Indebted Poor Countries (HIPC) initiative of the World Bank and the IMF offer some help, but it is *too late* (for many HIPC it has not even started), *too little* (only a portion of the debt is written off); *too rigid* (eligibility depends upon strict adherence to Structural Adjustment Programmes); *too limited* (only 41 countries are declared "eligible"); and *too unrealistic* (it does not consider social factors). Therefore, the most effective approach that can be employed is outright cancellation of debt under the philosophy of the Jubilee 2000 approach. For the 1.2 billion poorest people who are living on less than US$1 a day, 2050 will be much too late. The World Bank should aim to make its HIPC Initiative much faster, more flexible, and more comprehensive. Debt cancellation, not reduction, must be the aim.

However, debt cancellation alone will not be enough. If health inequalities are to be reduced, the distribution of income and assets across the population of each country must be made more even. And the priorities of rich countries about what they choose to spend their money on needs to be reviewed.

Interventions to Reduce Health Inequalities: Empowerment

We have seen that progress in reducing debt, poverty and early mortality has been slow, uneven and far from complete. Death gradients are persistent and universal. The vicious circle of poverty and ill-health is unbroken. What can be done to break it? Debt cancellation is a priority. Economic intervention is the best form of empowerment. Empowerment with "social capital" but no extra money will only raise false hopes. Genuine long-lasting improvements will only occur when the problems are removed at their root cause – poverty.

Interventions to reduce health inequalities can be applied at different levels of social organization: individual, community, health service, macroeconomic and cultural. The majority of effort within public health, psychology, and the social sciences has been directed towards the elimination of health inequalities in countries that are economically developed. Francome and Marks (1996) describe a general framework that can be used in the planning interventions designed to reduce inequalities. The framework includes direct and indirect effects linking environmental variables, employment, household income, housing, interpersonal processes (including social comparisons, social support, and community and family relationships), health-behaviour patterns and individual characteristics. These factors have a variety of impacts upon bodily systems, specifically the cardiovascular, pulmonary musculo-skeletal, nervous and immune systems. Sram and Ashton (1998) suggested the following measures to reduce the influence of income inequality on health:

At the Individual Level:

- Stress management (I1);
- Smoking cessation (I2);
- Counselling for people who become unemployed (I3).

At the Community Level:

- Social control of illegal activity (C1);
- Socialization of the young as participating members of the community (C2);
- Providing first employment (C3);
- Improving access to formal and informal health care (C4);
- Social support for health maintenance (C5);
- Allowing the exercise of political power to direct resources to that community (C6);
- Limiting duration and intensity of experimentation with dangerous and destructive activity (C7).

Improving Access to Essential Facilities and Services:

- Needs-based and Needs-driven provision (A1);
- Make equity the determining factor for provision (A2);
- Remove financial and geographical barriers to access and uptake (A3).

Encouraging macroeconomic and cultural change:

- Reduce income differentials at population level (M1);
- Sustain high levels of employment (M2);
- Improve working conditions (M3);
- Create conditions for social cohesion and stability (M4).

Nine of these 17 measures have relevance to developing countries: I2, C3–6, A2–3, M1 and M4. Probably C3 and the last four of these are the most crucial. Improvements to living and working conditions through improved access to water, sanitation, health services, education and the generation of income via economic development must all be the main priorities for the improvement of health and the reduction of inequalities. Breast-feeding instead of the use of formula feeding for infants needs to be more heavily promoted. Prevention of smoking through effective tobacco-control measures is necessary to complement smoking cessation. In addition, there is a need for sexual health education and health promotion through the widespread use of condoms, especially in Sub-Saharan Africa.

The World Bank's framework with pathways for improving the health, nutrition, and population outcomes of the poorest people is presented in Figure 4.3. Of particular interest to health psychologists and public health programmes are activities that come under the labels "Household behaviors and risk factors", "Household resources" and "Community factors". These factors are discussed in the light of two case studies given by Wagstaff and Yazbeck (2002) (Boxes 4.3 and 4.4).

One theme in Boxes 4.3 and 4.4 is that health is the outcome of processes within and between several systems: the health system, the environment, households and communities. At each stage of the lifecycle, there are risks to health and also preventive measures such as safe feeding and diet, hand-washing, safe disposal of faeces, safe sex, and non-smoking. Households are producers of health, receivers and demanders of health inputs, including services and benefits. Households are also subjected to rents, fees and taxes. Health outcomes at each stage of the lifecycle are influenced by health services – preventive and curative – and by a host of other factors that have nothing to do with the health care system, including food security, cooking methods, cuisine, water quality, hygiene, sanitation arrangements, transport, communications, and many others. For example, child deaths can be reduced by better nutrition, and by cleaner water and safer sanitation. Health services can deliver preventive and curative services, promote good nutrition, and encourage parents to wash

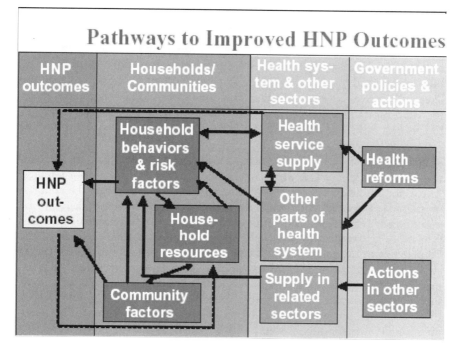

Figure 4.3 The World Bank's framework of pathways leading to improved health, nutrition and population outcomes (Source: Soucat and Yazbeck 2002)

their hands before food preparation and to dispose of faeces safely. They can also influence access to and use of food, water and sanitation. Better-off households have cleaner water, better sanitation and better transportation. They have better access to health services. They are the beneficiaries of a cycle of wealth, health, and yet more wealth. Worse off households suffer an opposite cycle of poverty, ill-health and yet more poverty.

Usage of health services influences impoverishment. High out-of-pocket spending on health services by households that are close to the poverty line may well push them below the poverty line. Better-off households use both private and public health services more. They have more income, more education, and more assets. They own more household effects that are likely to positively influence family health. For example, ownership of a refrigerator affects the household's capacity to translate spending into good nutrition while ownership of radios and TVs is important for receipt of health messages. Ownership of a bicycle or car affects ease of getting to health facilities, to school or college, and to market. Human assets include knowledge and skills – both general and health-specific.

Box 4.3   Case 1: Immunization in India

Immunization is a life and death issue in India. If current trends continue, only half of the 25 million children born every year in India are likely to be fully immunized by age one. Of the remaining 12 million children, half are likely to receive no immunization at all. A threefold difference occurs in the child mortality rate between the richest fifth of households in India and the poorest fifth. The income-related differences are similar for infant mortality. In concert with the data summarized above, the rate of death of children in poor families is much higher than those in wealthier families, and preventive life-saving services are not reaching the children from the poor families. Three household surveys in 1993, 1996 and 1998 confirm that the children of poor and socially vulnerable families in India are least likely to be immunized. Infants of the wealthiest 20 per cent of households in India are four times as likely to have received some vaccinations than children of the 20 per cent of the poorest families and three times as likely to have received all routine vaccinations. As noted above, there is an association between maternal literacy and children's vaccination coverage. The 1998 household survey asked households with unimmunized children why they did not seek this life-saving preventive service. While all three conditions listed above were mentioned, two specific answers – both related to knowledge – accounted for more than 63 per cent of responses. Thirty percentage of respondents were not aware of the need for immunization and 33 per cent were not aware of the time and place the immunizations were to be provided.

Source: Wagstaff and Yazbeck (2002).

The World Development Report (2001) proposed a three-pronged attack on poverty consisting of "promoting opportunity", "facilitating empowerment", and "enhancing security". The first and third of these are viewed as primarily economic in nature. The second is more psychological and social.

The specific role of the critical health psychologist is to provide a critique of the solutions being offered by institutions such as the World Bank and to argue for more structural changes. I would level three criticisms at the World Bank approach to poverty. First, the idea that people can become healthier by simply changing their behaviour in the form of safer feeding and diet, hand-washing, safe disposal of faeces, safe sex, and non-smoking is all very well, but until environmental, economic and structural improvements occur, there is a pernicious tendency to almost blame the victims of poverty for their habits and living conditions. Placing the responsibility for improvement at the level of individuals (mothers) and households is a convenient way of "passing the buck". If people are forced to live in squalid conditions, it is expecting more of them than of the Victorian working class, if we ask them to rise above the demeaning filth of everyday existence to become pillars of good health by

---

Box 4.4 Case 2: Malnutrition in Bolivia

Malnutrition is a life and death issue in Bolivia for a large proportion of the population. It is claimed that in economic terms alone the financial loss to the country will be US$1 billion for the eleven-year period covering 2000–2010 while only US$67 was spent annually by the public sector and NGOs on the malnutrition problem but that only 22 per cent of that spending covered proven and cost-effective solutions. Forty percentage of malnourished children are from the lowest 20 per cent of the population while only 4 per cent are from the richest quintile, a ratio of 10:1. Malnutrition is worse in rural areas and in households where indigenous language is spoken. Many Bolivian women are so malnourished that they will pass micronutrient deficiencies to their babies *in utero*. The poor have not benefited as much from overall economic growth as the non-poor. Malnutrition has generally dropped as GNP percapita has risen but the nutrition of the non-poor has improved far more than that of the poor, especially in the fourth quintile. Malnutrition is the product of individual and family choices, the cultural and natural environment, community processes, economic pressures, and national policies and programmes. Each of these is affected by poverty and can be alleviated or exacerbated by policies and programmes. Food security has three dimensions and three levels: availability, access and utilization at the national, household and individual levels. Disease is both a cause and an effect of malnutrition.

Source: Wagstaff and Yazbeck (2002).

---

indulging in hand-washing, bearing in mind that it may simply take six hours of walking to obtain one pot of water! It is neither fair nor reasonable to expect people to change their "lifestyle" (= living conditions) simply by informing them that their current habits are unhealthy. This is as true of the poor as it is of the rich. Elsewhere I have referred to this as the "Rationality Myth" (Marks 2002b).

Second, the call for "empowerment", "social cohesion", and "social capital" must also be questioned. It may well be the case that community-level processes that help produce health include intangible influences, such as cultural norms and social capital, but I would argue that the tangible influences in the form of the physical environment (pollution), the infrastructure (roads, water, sanitation, electricity, and so on) and the economy (GNP, income distribution) are the greatest determinants of health. Community organizations can mobilize action and resources. They can help develop new projects and services, and monitor and manage local health and social services. Community organizations can also provide information on the availability of health services and education on preventive care. But communities cannot do it alone. Social capital must be viewed as a local band-aid, not a structural change that prevents the poverty problem in the first place. The latter need to be tackled at its root cause, not by band-aids.

My third criticism of the World Bank approach to poverty is that it makes no attempt to critique the current resource uses of the rich countries. The World Bank focuses purely on what can be done within current budget allocations. While commenting on the gradual reduction in official development assistance as a percentage of GNP, and mentioning that strategic and political objectives have been more important as motives for aid than poverty reduction, it simply argues for more efficient use of aid, not for greatly increasing it (World Development Report 2001: 189–192). Yet, radical changes to current resource allocations by rich countries will be necessary if poverty is to be effectively tackled.

Social Justice as a Foundation for Health Work

Participation in the movement for social justice must be the foundation for revitalized health work. The current obsession with the organization of health systems in the richer countries of the West and the North provides a distracting diversion from the global human tragedy that is deepening everyday.

A set of international development goals have been set to improve health outcomes among the poor. These goals are:

- exclusive and prolonged breast feeding
- use of iodized salt
- no smoking
- hand washing
- waste disposal
- use of latrines
- safe handling of water (for example, use of a tap)
- safe sex
- home treatment of fever and diarrhoea.

The achievement of these goals across the world's entire poor population of two billion people is the most ambitious programme of health education and promotion ever contemplated. Facilitating population changes of this magnitude will require a concerted and focused effort across sectors, levels and nations and will involve a massive infrastructure of multidisciplinary teams skilled at effective community development and supported by the provision of multiple economic, health, educational and social resources. The latter will be crucial. As was the case in working-class London and Manchester in 1850, clean water and sanitation will bring massive improvements to a large proportion of the world's poorest and unhealthiest people. Literacy, breast feeding and safe sex are equally important.

But all of the above are the surface features of the underlying cause of ill-health which is poverty. Of the greatest importance is the redistribution of wealth between the rich and the poor and the elimination of poverty. The rich countries may well claim that they are already giving enough funds in the form of official development assistance (ODA). In 1998, members of the Development Assistance Committee of the Organization for Economic Cooperation and Development (OECD) consisting of 21 of the richest countries, gave an average of 0.24 per cent of GNP (Human Development Report 2000). The country giving the lowest percentage was the USA (0.10 per cent). The amount of ODA as a percentage of GDP is falling (World Development Report 2000/2001). In comparison, the high-income OECD countries are allocating an average of 2.2 per cent of their GDP on military expenditure. In absolute terms that is US$504.65 billion per annum on military expenditure and only US$55.05 billion on aid. These priorities must be re-evaluated.

One of the most significant causes of ill-health in the poor world is lack of clean drinking water. In discussing the world water shortage, Daudpota (2000) points out that only 2.5 per cent of the water on this planet is freshwater, two-thirds being locked in glaciers and icecaps. Less than one hundredth of 1 per cent is drinkable, and renewed each year through precipitation. As the global population climbs from 6 to 9 billion, the amount available per person will fall by 33 per cent. The increased shortage will affect mainly the poor where the water shortage is already most acute. More than a billion people lack portable water, and nearly 3 billion lack even minimal sanitation. As I reported, above under-5 mortality rates are significantly related to the proportion of households using bush, field or traditional pit latrines and negatively with the proportion of households having piped domestic water. The World Health Organization estimates that 250 million cases of water-related diseases such as typhoid and cholera arise annually, resulting in 5–10 million deaths. Intestinal worms infect some 1.5 billion people, killing nearly 100 000 a year. Tens of millions of farming families in poor countries cannot afford to irrigate their land, lowering their crop production and leaving them vulnerable to drought. More than doubling annual investment in water supply to US$180 billion (Parliamentary Office of Science and Technology 2002) is necessary, with the focus on sustainable use of water.

If the expenditure of the rich countries on defence was cut by 50 per cent, that would release US$250 billion per year for other uses. That is enough capital to buy every person on this planet clean water, and leave US$70 billion over for health and education. If President Bush and Prime Minister Blair really want to go down in history, this is how to do it. Not by another unnecessary war with Iraq, but by converting a substantial proportion of military expenditure into improving the supplies of water to those who most need it.

A New Approach to Tackling Poverty

The critical approach to health psychology is concerned with the analysis of social structures and of the social, economic and political issues that produce health, illness and health care. Critical health psychology considers health, illness and health care in social, political and historical context. A principal objective is to understand health and illness experience in the context of ideas about power, vulnerability and social justice. This chapter has followed that objective to its conclusion. To those who call this approach "idealistic" I say this – if we want a better world, what should we do but try to change it? If we can see a way of doing it, then let us say what it is and go for it.

This chapter could have followed the well-worn course of reviewing in minute detail the possible explanations for health gradients of British civil servants (Marmot *et al.* 1978; Ferrie *et al.* 1995). Instead it has focused on death gradients in the developing countries and their causes. I make no apology for that. Their huge scale and transparency puts the death gradients in a different league to that of British civil servants. The death gradients of the poor countries have been sorely neglected by western mainstream social science, medicine, and psychology.[1] The continued neglect of social justice on a global scale is a reflection of the ethnocentric, racist, sexist and superior stance of post-colonialism. Colonization, exploitation and the slave trade are mirrored today by the new slavery of unaffordable bank loans, unfair trading, sexual tourism and sweat shops.

In exploring poverty, we have travelled well outside the boundaries of psychology. But health and poverty are inter-related and it is foolish to pretend that we can tackle one without tackling the other. Throughout its history the discipline of psychology as a science has remained aloof from politics and economics. In this chapter, I have illustrated one domain in which these three fields are strongly interconnected – the world of health. Health and poverty are massive political issues and academic boundaries have to be crossed in all directions.

A new agenda for health policy fit for the twenty-first century must place rights and freedoms at the top of the list. Until this agenda becomes a reality, the Universal Declaration of Human Rights will remain nothing more than hollow words from a privileged minority of rich people and politicians. In a world that preaches *and practices* equality, there can be no bank loan slaves, illiterates, or third-class citizens living in prisons without bars called Poverty.

Key Points

- The Rich–Poor health divide is persistent and pervasive. It was tackled in Victorian England by Chadwick's health reforms. Similar issues are evident in global health today: poverty, housing, water, sewerage, the environment, safety, and food. Yet there is a lack of political will to take action to significantly improve a situation that is worsening daily.
- The specific role of the critical health psychologist is to provide a critique of the superficial solutions being offered by institutions such as the World Bank and to argue for more radical structural and economic changes.

- Community programmes and the strengthening of "social capital" can help to develop new projects and services, and to monitor and manage local health and social services. Community organizations can also provide information on the availability of health services and education on preventive care.
- However the health of local communities cannot be expected to improve over the longer term when the necessary capital investment to improve water supplies, education and health care are unavailable.
- A feasible two-step plan to eliminate global poverty is advocated:

  Step 1 – Rich countries release poor countries from 100 per cent of their debt.

  Step 2 – Rich countries cut expenditure on defense by 50 per cent and transfer the released funds to poor countries to improve water supplies, sanitation, health and education. The "Weapons into Water" Plan will require radical changes to current policies that determine resource allocation within the rich countries themselves. If we are serious about poverty, there is no other option. But do our political leaders have the will to make survival with dignity a reality? Or must we wait for famine and war to take the initiative from us?

Assignment Questions

1. Who was Chadwick and what did she or he do?
2. What was the Black Report and what did it show?
3. What are some of the specific causes of ill-health in the developing world?
4. Provide a critique of the World Bank's approach to human development.
5. What solution(s) can you offer for the elimination of poverty?

Note

1. The exceptions are anthropology, cross-cultural psychology and epidemiology where "exotica" have a privileged scientific status.

📖 Further Readings

Human Development Report 2000, *Human Rights and Human Development*, New York: Oxford University Press.

Published annually by the United Nations Human Development Programme, the Human Development Report is the best independent source of information concerning human development. Essential background reading.

Moore, M. (2001) *Stupid White Men*, London: Penguin.

A consciousness-raising polemic about some of the structural problems about the world's richest country from the point of view of one of its funniest dissidents. Strongly recommended, but treat some of the 'facts' and figures with a hilariously huge lump of salt.

Townsend, P. and Davidson, N. (1982) *The Health Divide: Inequalities in Health in the 1980s*, London: Penguin.

The original Black Report concerning health inequalities in twentieth century Britain. Essential background reading.

World Development Report 2000/2001 (2001) *Attacking Poverty*, New York: Oxford University Press.

Provides an overview of poverty from the point of view of the World Bank. Contains some excellent summaries of dozens of examples of why health and poverty are strongly linked and is full of suggestions about how to tackle the problem. A very useful reference source as long as one reads "between the lines".

CHAPTER 5

Feminist Contributions to Critical Health Psychology

Sue Wilkinson

Summary

Feminist work on health and illness is one of the key components of critical health psychology. Feminists have long been critical of mainstream medical science, including traditional health psychology, and have sought to develop alternatives which are less oppressive to women (and other marginalized groups), and which better reflect the wide diversity of human experience. Feminists have also made major contributions to theoretical and methodological debates about the ways in which health and illness may best be conceptualized and studied, as well as to policy decisions affecting the quality of health care provision. This chapter: (a) provides an introduction to some of the central features of feminist research and practice; (b) examines the oppressive role of traditional medical science; (c) documents feminists' resistance to this oppression, via activism and research; and (d) outlines the main traditions of feminist research in critical health psychology, illustrating these with contemporary examples of specific research projects, including my own work on breast cancer.

What is Feminism?

The terms 'feminist' and 'feminism' are often misrepresented or misunderstood. For example, it is commonly assumed that feminist work is work 'on women'. This assumption, however, while not entirely wrong, is both too broad and too narrow. It is too *broad* because not *all* work 'on women' is feminist – i.e., work 'on women' is not necessarily informed by a feminist political analysis, nor does it necessarily pursue feminist goals. Feminism (as a politics) acknowledges the oppression of women (and other social groups), and its central goal is to dismantle that oppression. Feminist research and practice, then, is research and practice which is underpinned by feminist politics (i.e., the recognition of women's oppression), and which is working towards feminist goals (i.e., the end of that oppression).

The assumption that feminist work is work 'on women' is also too *narrow* because feminism does not focus *solely* on women, and women's oppression. While addressing women's oppression is, of course, *key* to feminist research and practice, feminism *also* acknowledges that men may be oppressed too, albeit to a different degree, and in different ways, from women. In addition, feminism recognizes that gender, although central, is not the *only* axis of oppression. Rather, distinctions between people on the basis of (for example) social class, 'race'/ethnicity, religion, sexual identity, age, (dis)ability – and the intersections between them – provide further bases for the creation and maintenance of profound social inequalities. Feminism acknowledges, and aims to end, these oppressions too.

Feminist work is also typically assumed to follow a single, narrow, highly prescriptive 'party line'. This, too, is a misrepresentation. Feminist work is informed by a broad spectrum of political allegiances, and uses theories and methods derived from a wide range of academic disciplines. Rather than a single orthodoxy, contemporary feminist research and practice embraces a potentially dazzling array of different perspectives and different approaches – including positivist empiricism, experiential approaches and discursive research (cf. Wilkinson 1996, for a more extended 'mapping' of contemporary feminist psychology).

In the next section of this chapter, I will sketch out the broad context for feminist work on health and illness: the pervasive gender bias of mainstream medical science. Feminist analyses of medicine from the early 1800s on have shown it to be deeply oppressive of women, particularly working-class women, and ethnic minority women. Later sections of this chapter will focus on resistance to such oppression, in terms of feminist activism, and in terms of feminist research.

The Role of Medical Science in Women's Oppression

> Medical science has been one of the most powerful sources of sexist ideology in our culture. Justifications for sexual discrimination – in education, in jobs, in public life – must ultimately rest on the one thing that differentiates women from men: their bodies. Theories of male superiority ultimately rest on biology. (Ehrenreich and English 1973: 5)

The roots of gender bias in medical science can perhaps most clearly be traced back to the early nineteenth century (although, of course, they extend much further). This was the era when physicians replaced midwives in caring for women's reproductive health, and the prevailing medical orthodoxy was 'biology as destiny'. Medical writings of the time reveal that physicians regarded their female patients as little more than collections of organs designed solely for reproduction of the species. Further, *all* of women's illnesses were seen as traceable to their reproductive organs:

> the ovaries... are the most powerful agents of all the commotions of her system; that on them rest her intellectual standing in society, her physical perfection. (Bliss 1870, cited in Laurence and Weinhouse 1994: 14)
>
> The Uterus, it must be remembered, is the *controlling* organ in the female body... intimately connected, by the ramifications of its nerves, with every other part. (Hollick 1849, cited in Laurence and Weinhouse 1994: 14; italics in original)

Women with illnesses as various as indigestion, curvature of the spine, fatigue and depression were given treatments aimed at the ovaries or the uterus. These treatments included leeches applied to the vulva, chemicals injected into the uterus, and cauterization of the cervix with a white-hot iron rod. In the second half of the nineteenth century, doctors began removing ovaries to 'cure' a variety of ills: among the indications for such surgery were 'eating like a ploughman, masturbation, attempted suicide, erotic tendencies, persecution mania' and 'simple cussedness' (Barker-Benfield 1972: 52).

Women were also told that expending energy on non-reproductive activity of any kind (including mental activities) would threaten their reproductive capacities. Middle-class women were advised to stay in bed every month during their periods to protect their health (working-class women were never advised to take days off from factory work or other unskilled jobs):

> We cannot too emphatically urge the importance of regarding these monthly returns as periods of ill-health, as days when the ordinary occupations are to be suspended or modified... Long walks, dancing, shopping, riding and parties should be avoided... Another reason why every woman should look upon herself as an invalid once a month, is that the monthly flow aggravates any existing affection of the womb and readily rekindles the expiring flames of disease. (Taylor 1871, cited in Laurence and Weinhouse 1994: 14)

In these ways, then, medical science kept women 'in their place': i.e., within the home. It is, perhaps, less well known that many women rebelled against these misogynistic theories and practices by forming a popular health movement known as 'Ladies Physiological Societies'. These were groups, often led by women's suffrage workers, which met to teach themselves anatomy and hygiene (Ehrenreich and English 1973). In some ways, particularly in its emphasis on self-help, this mid-1800s movement can be seen as the precursor of the 1970s feminist health movement.

Mainstream medical science of this period was also responsible for the experimental abuse of women (particularly black women) as research subjects. For example, between 1845 and 1849, Dr J. Marion Sims, one of founders of modern gynaecology in the USA, developed his surgical 'cure' for tears between the bladder and vagina through experimental operations (without

anaesthesia) on black slave women in Alabama. The operations were performed without the women's consent – they were simply brought to Sims by
their masters, on the grounds that they were unfit for work. Sims later continued his work on indigent Irish women in New York (Barker-Benfield 1976).
This kind of abusive practice continued for at least another century: for
example, in 1971, Dr Joseph Goldzieher conducted experimental trials of a
contraceptive pill on Chicano women in Texas. Seventy-six of these women,
who all thought they were getting a contraceptive pill, received a placebo
instead – and ten of them became pregnant within months (Corea 1985).
Women, of course, are not the only ones to suffer abuse in the name of
medical science. Poor and ethnic minority *men* have also been frequent
victims – as in, for example, the notorious US army study in which black men
with syphilis were 'treated' with placebos and observed until they died
(Barker-Benfield 1976).

Contemporary medical science continues to oppress women, in particular.
Women are still subject to a great deal of unnecessary surgery, especially in
relation to reproduction. Rates for births by Caesarean section are soaring;
and around 85 per cent of the more than half-a-million hysterectomies performed every year in the USA are 'elective', rather than life-saving, with the
consequence that more than a third of North American women will not have
a uterus by age fifty (Laurence and Weinhouse 1994). Following the medical
redefinition of menopause as a 'hormone deficiency disease', millions of
(older) women have become unwitting participants in the massive, uncon-
trolled experiment of hormone replacement 'therapy' (HRT) – predicated on
the agenda of rendering women 'forever feminine' (Wilson 1966). And, as we
shall see below, women have been systematically *excluded* from a range of major
clinical trials on diseases considered (often erroneously) to be largely the province of men (for example, heart disease, lung cancer).

Feminist Resistance

Women have always resisted the oppressions of medicine and science – using
many different tactics. Sometimes, they have eschewed these oppressive professions, and the institutions that support them. Instead (as seen in the
example of the 'Ladies' Physiological Societies'), they have taken health care
into their own hands, forming self-help organizations, and producing their
own health care literature. This strategy was central within the 1970s 'second
wave' feminism – giving rise to the women's health movement (for example,
The Boston Women's Health Book Collective 1971) and to the lesbian health
movement (for example, O'Donnell *et al.* 1979). These movements, in turn,
led to the development of grass-roots, community-based health centres –
i.e., the Women's Cancer Resource Center in Berkeley, California and the
Lesbian Community Cancer Project in Chicago (Kaufert 1998).

As outsiders, women have also spoken out against medical and scientific orthodoxies, and have campaigned directly against the professions and institutions which perpetuate these. Pioneers of the feminist breast cancer movement, for example, include Kushner (1975), who was instrumental in changing surgical procedures, and black lesbian feminist Lorde (1980), who passionately refused to conceal her mastectomy, and frequently spoke out against environmental carcinogens. More recently, feminist journalists have provided some powerful exposés of the breast cancer 'industry', highlighting the profiteering of drug companies and cosmetic surgeons, questioning the safety of tamoxifen trials and silicone implants, and casting doubt upon the efficacy of mammography and genetic screening programmes (Batt 1994; Clorfene-Casten 1996).

Women have also campaigned for change from *within* the organizations of medicine and science (for a history of women's struggles for representation within the professional bodies of psychology, see Wilkinson 1990). In the nineteenth century, women fought hard for entry into the medical profession, in order to directly change it in ways that would benefit their own sex (for a history of women in medicine, see Walsh 1977). A great deal has subsequently been achieved by feminist activists working within the medical profession and the political establishment – both in developing health care services which better address women's needs, and in lobbying for increased funding for research and practice. For example, lesbian oncologist Susan Love established a state-of-the-art treatment programme at a leading (US) Medical-Surgical Oncology Center, and co-founded (with Susan Hester and Amy Langer) the National Breast Cancer Coalition – an umbrella organization which co-ordinates the campaigning activities of several hundred breast cancer groups (Love 1995). The Coalition has achieved some spectacular successes, building a network of breast cancer advocates across the USA, and obtaining a fivefold

---

Box 5.1 Feminism and resistance to oppression

Definition of feminist research and practice
Feminist research and practice recognizes the oppression of women – and other marginalized social groups – and aims to end that oppression.

Key ways in which feminists have resisted the oppressions of traditional medical science

- Remained outside its professions – formed their own institutions and produced their own literature;
- Spoken out against medical and scientific orthodoxies, and exposed their abuses;
- Campaigned for entry to the professions of science and medicine – and effected significant change from within;
- Undertaken feminist research, of various types.

increase in federal funds for breast cancer research – including the diversion of funds from the US Department of Defense (Kaufert 1998).

Feminist Research as Resistance

The development of feminist research is another key form of resistance to medical and scientific orthodoxy, including mainstream health psychology. Here, I will distinguish between three broad traditions of feminist research – positivist empiricism, experiential approaches, and discursive research – with examples of how each has been used in the service of exposing and dismantling oppression.

Feminist Positivist Empiricism

Positivist empiricism uses conventional scientific methods – particularly experiments, tests and scales – to produce knowledge about an objectively present external world (cf. Longino 1993). Key criteria for 'good' positivist empiricist research include the objectivity of the researcher, the standardisation of measures, and the replicability and generalizability of findings.

Some readers may be surprised to find a defence of positivist empiricism in a text on critical health psychology. In general, the critical movement within psychology (for example, Fox and Prilleltensky 1997; Ibanez and Iniguez 1997) has lambasted the traditional positivist empiricist paradigm – so foundational to the mainstream of the discipline – for its individualizing, objectifying, and decontextualizing tendencies, as well as for its inability to address issues of diversity and social inequality. But positivist empiricist research has been a crucial political tool for feminists in their fight against oppression. Feminist researchers have been able to critique mainstream research as 'bad science', and to develop their own 'better science'. Essentially, they have used the positivist empiricist tool to play the oppressors at their own game, on their own territory (Unger 1996).

Early uses of this strategy can be traced back to the first women to enter the professions of psychology and medicine – for example, Mary Putnam Jacobi, winner of the Boylston Prize at Harvard in 1876, for work showing 'bed rest' during menstruation to be medically unwarranted; and pioneering feminist psychologist Helen Thomson Woolley, whose laboratory experiments 'proved' that women's performance is not significantly impaired during menstruation (Unger and Crawford 1996). Others exposed the male bias of scientific and medical opinion as a serious threat to its purported scientific objectivity. In 1894, the *Women's Medical Journal* published this attack on ovariectomy by one of the first women to rise to prominence in medicine, Mary A. Spink:

> As for the removal of the ovaries the fact is, that women physicians object to the wholesale onslaught upon those innocent organs, which originated with so-called

reputable physicians and has been continued by men mountebanks to the degree that nearly every city in the land has several 'private homes' or 'sanitarioms' [*sic*] for the purpose of removing those organs, removing them for nervousness produced by a thousand outside causes, removing them because the husbands request it, removing them for everything but disease. (Spink 1894, cited in Laurence and Weinhouse 1994: 26)

More recently, feminists have critiqued mainstream health research as 'bad science' on a range of standard scientific criteria. First, they note that many studies have used only male subjects (Travis 1988; Johnson 1992). These studies include crucial areas of health psychology, such as: risk factors for coronary heart disease (Shumaker and Smith 1995); clinical trials on the prophylactic effects of caffeine and aspirin for heart attacks and migraine (Stanton 1995); psychosocial research on workplace stress (Fisher 1996); and, extraordinarily, the links between obesity and uterine cancer (Matlin 1993) and between diet and breast cancer (Tavris 1992).

Secondly, these findings using only male subjects have then been inappropriately generalised to women (Rodin and Ickovics 1990). For example, ideal blood-cholesterol levels have been determined in men and simply applied to women (Tavris 1992); in fact it appears that 'safe' cholesterol levels are much higher in post-menopausal women (Palumbo 1989). In medical schools, the 'paradigm patient' is a seventy-kilogram male, and medical students learn how to treat his allergies, appendicitis, diarrhoea and urinary problems, computing medication doses based on his weight (Tavris 1992).

Thirdly, health conditions that affect only, or predominantly, women (for example, osteoporosis, lupus, fibroids, ovarian cancer) have been under-researched, at least until recently (Travis 1988; Stanton 1995). Finally, feminists point out, when women's health *is* studied, it is likely to be the health of women who are (or who are assumed to be) middle class, middle-aged, white, heterosexual and non-disabled: there has been little attention to *diversity* among women, and its effects on their health (Reid 1993; Stern 1993; Chrisler and Hemstreet 1995; Stevens 1998).

Within the positivist empiricist tradition, then, there is a substantial feminist critique of mainstream health research as 'poor science'. This is not only for the (male) bias apparent in its *priorities*, but also for the (male) bias apparent in its *assumptions*. Just as Mary A. Spink challenged the 'so-called reputable physicians' for the assumption of a link between ovaries and disease, and the consequent practice of ovariectomy, so too have contemporary feminist researchers challenged psycho-oncologists for the assumption that women's major concern after breast surgery is anxiety about looking 'unattractive' or 'unfeminine' (for example, Holland and Mastrovito 1980) and the consequent practice of offering soft prostheses, make-up, and hairstyling immediately after mastectomy (for example, Pendleton and Smith 1986). Feminist psychologists have pointed out that, although it is important that women's possible concerns about appearance receive sympathetic understanding from health care professionals, little empirical evidence actually exists to support the primacy of concerns about appearance:

> At times, and without adequate data, the tendency has been to view these recommendations as meeting universal needs among patients, despite several studies that have called into question the belief that breast loss is the most important concern of patients. (Meyerowitz *et al.* 1988: 81)

Feminist positivist empiricists also conduct their own, better, scientific studies in pursuit of feminist goals. Feminist research on women's concerns after mastectomy, for example, has challenged the assumption that 'appearance' *is* the primary concern. In fact, in a study of 112 breast cancer patients, 'future health' was cited far more frequently than was physical attractiveness, and concerns about future health were found to be far more upsetting to patients (Meyerowitz 1981).

So, feminist positivist empiricism critiques mainstream science, on standard scientific grounds, for not being scientific *enough*. It exposes biased sampling, inappropriate generalization and unwarranted conclusions based on social stereotypes and sexist bias, rather than on objective evidence. And it may involve doing better – i.e., *more* scientific – research. The history of feminist health research shows that positivist empiricism is a pervasive and powerful strategy for pursuing, and achieving, feminist goals. Despite the various critiques of positivist empiricism produced by critical psychologists, including feminists (for example, Crawford and Kimmel 1999), it is still the dominant paradigm in North American 'psychology of women', including 'the psychology of women's health' (cf. Lee 1988; Adesso *et al.* 1994; Stanton and Gallant 1995).

Feminist Experiential Approaches

Experiential approaches are also a key tradition of feminist research, providing an influential counterpoint to feminist positivist empiricism. The key feature of this tradition is an emphasis on individual *experience*: individuals are regarded as 'experts' on their own lives, and as 'authorities' on their own experience. This feminist tradition sits very comfortably with qualitative health research based on individuals' own understandings and experiences of health and illness (for example, Bury 1988; Robinson 1990). Experiential approaches rely on a wide variety of qualitative methods, including one-to-one interviews, focus groups, life histories, narrative/storytelling approaches and autobiographies (see Murray and Chamberlain 1999b, for a review).

Feminists have emphasized how in mainstream research (and culture) the experience of women has systematically been ignored, trivialized or distorted. By contrast, feminist experiential approaches seek to 'listen to women's voices', expressing their *own* 'meanings', to *reclaim* women's experience as central (cf. Brems and Griffiths 1993). The arguments for 'listening to women's voices' can also be more generally applied to the experience of other marginalized and oppressed groups. Feminist experiential approaches seek to make visible the wide *diversity* of experience, in relation to differences of race, class and sexual identity, for example. In contrast to positivist empiricist research, which limits and constrains responses by means of standardized questions, scales and measures, and 'loses' the individual in statistical summaries, experiential approaches generate vivid, personal accounts of individual lives and experiences.

Feminist experiential approaches derive from a variety of feminist theory often called 'standpoint theory' (for example, Harding 1993), which, broadly speaking, holds that women see the world from a particular perspective, or standpoint, because of the specific experience of being a woman in a patriarchal world. Contemporary feminist theorists typically also emphasize the specificities of knowledge deriving from other standpoints/experiences (for example, a male standpoint, a working-class standpoint, a Jewish standpoint), and the interrelationships between standpoints (for example, Henwood *et al.* 1998). Such an approach challenges the positivist empiricist notion of a single, external reality, which can best be apprehended by means of objective scientific enquiry. Rather, knowledge is seen as contingent upon the standpoint of the knower, and as dependent upon the specificities of her/his experience.

Feminist experiential approaches aim particularly to 'give voice' to those whose experience has traditionally been ignored, muted or silenced by oppressive institutions and practices. So, for example, in the context of a study of women's narratives of recovery from disabling mental health problems in Aotearoa/New Zealand, Lapsley *et al.* (2000) present Maori (indigenous) women's narratives alongside those of Pakeha (settler) women. Similarly, Marshall and Yazdani (2000) determine the meanings of self-harm for young South Asian women living in East London themselves, rather than inferring such meanings from the 'homogenizing' health and counselling services to which they have access.

I will give two more extended examples of experiential research. The first is drawn from my own work on lesbians and breast cancer. Although lesbian and gay health has become a distinctive specialism within the broader field (see Solarz 1999; Wilkinson 2001 for recent research reviews; and White and Martinez 1997; Wilton 1997, 2000 for more 'popular' treatments), breast cancer has been little studied in relation to lesbians. This is all the more surprising because it is widely believed that lesbians are more at risk of contracting breast cancer than are heterosexual women (for example, Rankow 1995), although recent reports that lesbians have a three times higher risk of breast cancer than heterosexual women are not well-founded (cf. Yadlon 1997). Apart from a few moving autobiographical accounts (for example, Lorde 1980; Butler and Rosenblum 1994), little is known about lesbians' experiences of breast cancer. My own small-scale study, using interviews and focus groups, explores this neglected area.

As one might expect, in the context of a life-threatening illness, many of the issues raised by lesbians are very similar to those raised by heterosexual women. But there are some important differences. Although lesbians with breast cancer may suffer just as much anxiety, fear and pain as do heterosexual women, they do so in a context in which the *expectations* they face are very different. The literature on breast cancer is suffused with heterosexist assumptions (see Wilkinson and Kitzinger 1993, for a feminist critique). As we have seen, women are assumed to be obsessed with their personal appearance, and to feel 'unfeminine' or 'unattractive' to men after surgery. Equally, lesbians (and older heterosexual women) are assumed not to care about their appearance and, it seems, are even told by some surgeons that they do not 'need' their breasts, presumably because breasts are primarily for attracting men and for satisfying them sexually (and maybe occasionally for breastfeeding babies). As one focus group participant said, 'it's very easy for them just to whip it off and think it doesn't matter'. But, of course, lesbians' breasts also have a sexual role (and sometimes a maternal one, too) and the appearance, touch and feel of breasts are often central to lesbians' sex lives, as many of my research participants emphasized: 'I really like my breasts a lot and I have a really erotic relationship to them'; 'I just love [my partner's] breasts and they do turn me on'; 'I think sexually my nipples are very sensitive; when that's the most exciting part of sex, I get so bloody turned on it can drive me up the wall'; 'I must say I think that breasts are, you know, one of the most attractive parts of a woman's body'; 'I love my breasts'; 'they're erotic'.

Not surprisingly, then, the loss of a breast was also described by many lesbians as 'devastating'. One lesbian who had had a mastectomy told me: 'I thought, "Well, you know, this is the end of life as I know it", and I actually, I sort of mourned for the loss of my breast... I was really very disturbed and distressed about it.' Another woman, whose lover had developed breast cancer, found it extremely difficult to come to terms with her lover's appearance after her mastectomy: 'I thought it was horrific what the body looks like without a breast...she looked like she'd been butchered...the fact she was flat-chested wasn't the issue, it's the scars.' Lesbians contemplating the possibility of mastectomy said 'I would just feel so mutilated'; 'it's something that is sexual'; 'in my sex life I would miss it'; 'it's not just your breasts, it's your whole body image – it's the way you feel about your body afterwards'. There was no suggestion at all that breasts are unimportant or irrelevant to lesbians or that the loss of a breast (or breasts) would be anything other than traumatic. These preliminary findings suggest how important it is to listen to lesbians' own voices in order to develop health services and support facilities better attuned to their specific needs and concerns.

My second example is drawn from the relatively new interdisciplinary field of 'men's health studies', which is heavily influenced by critical feminist theory. Broadly speaking, it is now recognized that traditional notions of 'macho' masculinity can be dangerous to men's health (for example, Harrison *et al.* 1995); and that there is substantial diversity among *men's* experiences, including their experiences of health and illness (cf. Sabo and Gordon 1995). Experiential approaches are being used within 'men's health studies', in particular, in order to understand better and theorize the specific experience of non-traditional and low-status men (for example, gay men living with HIV, men with physical disabilities). In a study of the ways in which having testicular cancer affects men's sense of themselves as men, for example, Gordon (1995) found that having a clear-cut masculine identity of some kind was very important. His interviewees employed two different strategies in thinking about their masculinity. The first was to define the cancer experience as reaffirming a traditional view of masculinity (the 'John Wayne' attitude):

> It is very much that kind of defiance of castration. And I like that . . . I like being able to say to myself, You know, you've had cancer and you beat the son of a bitch . . . (College professor, cited in Gordon 1995: 255)

Men who used this approach to make sense of their experience interpreted their survival as a fight they had won by displaying courage and toughness. This enabled them to feel more self-confident and more (traditionally) masculine.

The second, less common, strategy was to define themselves in non-traditionally masculine terms:

> I think you start thinking more about yourself as to how you are as a person in your relationships to other people. It's not so much of a me attitude. It's us. And you know we all count in this world. I remember, I don't think I ever hugged anybody all that much. My father was never a hugger. But I'll tell you, since I've been through this, I've hugged more people in the past six years than I had in my entire life. (Administrator, cited in Gordon 1995: 260)

Men who employed this strategy interpreted the cancer experience as having changed them in one of three ways: becoming more emotionally expressive, becoming more concerned about personal relationships, and becoming more empathetic to others. They did not report feeling *less* masculine, but rather *redefined* masculinity to include these characteristics. They also reported feeling better about themselves and about life in general than before the cancer experience. Gordon (1995) concludes that the non-traditional strategy promotes more effective coping with the experience of testicular cancer.

So, feminist experiential approaches offer a 'window' on the richness and complexity of individuals' lives, particularly those whose voices have not traditionally been heard. Listening to participants' articulations of their own meanings and identities may afford feminist researchers a radical opportunity to understand individuals' lives in their own terms. 'Speaking' and 'listening' are fundamentally feminist political acts.

Feminist Discursive Research

A third key tradition is feminist discursive research. The term 'discursive' covers a variety of approaches, including those which draw relatively heavily on

---

Box 5.2   Key traditions of feminist research

Feminist positivist empiricism

- Uses conventional scientific methods to discover 'objective' truths about the external world;
- Critiques mainstream science for its biases – i.e., not being 'scientific enough';
- May involve doing better, i.e., 'more scientific, research within the same tradition.

Feminist experiential research

- Uses qualitative methods to generate vivid personal accounts of individuals' own experience, in their own words;
- Aims to make a wide diversity of experience visible;
- May highlight, in particular, the 'voices' of those whose experience has, to date, been largely ignored or invisible.

Feminist discursive research

- Focuses on the study of talk, seen as a form of action (i.e., as doing things);
- Emphasizes individuals' own understandings of what their talk is doing, in its interactional context;
- May be used to study issues of accountability and the moral order, as co-constructed in, and through, social interaction.

---

poststructuralism or postmodernism – sometimes referred to as 'critical discourse analysis' (CDA) or 'Foucauldian discourse analysis' (cf. Burman and Parker 1993) – and those which draw more extensively on the interdisciplinary field of conversation analysis – sometimes referred to as 'discursive psychology' (DP) (cf. Edwards and Potter 1992). Although feminists work within both the CDA and the DP traditions, it is the second of these I will highlight here (see Chapter 9, for a focus on CDA).

There are three key features of the DP approach. First, it is the study of *talk* – not the thoughts, emotions, attitudes, beliefs or life experiences presumed to lie behind (and to be expressed through) talk. Second, it treats talk as a form of *action* – i.e. *doing things* (like disagreeing, complaining, or presenting a particular identity). Third, it focuses on how the people involved in the talk understand what their talk is doing, as those understandings *are displayed in the talk itself*. A discursive approach draws on analytic resources 'intrinsic to the data themselves' (Sacks *et al.* 1974: 729): i.e., rather than depending on the *researcher's* analysis, it prioritizes the *participants'* analysis of the interaction, as manifest in their talk, through the conversational practices they use.

I will give two examples of DP research that is of importance to feminists, focusing, in particular, on issues of accountability and the moral order. Note that there is no assumption here (as in CDA) that the external world 'imposes' a pre-existing moral order upon interactants. Rather, the emphasis of DP is that interactants themselves co-construct a moral order, moment by moment, by and through the processes of their interaction. Any communicative action is seen as *context-shaped* (i.e. as understandable – by participants – only by reference to the ongoing sequence of actions of which it forms a part) and as *context-renewing* (i.e. contributing to the immediate context within which the next action will be understood). Each action also contributes to (i.e., maintains, alters, adjusts) the more generally prevailing sense of context that informs the participants' orientations and actions (for a more extended, accessible introduction to the key assumptions of conversation analysis, see Heritage 1984, Chapter 8).

The first example is drawn from a study of health visitors' interactions with first-time mothers, during the course of the health visitor's initial visit to the mother's home (Heritage and Sefi 1992). In the following extract, both the mother and father of the baby are present when, early on in the visit, the health visitor makes an apparently casual observation (the baby is – presumably – engaged in some kind of 'sucking' or 'mouthing' behaviour):

```
[4A1:1]
  1   HV:              He's enjoying that [isn't he.
  2   Father:                            [ °Yes he certainly is=°
  3   Mother:          =He's not hungry 'cuz (h)he's ju(h)st (h)had
  4                    'iz bo:ttle .hhh
Heritage & Sefi, 1992: 367¹)
```

The health visitor's observation ('He's enjoying that, isn't he?') elicits contrastive responses from the baby's father and the baby's mother. While the father apparently takes the remark at face value and responds with an agreement, the mother's response is notably defensive. She treats the health visitor's observation as implying that the baby may be hungry, and, further, that this might possibly imply some failure on her part to provide him with adequate nourishment. She quickly – and explicitly – denies that the baby is hungry, and goes on to produce an account that justifies her claim (i.e., he cannot possibly be hungry 'cuz he's just had 'iz bo:ttle'). This account is delivered with laughter infiltrated: which could perhaps be read as 'doing laughing off' the very possibility that such an implication could be made. On the other hand, in a medical context, reports of 'misdeeds' (i.e., breaking a dietary regime, or recommencing smoking) are often inflected with laughter (Heritage, pers. comm.), so perhaps she is acknowledging culpability (or at least uncertainty) of some kind. In either case, the mother's response indicates that she sees herself as accountable to the health visitor – i.e., she treats the health visitor as someone who, whatever else her job may entail, is here evaluating her competence in child care, her very adequacy as a mother.

Heritage and Sefi note that this orientation towards the health visitor as someone who may 'stand in judgement' on the mother's competence (irrespective of whether the health visitor does, or does not, make such judgements) render the requesting and receiving of advice highly problematic in these early home visits. A request for advice from the mother constitutes an admission of uncertainty, and may further imply – or display – a lack of knowledge, competence or ability to cope. At the same time, such a request, in the very process of its being made, constitutes the recipient (i.e., the health visitor) as the knowledgeable, competent and authoritative party to the interaction.

This small fragment of data offers the analyst a glimpse of the moral universe inhabited by participants. It is possible to infer, from data-internal evidence, that this is a universe in which mothers are expected to provide adequate care for their infants (in a way in which, perhaps, fathers are not) and that, further, mothers consider themselves accountable (to specified medical authority figures) for any – imputed – failure of care (again, in a way in which, perhaps fathers do not). Through the very action of responding to the health visitor's observation as an (implied) criticism of her mothering skills with an account which addresses this implied criticism, the mother (re)produces *herself* as someone who is accountable for the adequacy of her mothering, and co-implicates the *health visitor* as someone who is in the business of assessing this adequacy. Examining the constitution of women (and perhaps only women) as mothers, and the (re)production of this role through the day-to-day business of doing-being-a-mother is a powerful way to study the conditions of oppression.

My second example comes from my own data set: a series of discussions between women with breast cancer, audiotaped and subsequently transcribed (cf. Wilkinson 2000 for more details). In reading through the transcripts, I noticed a great deal of talk about 'thinking positive' or 'positive thinking'. Rather than taking this as empirical evidence for the existence of thinking positive (the positivist empiricist approach) or as telling us something about women's experiences of positive thinking (the experiential approach), I was interested, from a feminist discursive perspective, in looking more closely at what such talk is doing, as a form of action, in the context of these discussions.

There are many ways in which thinking positive *could* be talked about: as something that participants happen to do and are therefore reporting; or as something they have found helpful; or as a way of dealing with their cancer that they are planning to adopt. But thinking positive is most typically talked about as a *moral* obligation, as something you 'have' to do. Moral exhortations (imperatives and injunctions) are commonplace in the data: for example, women say 'you just have to think positive'; 'you've got to think positive, a'n't you?'; 'you've got to think positive'; 'you *have* to be positive'; 'you have to think positive'. In the following extract, for example, Betty and Yvonne are discussing thinking positive *not* as a natural reaction to having cancer (the natural reaction is that 'obviously you're devastated because it's a dreadful thing'), but as a moral imperative ('you've got to have a positive attitude'):

[TP1, G3]

1	Betty:	When I first found out I had cancer, I said to myself, I said,
2		right, it's not gonna get me. And that was it. I mean
3	Yvonne:	Yeah
4	Betty:	obviously you're devastated because it's a dreadful thing
5	Yvonne:	(overlaps) Yeah, but you've got to have a positive attitude
6		thing, I do
7	Betty:	(overlaps) But then, I was talking to Dr Purcott and he
8		said to me the most helpful thing that anybody can have
9		with any type of cancer is a positive attitude
10	Yvonne:	A positive outlook, yes
11	Betty:	Because if you decide to fight it, then the rest of your
12		body will st-, will start
13	Yvonne:	Motivate itself, yeah
14	Betty:	to fight it

Like Betty, women with breast cancer often report that it was a medical professional who advised them to think positively (here – lines 7–9 – 'Dr Purcott', the women's consultant oncologist). However, from a discursive perspective, such reports are not taken as transparent evidence that a medical professional *was* the source of this advice. Rather, Betty is seen as attributing this recommendation to an 'expert' in order to render her conduct accountable: perhaps to distance herself from a *personal* belief in the efficacy of positive thinking (with the attendant possible implication of gullibility), for example, by presenting it as a *medical* recommendation. Notice also how delicately Betty and Yvonne negotiate (while leaving rather vague and understated) what will happen 'if you decide to fight it' (i.e., if you have 'a positive attitude' or a 'positive outlook'). Nonetheless, the two women are broadly aligned in their assessment that the consequences of this will be good ones: Yvonne completes Betty's statement before Betty herself does (lines 11–14). Elsewhere in these discussions, women are careful to emphasize that in advocating positive thinking they do not subscribe to a simple belief in 'mind over matter' – for example, 'It's *not* mind over matter, no' (see Wilkinson and Kitzinger 2000 for a more extended analysis).

More broadly, these frequent moral exhortations and injunctions point to the existence of a moral order for breast cancer patients: that they *should* be thinking positively, that this is the right attitude – indeed the expected attitude – of patients if they are to be seen as co-operating with medical treatment and giving themselves the best chance of recovery. The most devastating implication of this moral order is that cancer patients *themselves* are to blame if they don't get well (cf. Hay 1984; Richardson 1988) and that this must be because they failed to 'let go' of their 'negative thoughts' or 'negative attitudes' (see Wilkinson and Kitzinger 1993 for a more extensive critique of the cancer 'self-help' literature).

There is plenty of evidence for this moral order in both the self-help and psycho-oncology literatures. Self-help books with titles like *The A–Z of Positive Thinking* (James 1999) or *The Power of Positive Thinking* (Peale 1998) are readily available, and health professionals are likely to draw on the work of Steven Greer and his colleagues (for example, Greer *et al.* 1989), claiming an association between thinking positive and cancer morbidity and mortality rates. Critics have even referred to this state of affairs as the 'moral oppression' (de Raeve 1997) of positive thinking in cancer care.

Little wonder, then, that *talk* about thinking positive is so pervasive. From a discursive perspective, however, these women's talk does not simply reflect the existence of a 'moral order of thinking positive' out there in the world – rather, that moral order is 'talked into being' in and through their discussions. The discussions themselves provide local contexts within which this moral order can be affirmed, or resisted (see Kitzinger 2000a, for an analysis of resistance to 'thinking positive'). Identifying the role of moral injunctions – i.e. 'think positive' – as powerful and pervasive components of oppression is central to the feminist project. Identifying, and facilitating, acts of resistance to such potentially harmful injunctions is equally crucial.

So, feminist discursive research focuses on talk *itself*; it treats talk as a form of *action*; and it prioritizes speakers' and listeners' *own* understandings of what their talk is doing (rather than those of the researcher). As a form of feminist research, then, it shares with experiential approaches a commitment to 'hearing participants' voices', but it takes what they say still more seriously. Rather than the *researcher* offering an interpretative 'gloss' on what participants 'mean' (as in experiential research), the focus is on participants' *own* understandings, *as displayed in their talk*. Feminist researchers (for example, Kitzinger 2000b) are enthusiastic about the value of such an approach for furthering the feminist goal of exposing, and dismantling, oppression. Although feminist discursive approaches have, as yet, been relatively little used in the context of researching health and illness, they offer considerable potential for the future development of feminist contributions to critical health psychology.

Conclusion

Although their approaches are very different, all three of these research traditions – feminist positivist empiricism, feminist experiential approaches, and feminist discursive research – have been used within critical health psychology to pursue the political goals of feminism. Just like feminist activism, feminist research seeks to expose and dismantle women's oppression (and that of other marginalized social groups). *All* of the feminist contributions to critical health psychology – feminist analysis of gender bias in mainstream medical science, feminist resistance through activism, and feminist resistance through research –

which I have outlined in this chapter, share the central feminist goals of better reflecting the wide diversity of human experience, and of improving the conditions of all our lives.

Key Points

- Feminist work is a central component of critical health psychology.
- Feminist research and practice recognizes the oppression of women (and others) and aims to end that oppression.
- Feminists have exposed pervasive gender bias in mainstream medical science.
- Feminists have resisted such oppression through various kinds of activism and various kinds of research.
- Feminist activism includes: forming organizations outside the mainstream professions; speaking out against medical and scientific abuses; campaigning for entry into the professions in order to change them from within.
- Feminist research traditions include: feminist positivist empiricism; feminist experiential approaches; and feminist discursive research.
- Feminist research and activism have both been used to improve the lives not only of women, but of other oppressed and marginalized social groups.

Assignment Questions

1. What is feminist research – and how can it contribute to critical health psychology?
2. In what ways has traditional medical science oppressed women; and in what ways have they resisted this oppression?

Note

1. For data extracts included in this section, the notation at the top locates the specific extract within a larger corpus of data, and the transcription conventions used are as follows:
   underlining indicates emphasis
   [indicates start of overlapping talk
   ° indicates talk noticeably quieter than the talk surrounding it
   = indicates that the talk is 'latched' (i.e., follows the preceding talk without a break)
   (h) indicates that laughter infiltrates the talk
   : indicates a sound stretch on the preceding syllable
   .hhh indicates an inbreath
   a dash indicates that a word (or sound) is cut off abruptly
   transcriber's comments are enclosed in parentheses

📖 Further Readings

Dan, A.J. (ed.) (1994) *Reframing Women's Health: Multidisciplinary Research and Practice*, Thousand Oaks, CA: Sage.

An eclectic 'reader', emphasising diversity – contributions span a range of feminist theoretical perspectives, methodologies, research participant/client groups and geographical areas.

Ehrenreich, B. and English, D. (1978) *For Her Own Good: 150 Years of Experts' Advice to Women*, New York, NY: Anchor Doubleday.

One of the most accessible, informative and entertaining introductions to the history of women's health care in the nineteenth and twentieth centuries.

Laurence, L. and Weinhouse, B. (1997) *Outrageous Practices: How Gender Bias Threatens Women's Health*, New Brunswick, NJ: Rutgers University Press.

An excellent introduction to, and overview of, sexist bias in health research and medical practice (both historical and contemporary).

Sabo, D. and Gordon, D.F. (1995) 'Rethinking men's health and illness: the relevance of gender studies', in D. Sabo and D.F. Gordon (eds), *Men's Health & Illness: Gender, Power and the Body*, Thousand Oaks, CA: Sage.

Demonstrates the value of a feminist theoretical and political framework for developing new understandings of men's health.

Wilkinson, S. (2000a) 'Feminist research traditions in health psychology: breast cancer research', *Journal of Health Psychology*, 5, 359–372.

Outlines the three main approaches to feminist research in health psychology (positivist empiricist, experiential, and discursive), and illustrates the use of each in relation to breast cancer.

Wilkinson, S. (2001) 'Lesbian health', in A. Coyle and C. Kitzinger (eds), *Lesbian and Gay Psychology: New Perspectives*, Oxford: Blackwell.

Briefly reviews the field of lesbian health, and highlights two different, and contrasting, projects: a large-scale (UK) national survey of lesbian health and a small-scale qualitative project on lesbians and breast cancer.

CHAPTER 6

Culture, Empowerment and Health

Malcolm MacLachlan

Let us think for a moment of the expatriate relief worker arriving for his morning clinic at the refugee camp. The cloud of approaching dust announces the arrival of the Landrover, with our relief worker, the sole occupant, at the wheel. He doesn't know it, but he's not alone. With him he brings cross-cultural transference and counter-transference: In the back of his Landrover are White Colonial Masters, Eurocentricism, parentalism, professionalism, reductionism, capitalism, and other 'isms', which he, and I, are simply unaware of. The point is, no matter his intentions, he is a symbol. Even if he does not embody that which he symbolises to others, he is never, himself alone. (English translation from German; from MacLachlan 2002: 242)

Summary

This chapter is concerned with the interplay between culture and health. This is a vast area and there are several comprehensive reviews of the literature available (see for instance, MacLachlan 1997; Swartz 1997; Helman 2001). My interest here is to develop a taxonomy of the ways in which culture can influence health. To begin we will consider three, what could be termed, conventional approaches. First, 'Cultural Colonialism' is rooted in the sort of colonial intrigue that stuffed our natural history museums with exotic beasts. Here the interest is to compare 'ourselves' with those who are different. Second, 'Cultural Sensitivity' is not about managing the health of 'those people' over there, its about managing the health of 'those people' here. The key concern is how services should be adapting to meet the needs of cultural minorities amongst 'us'. Third, the 'Cultural Migration' approach is concerned with managing the health of people migrating to a new country, in such a way as to enhance their well-being, and to 'protect' the well-being of nationals. We will only briefly review literature pertaining to these three areas, because the major focus of the chapter is on the other, somewhat less conventional, and more 'critical' categories.

Perhaps bridging the conventional and the less conventional approaches to the relationship between culture and health is what could be called 'Cultural Alternativism'. While alternative (or complementary) therapies have been around for some time, we are interested in what accounts for their recent surge in popularity? What is it that people 'get from them'? The Fifth approach we will consider is, 'Cultural Empowerment', which sees health as an index of the social well-being of a cultural group and advocates cultural reawakening as a form of therapy. The sixth approach, 'Cultural Globalisation', can be seen in some ways as the re-introduction of Western colonialism under a commercial banner. In many ways, this approach is the antithesis of the previous one and may have dire consequences for the health of the under-privileged. The final approach in this typology, 'Cultural Evolution', examines the effects of culture change, within the same society, on health. The large number of societies undergoing rapid change makes many of us 'transitional people' who, at times, may have similar acculturation problems as cultural migrants.

This typology is a sketch and is intended to be neither comprehensive nor mutually exclusive. One type of research may be categorised under more than one category, and research from several categories may be brought to bear on similar issues. After describing in more detail this taxonomy, I conclude with the 'so what' question: 'What are cultures for?' Drawing on the work of Ernest Becker and of the more recent research on Terror Management Theory, I conclude that culture is the glue of our identity, and *maintaining our identity is what we need our health for*. Before all of this, let's start by considering why a chapter on culture is important in a book on critical health psychology.

What's Critical about Culture?

Critical psychology is concerned with counteracting approaches to psychology that portray people in an individualistic, reductionist, or abstract manner (Guba and Lincoln 1994; Murray and Chamberlain 1998b) and denude them of their humanity and the legitimacy of their subjectivity. Health psychology's adoption of the biopsychosocial model (Sarafino 2001) was supposed to counter an overly biomedical and reductionist perspective on health, but the biopsychosocial model has tended to be used as a multiple rather than integrative framework (Cooper *et al.* 1996). Critical health psychology places the person's experience, and the meanings they adopt, at the core of health and illness. Furthermore, it acknowledges the importance of our consciousness, or our ability to reflect on our own behaviour and our attempts to make meaning (Crossley 2000). In the postmodernist sense, critical health psychology therefore acknowledges, that the 'viewer is always a part of their view' and that views (or meanings) are, constructed through and influenced by, the social, political and economic fabric of people's lives.

Once we get to acknowledging a degree of subjectivity, and the influence of those around us, on how we understand important health-related events in our lives (see for instance, Stainton Rogers 1991; Radley 1994), we are by default acknowledging the importance of culture. However, the interest of critical psychologists in culture goes beyond validating the alternative perspectives to health and illness. It acknowledges that because of political and economic forces all perspectives are not equal – not because of inherent benefits or flaws within these perspectives *per se* – but because those espousing predominately 'Western' approaches to understanding health and illness are usually in a much more powerful position than those espousing, for instance, aboriginal understandings (Carr *et al.* 1998). Psychology cannot be, and never has been, neutral on such matters. Indeed the 'science' of psychology, and in particular psychometrics, has been used to discriminate against disempowered groups, even to the extent of justifying the creation of apartheid in South Africa (recall that H.F. Verwoerd, the 'architect' of apartheid, was formally the head of a well respected university department of psychology).

The 'New World Order' suits mainstream psychology well. With only 4 per cent of the world's population, North America dominates the world of psychology to such an extent that alternative psychologies are termed 'indigenous psychologies'. While 'critical psychology' is not a unified whole and there are different perspectives within it, a common theme is its concern with the alleviation of suffering associated with exploitation and oppression, and an acknowledgement that the implicit individualism of mainstream psychology prohibits its effectiveness in combating social problems (Prilleltensky 2001).

Cultural considerations are therefore central to a critical health psychology not only because they give legitimacy to alternative views, but also because they help to elucidate how the predominant worldview dissempowers those outside of it (and often many within it too). Before considering the typology described above it is important to sound a cautionary note. Because culture, empowerment, racism and illness are *things that matter to people* on a personal level, they arouse great emotions, *and so they should!* A health psychology, which is of no emotional consequence, is redundant in a world where two billion people live in poverty and 20,000 people die each day from hunger (Concern 2002; Sloan 2002; Carr and Sloan 2003). Yet, in describing this typology and considering how culture, empowerment and health are related, it is important to bear in mind that this classification is systemic. There are many well meaning *individuals* who are not part of any great plot to undermine anybody, but who may lack an understanding of how working in the way that they do, contributes to a *system* that diminishes the value of others. Such individuals may be rather unreflective cogs in the well-greased machinery of cultural oppression – indeed to the extent to which we do not rage against such inequity, we all are.

Cultural Colonialism

In the 19th-century heyday of multiple European colonial powers (for example, Britain, France, Belgium, Portugal, Holland, Italy), Europeans sought to 'farm' South America, Africa and Asia for the benefit of the European ruling classes. An important aspect of this venture was not only to understand 'the mind of the savage', but also to make sure 'he' was healthy enough to be productive. Anthropologists did good trade in identifying any number of 'culture bound syndromes'. The implicit ethnocentricity in this perspective was that the term 'culture bound syndromes' was used to describe disorders or illnesses with which the people making the classification were not familiar. Thus, if an array of symptoms was not familiar to Europeans, and yet occurred in sufficient cluster to be called a syndrome, then it was thought to be a condition bounded by the culture in which it was exhibited. Dubow (1995) suggests that as part of the Colonial research agenda Africans became the 'objects' of three distinct 'scientific' projects: accumulating scientific knowledge of 'primitive minds'; Africa as a laboratory for the discovery of psychological universals; and the design of psychometric devices for the selection and training of African workers. As Nsamenang and Dawes (1998) assert, all these endeavours were exploitive and their primary relevance was to the academic, government and industrial communities of the time, and not to Africans.

The 'dramatic exotica' (Simons 1985) so classified, does without doubt provide us with some colourful and bizarre conditions. These include *koro*, where people believe their genital organs are shrinking, and for instance, a man may anchor his penis with some sort of clamping device, or a woman may insert iron pins through her nipples, all to stop them contracting (see MacLachlan 1997). In the case of *latah*, a person who is startled by an unexpected event may throw or drop an object which was being held, utter obscenities, carry out actions suggested to them, in an apparently automatic fashion, and mimic the word or movements of someone close by at the time (see MacLachlan 1997). However, both of these syndromes – and there are many, many more (see Simons and Hughes 1985) – when considered in the sociocultural context in which they occur, can be understood not as oddities, but to have a meaningful *order* and a valuable social *function*.

While the 'collecting' of culture-bound syndromes by European colonialists may have been part of the machinery of oppression, and a means of reassuring them that the people they were oppressing, were not like themselves, these syndromes are undeniably intriguing. It is perhaps less that they were wrong in their linking cultural factors to health, and more that they were wrong in doing it so selectively: the European colonialists were somewhat 'construct bound'. It is now increasingly accepted not only that the 'West' has culture-bound syndromes (for instance, anorexia nervosa, exhibitionism, Type A behaviour), but in fact that all disorder is influenced by cultural factors, and sometimes a direct product of them (for example, Weisz *et al.* 1987).

Cultural Sensitivity

This approach to health care is typical of the situation where ethnic minorities have particular requirements within a health system. Sometimes these minority groups will be constituted of several generations of immigrants (with migrants continuing to come to the country), for instance, the Latino community in the United States. However, such minorities may well be indigenous peoples whose culture has existed only on the periphery of mainstream society (for instance, 'Native American' or First Nations people in North America). The emphasis in this approach is to essentially try and provide the same sort of health service as to mainstream society but to take into account the cultural 'peculiarities' of ethnic minorities.

Rogler *et al.* (1987), in addressing the question 'What do culturally sensitive mental health services actually mean?', outlined a hierarchical framework. At the base of their three-levels hierarchy is the need to increase the *accessibility* of treatment to cultural minorities. Next, is the *selection* of treatments to fit particular cultures and finally, they recommend the *modification* of treatments to fit particular cultures. Suggested mechanism for encouraging cultural sensitivity have ranged from trying to increase cultural awareness with specific taught modules during the training of health professionals, to using paid 'minority mentors' who teach and supervise clinicians who are working with minority groups, to Traditional Healers from the client's culture working alongside clinicians, as co-therapists (Casimir and Morrison 1993). Sometimes these models of training will be contentious because, in effect, they question the validity of the predominant Western individualised biomedically orientated ethos. If, for instance, one is trained in a scientific psychology that is concerned with discovering universal principles underlying human behaviour, it can be difficult to accept that your 'universals' do not apply universally! The proponents of such contrary views can be dismissed as unscientific, underdeveloped, ignorant and so on, when in fact they may simply be expressing a different (and often equally culturally encapsulated) psychological rationale.

The sort of conflict described above can be constructive and informative to all involved, if they feel equally able to express their views. The clash becomes more insidious when, for example, in an attempt to help identify service needs, an ethnic minority group is surveyed for mental health problems and they are shown to have a high need for services, not because of inherent mental health problems, but because of the cultural insensitivity of the instrument. If one considers the DSM-IV criteria for personality disorder, there are behaviours characteristic of certain ethnic groups which increase the likelihood of such a diagnosis, *in the absence of mental health problems* (Alarcon and Foulks 1995). Ultimately, cultural sensitivity has to be more about an approach to human problems that is accepting of alternative causal models, than it is about modifying a mainstream theory or ethos, to take account of cultural peculiarities. We must not however run away from the very real ethical responsibility of any clinician to facilitate action or treatment in a direction which accords with their own personal and professional beliefs about what will be of benefit to someone who is suffering.

Cultural Migration

The focus here is on people who have left their own country either as temporary sojourners or permanent migrants, sometimes as *forced* (involuntary) migrants, or refugees. The major concern, particularly for permanent migrants, is how the stresses and strains of adjustment are dealt with. Berry's (1990, 1997) framework, one of the most influential in this field, posits four distinct acculturation strategies determined by the extent to which people value their heritage culture relative to the one they have migrated into. When distress results from this individual–culture interaction, *acculturative stress* may be observed with consequences ranging across each of physiological, psychological and social aspects of health (Searle and Ward 1990). A number of studies have now demonstrated that *integration* (wishing to identify with the host culture and the culture of origin) is a more beneficial strategy in terms of maintaining mental health, than *marginalisation* (wishing to identify with neither), with *assimilation* (identifying only with the host culture) and *separation* (identifying only with the culture of origin) being associated with intermediate levels of distress (Berry and Kim 1998).

Programmes set up to screen migrants for physical disease and mental disorder are not only for the well-being of the migrants, but also often to reassure host communities, and can at times indirectly support racist attitudes to immigrants. It is ironic that those who are xenophobic and oppose migrants being allowed to settle in their own community often create the very circumstances that are more likely to cause difficulties for the migrants – and themselves. There are many changes associated with migration, for instance, loss of familiar social networks and roles, communication difficulties, different attitudes regarding the relative status of older and younger people, vocation changes, and changes in religious practices.

While the mental health effects of migration may be apparent, migration can also have serious effects on physical well-being. However, it is important to recognise that cultural change occurs in a much broader social context than is often considered by many health psychologists. Between 1989 and 1992 over 380,000 Jews from the former Soviet Union emigrated to Israel, leaving behind them economic hardship, political instability, national conflicts and fear of increasing anti-Semitism. In Israel, they confronted severe housing shortages and high level of unemployment, along with the radically different Israeli culture. Baider *et al.* (1996) compared 116 immigrants who had cancer with 288 physically healthy immigrants. All immigrants reported significant adjustment problems. Sixty percentage of the healthy immigrants reported that their employment, economic and social situation was worse than it had been in Russia, while 80 per cent of those with cancer judged their social situation in Israel to be worse than it was in Russia. Both groups scored highly on measures of mental distress. The majority (almost 90 per cent) of the cancer patients had been diagnosed since arriving in Israel. Putting all of these factors together – recent serious diagnosis, being older, recently arriving in a new country, being out of work, economically worse off and often having less social support – it is clear that the health of these migrants was influenced by many more factors than having to adapt to different cultural values and customs. Thus, while it is important to consider the migration experience in terms of cultural change, it is also important to ground this in terms of a possibly more significant change in political, economic and social context.

Cultural Alternativism

Kleinman (1980) has suggested that there are three overlapping sectors in health care – the popular sector (where 'everyday' ideas about health and illness are discussed), the professional sector (comprised of conventional health professionals) and the folk sector (combining aspects of the first two). The folk sector includes sacred and secular healers, incorporating faith healers, mediums and herbalists, for instance. With increasing international migration, those who would be thought of as 'traditional healers' in their own society are seen as alternative practitioners in host societies (offering for example, reflexology, shiatsu, yoga). If you add to the 'folk sector' a range of more 'New Age' therapies (such as, crystal and gem therapy, therapeutic touch and sound therapy), you have a plethora of approaches to healing which are attracting an ever increasing number of followers (Furnham and Vincent 2001). While many of these approaches may be beneficial in their own right, it may also be that they are attractive to people because they offer a different 'culture' of health care. If this is so, what distinguishes them from conventional health care?

Gray (1998) has characterised the biomedical perspective as being concerned with the curing of disease and the control of symptoms. The physician is seen to be a scientist working technically with high-level skills to correct physiological problems. In contrast, Gray (1998), while noting heterogeneity in complementary therapies, suggests that they tend to share a concern with life domains beyond the physical domain; view disease as symptomatic of underlying systemic problems; have a reliance on clinical experience to guide practice; and are critical of the limits of a biomedical approach. Furnham and Vincent (2001) suggest that a centrally attractive – and probably therapeutic in itself – feature of complementary medicine is the consultation process. In contrast to the brief encounter with an overworked general practitioner, complementary consultations are much longer; tend to include all aspects of a person's life and therefore be more holistic; emphasise the importance of understanding 'the person' rather than 'the problem'; involve touching and examining the patient/client which helps to build a trusting relationship; involves a discussion of options, uncertainties and prognosis; and show a greater willingness to discuss emotional problems and spiritual perspectives on health and illness.

In short, conventional medicine seems to focus increasingly on the clinician finding technical outcomes that will create better health, while alternative practitioners are more aware of the process of healing and using this to facilitate better health. The latter is about making people feel valued in the process, when often in wider society they may be afforded little respect. Feeling valued is, as we will see later, one of the most important functions that a culture has to perform. While recognising that not all alternative therapies are complementary (for example, St John's Wort and some antidepressants are antagonistic), I use the term 'cultural alternativism' in the sense that those not choosing to stick solely with conventional health care are entering into an ethos of 'pick and mix', which offers many alternatives to orthodoxy, some of which may be complementary.

Cultural Empowerment

> Psychologists cannot deny, and should not deny, the ethical, moral, and political ideological dimensions of our psychologies (Marsella 1998: 1286)

In describing the first category in this typology – Cultural Colonialism – we considered how the colonial worldview had sought to re-fashion local experiences into an account which made sense to the Colonials. As with any conquering tribe or nation, 'the conquered' were re-orientated to consider the world from the perspective of those who conquered them. This re-orientation effectively stripped people of the value of their own culture and resulted in them being second- or third-class citizens of a culture they did not ask for, identify with or have any prospect for achieving self-worth through. Even after the 'independence' of many former colonies, which had been culturally denuded of their traditional practices and customs, there remained a diminished sense of cultural worth. It was not, after all, so much that the colonials were giving up control, more that they were giving up residence, but often maintaining strong economic and political influence. Sloan (1996) has cogently argued that psychology so embodies Western cultural assumptions that it primarily performs an ideological function, to sustain a status quo characterised by economic inequality, and other forms of oppression such as sexism and racism. He believes that the core assumptions of Western psychology responsible for this are individualism and scientism.

Recently indigenous psychologies have sought to give credence to more traditional and localised ways of understanding people, as an equally legitimate alternative to European and North American 'mainstream' psychology (Holdstock 2000). While indigenous psychologies, may or may not, be an important stage in nation-state building, they do have an important role to play in building nations within nations. The North American 'First Nations' and the Australian Aborigines constitute a plethora of cultures subjugated by (at least originally) white Europeans. Unfortunately, alcoholism and drug abuse are a major problem in many of these communities. These problems may be attributed to social deprivation and the erosion of cultural integrity. Thus the individual alcoholic may be seen as a social expression of the experience of cultural repression. If this analysis is correct, then reconnecting individuals with their cultural heritage not only provides a medium for intervention, but also regenerates traditional values that in the case of First Nations are being increasingly portrayed as counter drug abuse (Brady 1995). The use of sweat lodges is the most common feature of native alcohol treatment programmes in North America. As a mechanism of treatment the sweat lodge has many advantages: it is a symbol of 'Indianness'; it creates a sense of detoxification and cleansing (physical, psychological and spiritual); its inherent drama and the fortitude it requires provides a rite of passage and commitment to a new way. The sweat lodge is thus a vehicle for both a cultural reawakening and an individual's re-enculturated awakening. This is only one example of the many ways in which we can see *culture as treatment*, in and of itself (MacLachlan 1997).

An important element in the empowerment of North American First Nations peoples has been the Indigenous People's Council on Biocolonialism (IPCB). Recently they released the Indigenous Research Protection Act intended to help American Indian tribes protect their genetic resources and peoples from the potentially harmful effects of scientific research. Essentially the act should allow them to become research 'partners' as opposed to research 'subjects', and represents an important initiative in valuing the resources and being of indigenous peoples (see www.ipcb.org/pub/irpaintro.html). For many indigenous groups who are marginalized by mainstream society, they are often presented with an implicit trade-off between integrating into the mainstream and enjoying its health, welfare, social and material benefits, or remaining culturally 'stuck' in another time when these benefits were not available. However, as Dobson (1998: 8), a prominent Indigenous Australian has said of domestic welfare: 'We want health, housing, and education; but not at the expense of losing our soul; our own identity; a say in our lives. We refuse to sacrifice the essence of what makes us Aboriginal people.'

Nsamenang (1995) argues that, 'African social thought and folk psychology are structured by ethnotheories and epistemologies that differ in remarkable ways from those that drive Western thought and psychology . . . Psychology cannot successfully develop in a society without having the local reality as the basis for its growth. Indigenization as a process of deriving theories, concepts, tools, and assessment techniques from a sociocultural system and feeding them back into it has become an acceptable and legitimate research goal' (p. 735–736). However, Nsamenang goes onto suggest that the development of indigenous psychology should not be an end-goal in itself because it could come to be 'as parochial and ethnocentric as mainstream psychology is at the moment' and suggests a need to realign and integrate locally developed psychologies with mainstream psychology.

Over the past ten years, having been criticised (by different authors) for being both Eurocentric *and* Afrocentric in our writings, it would be fair to say that Stuart Carr (Massey University) and myself are acutely aware of the epistemological and 'emotional booby-traps' awaiting any attempt to integrate mainstream and more local psychologies. We have argued that the application of psychology in developing countries has often met with a poor reception because 'psychologists have sought to apply psychologies from "somewhere else"' (MacLachlan and Carr 1994: 21); and we have set out a framework for a psychology 'which will address the local "settings and conditions"' (p. 22). We suggested that local psychologies may interact with mainstream Western psychology by refuting it, restating it, reconstituting it, or on occasion, realising that it applies quite nicely! (see also Carr *et al.* 1998; Carr 2002).

The indigenisation of psychology, while important in its own right, may also be understood as a reaction against the apparent hegemony and insensitivity of Western psychology (Carr and MacLachlan 1998). Often, it will not be possible to transpose Western psychology onto non-Western problems. Sometimes indigenous psychologies will be such an inseparable part of the context of a health problem that any dissolution of them, or any importation of an external perspective, will fail to achieve the desired ends. At other times, ideas, materials or methods from elsewhere may provide acceptable solutions to health problems within a community and therefore be welcomed by them when presented with regard to cultural mores (see for example, Meegan *et al.* 2001). Sometimes a mixture of ideas will work best. I have called this approach to cultural psychology 'pragmatic vernacularism' (MacLachlan 2001), drawing on developments in architecture. There, post-modern vernacular architecture has shunned classical or symbolic forms to create what people actually like – what works for them, at a local level. 'What works' may combine local and 'universal' forms. Similarly cultural empowerment should ideally give people the strength of a (local) collective identity, but not at the cost of having to neglect their (universal right to) health and welfare.

Cultural Globalisation

If you think you are too small to make a difference, try sleeping in a closed room with a mosquito – African Proverb.

Just when you thought we were finished with colonialism, it is back again! This time it is not in the guise of nation-states, but portrays itself as a 'global age'. 'Globalisation is restructuring the way in which we live, and in a very profound manner. It is led from the West, bears the strong imprint of American political and economic power, and is highly uneven in its consequences' (Giddens 1999: 4). Giddens goes on to say that we 'must find ways to bring our runaway world to heel' (p. 5). While there are many facets to globalisation (technological, cultural, political, economic), some of which may be quite positive, there are also many victims, especially of economic globalisation. For instance, in 1989 the poorest fifth of the world's population had 2.3 per cent of global income, whilst by 1998 this had dropped to an alarming 1.4 per cent; and in sub-Saharan Africa 20 countries now have lower per head incomes in real terms than they had 30 years ago (Giddens 1999). To put it another way, the three wealthiest people in the world (Bill Gates, Warren Buffet and Sultan Hassanal Bolkiah, with a combined wealth of US$117 billion) are a few million ahead of the combined Gross National Product (GNP) of the world's 45 poorest countries, whose population is close to three hundred million (Hopkin 2002).

World Bank loans to developing countries have become virtually conditional on the recipient country's agreement with the International Monetary Fund (IMF) on a fund programme (Cassen 1994). Often countries will be required to invest in cash crop production to be traded on the world market under 'free trade' regulations. This creates bizarre situations such as during the height of the 1984 Ethiopian famine, when oilseed, rape, linseed and cottonseed was being grown on prime agricultural land to be exported as feed for livestock to Europe Corner House Briefing (Sexton *et al.* 1998). Similarly, in 1997 the UN Development Report stated that in Africa alone, the money spent on annual debt repayments could be used to save the lives of about 21 million children by the year 2000. Indeed it has been argued by many that debt is now *the new colonialism* (see for example, George 1988; Somers 1996). In fact, 'Third World' debt and globalisation are different branches of the same tree.

So what has this got to do with critical health psychology? The major emphasis in 'development' circles is on macroeconomic policies and there is little recognition that a well-educated healthy population is an important resource for sustainable development. Somers (1996: 174) quotes the following emotive statement from UNICEF: 'Hundreds of thousands of the developing world's children have given their lives to pay their countries' debts, and many millions more are still paying the interest with their malnourished minds and bodies.' So, for instance, Somers reports that in Nicaragua overall budget spending on health is now less than half the level of the early 1980s and infant mortality rates are increasing after declining steadily for more than a decade. The same is now true in many other 'Third World' countries who have had to cut back spending on health and social welfare, liberalise their markets and invest in cash crop production – all in order to compete on the global market, in order to meet the requirements for Structural Adjustment Loans (SALs) from the World Bank.

A critical health psychology that seeks to consider cultural context, inequity, and oppression, along with social, economic and political factors, must also try to address the negative effects of globalisation. The 'cultural' element being examined here is the selling of globalisation (with all its political and economic baggage) as if it is synonymous with improvement. Behind the rhetoric of democratisation (such as, our type of democracy), free trade (such as, states do not restrict trade, conglomerates do!), and equal standards throughout the world (such as, CNN, McDonalds and Coke!), there are costs to be paid, not by those in the 'First World' but by those who will never know such a world. Some have already risen to this challenge. Marsella (1998: 1284) advocates a 'Global-Community Psychology' which he defines as 'a superordinate or metapsychology concerned with understanding, assessing and addressing the individual and psychological consequences of global events and forces by encouraging and using multicultural, multidisciplinary, multisectorial and multinational knowledge, methods and interventions'. While this sounds very ambitious, it is, I believe, what critical health psychology must also advocate. It is more important to do the right thing than to do the easy thing. And remember, 'try sleeping in a closed room with a mosquito!'

Cultural Evolution

Cultural evolution refers to the situation where values, attitudes and customs change within the same social system, over time. Thus, different historical epochs, although being characteristic of the same 'national' culture (for example, Victorian England compared to contemporary England), actually constitute very different social environments – cultures. Peltzer (1995, 2002), working in the African context, has described people who live primarily traditional lives, those who live primarily modern lives, and those who are caught between the two – transitional people. Peltzer argues that socialisation is powerfully influenced across three dimensions: the authority dimension, the group dimension, and the body-mind-environment dimension. The transitional person, on their way to becoming a 'modern' person, is no longer so influenced by traditional authority figures, is less under the influence of group norms so that rites of passage seem empty rituals that fail to fulfil their reassuring and integrating roles, and technology and the emphasis on 'the mind' diminish the importance of the cycles of nature and of physical contact between people. It seems to me that what Peltzer describes as 'transitional' people can be found throughout the world, including in its most 'advanced' industrial societies. Are such 'transitional people' simply caught in a temporal limbo between two end points on a scale of cultural evolution, or are there particular characteristics of their identity, independent of these end points? In the future, will transitional people be a thing of the past, or in a post-modern world, will we all be transitional people?

Inglehart and Baker (2000) examined three waves of the World Values Survey (1981–1982, 1990–1991 and 1995–1998), encompassing 65 societies on six continents, and apparently representative of three quarters of the world population. Although the time span covered is relatively short, Inglehart and Baker (2000: 49) argue that the results provide strong evidence for both massive cultural change and the persistence of distinctive traditional values: 'A history of Protestant or Orthodox or Islamic or Confucian traditions gives rise to cultural zones with distinctive value systems that persist after controlling for the effects of economic development. Economic development tends to push societies in a common direction, but rather than converging, they seem to move on parallel trajectories shaped by their cultural heritages. We doubt that the forces of modernization will produce a homogenized world culture in the foreseeable future.'

Hermans and Kempen (1998) have argued that the emphasis of conventional cross-cultural psychology on geographical location is becoming increasingly irrelevant. Instead they emphasise the influence of interconnecting cultural and economic systems, of cultural hybridisation creating multiple identities, and of increasingly permeable cultural boundaries, all producing a multiplicity of meanings and practices and contributing to greater uncertainty. As Hermans and Kempen (1998: 1119) state 'uncertainty is not primarily in a culture's core but in its contact zones'. Yet surely every age has its uncertainties and perhaps also its hysterias. Showalter (1997) uses the term *hystories* to describe cultural narratives of hysteria, and includes among her contemporary examples, chronic-fatigue syndrome, Gulf-war syndrome, recovered memories, multiple personality disorder, Satanic ritual abuse, and alien abduction. These conditions, which Showalter sees as psychogenic, it is argued, reflect the anxieties and fantasies of the cultures that harbour them. They may indeed, like their predecessor – hysteria – come to be seen as largely time-bound syndromes. Perhaps we are in the 'age of insanity' where the forces of modernity have also produced a mental health crisis (Schumaker 2001). Or perhaps the health consequences of change and uncertainty depend on our style of what might be called 'temporal acculturation'.

Berry's framework for geographical acculturation, describes four accultur-ation strategies (assimilation, marginalisation, separation and integration) in terms of the extent to which migrants wish to identify with their host or heritage culture (see Berry 1997, for a review). Smyth, MacLachlan, Breen and Madden (submitted) investigated how Irish people have acculturated from the 'traditional Ireland' to the 'Celtic Tiger' Ireland of unprecedented immigration, increasing secularisation, economic prosperity and liberalisation of social attitudes (MacLachlan and O'Connell 2000; O'Connell 2001). As an innovation to Berry's framework we also allowed for an 'uncertain' or a 'cultural ambivalence' classification, where participants gave mid-range responses to their desire to identify with the culture of 'old Ireland' and 'new Ireland'. Eighty-eight percentage of over seven hundred respondents agreed that there had been a 'big change in Irish culture over the past ten years', and it was those people in this uncertain, or ambivalent, group who had the worst mental health.

My use of the term 'cultural evolution' does not necessarily carry the connotation of biological evolution; that those fittest for the changing envir-onmental niche will prosper while those who do not 'fit' will perish. Yet, the rate of change in many societies makes it clear that adapting to culture change within one's own culture may be every bit as demanding as adapting to cultural change across geographical boundaries, even when the changes within a culture are broadly welcomed (see for instance, Gibson and Swartz's (2001) account of the difficulties some people in South Africa have faced in making sense of their past experience under apartheid in the context of their current democratised experience). Durkheim's (1897) classic description of anomie and its potentially suicidal consequences for those who feel out of touch with their own society may become an increasingly distressing consequence of cultures that rush to change without considering the social consequences of the values which they then engage (Smyth *et al.* 2003). The typology described above is summarized in Box 6.1.

Box 6.1   A typology of themes relating culture, empowerment and health

Cultural Colonialism
Rooted in the 19th century when Europeans sought to compare a God-given superior 'us' with an inferior 'them' and to determine the most advantageous way of managing 'them' in order to further European elites.

Cultural Sensitivity
Being aware of the minorities among 'us' and seeking to make the benefits enjoyed by mainstream society more accessible and modifiable for 'them'.

Cultural Migration
Taking account of how the difficulties of adapting to a new culture influence the opportunities and well-being of geographical migrants.

Cultural Alternativism
Different approaches to health care offer people alternative ways of being understood and of understanding their own experiences.

Cultural Empowerment
As many problems are associated with the marginalisation and oppression of minority groups, a process of cultural reawakening offers a form of increasing self- and community-respect.

Cultural Globalisation
Increasing (primarily) North American political, economic and corporate power reduces local uniqueness and reinforces and creates systems of exploitation and dependency amongst the poor, throughout the world.

Cultural Evolution
As social values change within cultures, adaptation and identity can become problematic with familiar support systems diminishing and cherished goals being replaced by alternatives.

So What ... is Culture for?

Marin (1999) has described how the U'wa (meaning intelligent people who know how to speak) of Columbia, a traditional indigenous society, have responded to the continued diminishment of their lands. In response to new plans for oil exploration, they responded with an astonishing threat that should the plans go ahead they would collectively commit suicide: 'To be severed from their place, to be removed from the context of the stories which they have passed down from generation to generation, is to be killed as a people, and is, as they have made very clear, a fate worse than death' (p. 43). A statement by the U'wa does in some way explain this stance: '...We must care for, not maltreat, because for us it is forbidden to kill with knives, machetes or bullets. Our weapons are thought, the word, our power is wisdom. We prefer death before seeing our sacred ancestors profaned' (cited in Marin 1999). If people will die for their culture, then what is it for?

For me, Ernest Becker is one of the great unsung intellectual heroes of the last century. Hopelessly out of touch with the contemporary penchant for reductionism, Becker, an anthropologist who embraced the breadth of the social sciences, dared to ask 'big' questions about the meaning of life (see, for instance, Becker 1962, 1968, 1975). Over the last 15 years a trio of experimental social psychologists have developed and demonstrated the value of Terror Management Theory (TMT) based largely upon the writings of Becker (for a review, see Solomon *et al.* 1991, 1998). A review of either Becker's work or of the deft experimental evaluation of TMT is beyond the scope of this chapter. However, the central premise of TMT is that our concerns about mortality play a pervasive and far-reaching role in our daily lives. The intelligence of human beings, coupled with their capacity for self-reflection, and the ability to think about the future, gives them the unique capacity to contemplate the inevitability of their own death.

Like Sigmund Freud and Otto Rank, Becker believed that humans would be rooted to inaction and abject terror if they were to continually contemplate their vulnerability and mortality. Thus cultural worldviews evolved and these were 'humanly created beliefs about the nature of reality shared by groups of people that served (at least in part) to manage the terror engendered by the uniquely human awareness of death' (Solomon *et al.* 1998: 12). The visions of reality created by cultural worldviews help terror management by answering universal cosmological questions: 'Who am I? ...What should I do? What will happen to me when I die?' (Solomon *et al.* 1998: 13). In effect then, cultures give people a role to play, thus distracting them from the anxiety of worrying about what they fear most. Coincidentally, this is, of course, exactly what psychologists recommend for socially anxious people. Cultures provide recipes for immortality, either symbolically (such as amassing great fortunes that out-survive their originator) or spiritually (such as going to heaven). Abiding by cultural rules can ensure immortality, but perhaps even more important, is its here and now function: 'The resulting perception that one is a *valuable* member of a *meaningful* universe constitutes *self-esteem*; and self-esteem is the primary psychological mechanism by which culture serves its death-denying function' (Solomon *et al.* 1998: 13, italics in the original).

The U'wa's dramatic stance perhaps only seems so dramatic to us because we do not share with them a fully conscious appreciation of the life-saving and death-denying function of culture. Too often and for too long psychologists have stripped hapless mortals of their shaky beliefs and sent them out to discover their 'true self' and their apparently obligatory enormously creative potential (I know it is meant to be a mouthful!) When I lecture on Sheldon's Kopp's (1973) 'If you see the Buddha on the road, shoot him', I insert a dirty big red DON'T sign, before 'shoot him'. Swinging between a pluralistic liberalism and a scientific fanaticism, health psychology will have to embrace the consequences of being human. These may be ugly and horrendous such as when cultural worldviews clash, or humbling and inspiring when individuals seek to become more than their biological substrate.

Key Points

- Critical health psychology's challenge to mainstream psychology emphasises the importance of acknowledging other people's realities. Social constructions of reality differ across cultures and so when people from different cultures interact, understandings of reality may differ.
- When people from different cultures interact it is rarely on an 'even playing field'. Usually one group is empowered (politically, economically or socially) and this will have consequences on how they relate to one another.
- A typology of seven kinds of relationships between culture, empowerment and health is outlined.
- Traditionally psychologists have recognised the interplay between culture and health in colonialism, through sensitivity to minority groups and in the acculturation issues of migrants. The recent enthusiasm for alternative medicine can be seen as introducing more pluralism into health care.
- Distinctive relationships between culture and health are also played out in the renewed enthusiasm for cultural empowerment, especially among marginalised indigenous groups; in the globalisation of a singular politico-economic system based on North American values; and in the rapid social and cultural change within many societies.
- The function of culture is to provide a meaningful self-identity and to provide a belief system that is capable of distracting us from the prospect of our own inevitable mortality. Without a belief in oneself and an identity with some coherent account of life, 'we are only food for worms!'

Sample Questions

1. If globalisation is the new colonialism, what are the implications for health?
2. Does socio-economic context or local culture have a greater influence on people's health?
3. Are cultural clashes inevitable consequences of our need for self-esteem and the avoidance of our own mortality?
4. What aspects of health are independent of cultural factors?

📖 Further Readings

MacLachlan, M. (2004) *Culture & Health* (Second Edition), Chichester: Wiley.

Written by a clinical and health psychologist, this book covers cultural influences on both mental and physical health, provides interesting case studies and useful guidelines for practitioners, along with web addresses.

Helman, C.G. (2001) *Culture, Health and Illness*, London: Arnold.

Written by a medical anthropologist, this book places greater emphasis on physical than mental health and provides useful qualitative questions concerning the topic of each chapter that may be followed up for research or clinical purposes.

Regan, C. (ed.), *80:20, Development in an Unequal World*, Bray, Co. Wicklow, Ireland: 80:20, Educating and Acting for a Better World (E-mail: info@8020.ie).

This outstandingly accessible and engaging introduction to development issues is now in its third version. It covers much that will be of interest to critical health psychologists including human rights, gender, culture, sustainability and globalisation, to name but a few.

PART III

Research Methods and Health Psychology

CHAPTER 7

Qualitative Research, Reflexivity and Context

Kerry Chamberlain

Summary

This chapter examines the turn to qualitative research that has recently taken place in health psychology, and discusses some of the implications for researchers conducting research from this perspective. One important issue considered is how the move to qualitative interpretative research repositions the researcher, and the major focus of this chapter is on reflexivity – being aware of the researcher's assumptions behind research and how they shape and direct the research. The chapter considers the variety of reflexivities, but focuses particularly on the researcher's perspective and its impact on research practices and outcomes. Discussion of these issues opens up consideration of ethical concerns and the value of a critical approach to research.

Background

Almost from the beginning of its modern inception about 150 years ago, psychology has adopted and promoted a view of itself as a science. Although the terms 'science' and 'scientific method' are open to broad interpretation, the general model of research promoted within psychology has been the scientific method, based on a positivist conceptualisation of the world, and valuing 'objective' empirical methods (see Danziger 1990). Although alternatives to this view have existed throughout the history of psychology, the 'received view' of the nature of psychology (as a science) and its research approach (the scientific method) has prevailed throughout psychology's short history.

However, more recently this view has been the subject of challenge and debate, questioning whether the natural science view can provide a legitimate model of research for the investigation of psychological concerns. Rather, it is argued, psychology should be viewed as a social or human science and should adopt research practices that are more commensurable with the investigation of human activity and thought. Further, this argument is proposed to have even greater force when we acknowledge that the 'object' of investigation is ourselves.

Critiques of the nature of psychology, and consequently of the appropriateness of its research techniques, have come primarily from the arena of social psychology, although not exclusively so (for example, Fox and Prilleltensky 1997). Health psychology, for a variety of reasons (see Chapter 1) has been slow to hear and apply these critiques to its own practices until very recently. One important outcome of this more critical view of the sub-discipline has been the turn to the use of qualitative methodologies for research (for example, Murray and Chamberlain 1999a).

The Turn to Qualitative Research

Although I am using the term 'qualitative research' here, it should be noted that this label embraces a considerable variety of methodologies and specific methods, and that strictly there is no single entity that can be labelled as qualitative research *per se* (see also, Kidder and Fine 1997). However, many qualitative methodologies are now being adopted and used in health psychology research, and we can identify several reasons for this turn to qualitatively oriented research practices. An integral part of the critical argument has been dissatisfaction with the limitations of the positivist quantitative approach, especially in regard to its assumptions about the nature of variables, the preoccupation with their measurement, and the statistical analysis of data (Chamberlain 2000; Crossley 2000). The use of qualitative methodologies, with different assumptions and methods, can provide a means to counter this.

Alongside this is a growing recognition that we frequently want to ask questions about health issues that cannot be adequately answered by a positivist, quantitative approach. We want to understand the experience of having a disease like diabetes or of receiving a treatment like chemotherapy. We want to understand how interactions with health professionals are changing, and how it is that the active health consumer is replacing the passive, accepting patient. We want to understand the processes that parents go through in deciding to seek health care for their children. We want to understand how illness is reflected in people's daily lives, and how they represent themselves to healthy people around them. We want to understand how different socio-cultural groups construct their understandings of the relation between medications, herbal remedies and health. We want to understand the discursive construction of the relationship between healthy eating and preventing illness. The complexities of such questions are not readily investigated by a positivist approach requiring participants to circle numbers or check response categories in response to predetermined, researcher-driven questions.

For many psychologists, given a background and training which emphasises positivist 'scientific methods', the move to qualitative methodologies can be difficult to make. As I have argued elsewhere (Chamberlain 2000), such a background channels health psychologists into methodolatry, leading them to place methods in a privileged position relative to other research issues, and to minimise epistemological and theoretical considerations in their research as they strive to ensure that they use the correct methods for data collection and analyses.

Epistemological Concerns

One major issue arising out of the turn to qualitative research is the nature of the assumptions that underlie research practices. All research is based on assumptions and decisions about which ways to proceed. These assumptions and decisions necessarily drive our research practice and work to preclude other ways of researching. In short, they determine what may and may not be accomplished in the research. Most, although not all, qualitative research seeks to move away from a positivist or post-positivist epistemology. Much qualitative research in psychology, although again not all by any means, adopts a social constructionist epistemology, and works with the assumption that the meanings of the objects of our research (hospital patients, doctor–patient interaction, the narrated experience of chronic illness, the processes of seeking care after a heart attack, understandings of healthy diet and exercise, and so on) are constructed by the researcher in interaction with these 'objects'. Allied to this, researchers carrying out qualitative research also adopt an ontological position, making assumptions about the nature of reality and adopting a stance on how 'real' the objects of their research are considered to be. Detailed treatment of these issues is beyond the scope of this chapter, but Crotty (1998) gives an excellent overview of epistemological assumptions in research practice and Nightingale and Cromby (1999) provide a critical treatment of social constructionism. For our purposes here, we need to note that taking a position on these issues requires researchers to make assumptions about the nature of their research, how it can be conducted, and what outcomes it seeks.

Let us take an example and examine how this comes about. For our data, we have interviews that we have conducted with a number of asthma sufferers about managing their illness. A number of concerns arise. How many people do we need to interview? How should we sample them? Can we generalise from this sample? These questions are driven largely from a positivist orientation. Under a social constructionist orientation, we may not be at all concerned about generalisation, especially of the specific findings, as we would assume that all research is historically, socially and culturally located, and accept that generalisation of research findings is not the goal. Similarly we could ask whether what we were told in the interviews is accurate or true. How valid is it? How reliable is it? Once again, these questions reflect positivist assumptions about research. Under a social constructionist approach, in contrast, we could assume that the talk is constructed for a purpose – to represent the person and their experience to the interviewer in a particular way – and is obviously constrained and produced within the dialogical interaction between the interviewee and the interviewer. Under these assumptions, issues of truth, validity and reliability take on completely different connotations. Taking this further, under a framing of discourse analysis, if that was to be our methodology, issues of sampling are considerably minimised, as it is assumed that participants will draw on culturally shared linguistic resources to produce this representation. If action research was our chosen methodology, the site and the group of participants would most likely be pre-determined, and again sampling and generalisation would not be relevant concerns.

Taking this in another direction again, what should we do with the interviews during analysis? Should we transcribe them, and in so doing, possibly lose some of the rich detail of the spoken account? Should we show the transcripts to the participants for 'member checking' to determine the accuracy of their account? What are we assuming about truth and accuracy if we do this? Should we show the specific interpretation of each person's data, or perhaps the overall findings that we have produced, back to the participants? Again, the reasons for doing this are driven by our assumptions about the nature of the findings and how these are therefore amenable to input from participants. Returning findings to participants for checking individual transcript correctness, for checking the overall interpretation, for information, or to empower the participants with the findings, all have different implications and rest on differing assumptions about the nature of the research and the participant's role(s) in data analysis and interpretation. This does not mean that there is anything wrong with doing any or all of these in a particular study; the point is that we need to be clear about why we would do this, and about the assumptions underlying it. The example could be continued further, as every specific method we adopt for data collection and analysis gives rise to similar matters.

One further issue to recognise here is that epistemological concerns are not just importantly related to methodologies and methods, but that these need to be carefully aligned to ensure good research practice. Methods only make sense in the service of methodologies and these in turn rely on epistemological assumptions about practice (see Crotty 1998). We cannot avoid epistemological assumptions as all research rests on these; however, we need to ensure that we are aware of them and explicate them, if only to ourselves, and that they are related consistently to the practices of our research.

Although research is replete with assumptions and decisions that shape it, in this chapter I will focus specifically on those aspects that are brought into the research by the researcher. Assumptions and decisions taken by the researcher relate to all aspects of the research; the epistemology chosen, the theoretical framework adopted, the methodology implemented and the specific methods used to collect and analyse the information. Being aware of these assumptions and being reflexive about how they shape and focus the research is termed reflexivity. Unfortunately, this topic is rarely included in the texts in which research findings are presented. Publication conventions, both of the discipline (for example, the expected headings, content and presentational style of a research article) and of the publishers (for example, space limitations), work to limit opportunities for disclosure and discussion of this material. When these issues are discussed, it is usually within specific articles or book chapters offering more general commentaries. This means that connections between context and practice in this arena are often obscured and consequently minimised.

Being Reflexive

The key issue here is that researchers are not independent of their research and are, in fact, part of the social world that they seek to investigate; they are intimately involved in the research practices that they conduct. This raises questions about the nature and effect of their involvement, and reflexive researchers attempt to address such issues – who is the researcher (female, black, middle class, etc.), what do they bring to the research (values, assumptions, etc.), and how has all that impacted on the practices, findings and outcomes of the research?

Reflexivity is complex and multi-faceted and may be considered and described from a number of different perspectives. For example, Willig (2001) suggests that reflexivity can be usefully divided into two types: *epistemological* reflexivity, relating to the assumptions underlying the research and how these have shaped the research practice and outcomes; and *personal* reflexivity, relating to ways that issues such as the researcher's values, experiences, interests, personal identities have shaped the research, and conversely, how carrying out the research has lead to changes in these. Earlier, Wilkinson (1988) had suggested three different types of reflexivity: *personal*, accounting for the interests, values and individuality of the researcher; *functional*, examining the values and assumptions around the research processes and practices; and *disciplinary*, examining the practices at a more critical level as influenced by context and disciplinary constraints within which the research is conducted. Lynch (2000) takes this further, identifying six different types of reflexivity. These include mechanical, methodological, and interpretative reflexivities, along with several subtypes of each, and he also comments that this does not provide an exhaustive enumeration. Box 7.1 outlines several different types of reflexivity that can be usefully identified. These are best considered as overlapping rather than independent of one another, and a researcher may engage with several of these within a single research project. Unfortunately, many research articles do not address any of these reflexivities directly, and reflexive concerns are often left unstated and unexamined. Sometimes, reflexivity issues form the focus of specific reports that are written as commentaries from outside the research (for example, Bannister 1999; Sword 1999; Järvinen 2000).

Of course, to note that reflexivity is not addressed in much research publication should not be taken to suggest that researchers go about their research unthinkingly. Good researchers are necessarily engaged in thoughtful considerations of how best to engage with the field and how best to find an answer to their questions. This level of introspective reflection, however, tends not to open space for considerations of the assumptions, positionings, and relationships

---

Box 7.1   Types* of reflexivity in research

Reflection: Self-reflective activity or reflexive introspection about the processes of research that does not impact on the research activity or appear in the published account of the research.

Methodological reflexivity: Reflection about the methods and practices of the research, involving active consideration of the role and values of the researcher in shaping the practices of the research, and of the relation between the researcher and the researched.

Epistemological reflexivity: Reflection about the epistemological and ontological assumptions underlying the research, and how these shape the research practices and interpretations.

Meta-theoretical reflexivity: Stepping back from the research activity and considering its place and role as a social activity; disengagement from the research for the purposes of critically examining the activity; deconstruction of the research and/or the researcher's role to determine taken-for-granted assumptions; using deliberate variation and disruption of the activity and undertaking an examination of the consequences arising.

Textual or hermeneutic reflexivity: Consideration of the meanings and possible alternative interpretations of the representations offered in texts about the research.

* These should not be considered as levels of reflexivity as reflexive practices may combine several of these within a single project.

---

surrounding the research and its interpretation and representation. As Taylor and White (2000) note, there is an important difference between engaging in reflection and being reflexive. They suggest that it is one thing to reflect on 'our practice at the time (reflection-in-action) or after the event (reflection-on-action)' (p. 198), and quite another to be reflexive. They argue that reflecting on our practice may operate to make us better practitioners, but being reflexive about our practice means to interrogate our practices at a deeper level – to analyse them for the underlying assumptions, to question our knowledge, and how our practices shape our knowledge, and more broadly again, how they shape our discipline. This notion of reflexivity conflates several of the types identified in Box 7.1, demonstrating how different aspects of reflexivity, methodological, epistemological and meta-theoretical, may be distinguished conceptually but are heavily interrelated within research practices.

   A first step towards engaging in reflexive practice is to include some commentary in the research report as to the standing of the researcher in relation to the researched. For example, if the research is concerned with the phenomenology of living a drug-dependent life, it may make a difference to the research practice if the researcher is a reformed 'junkie', a drug agency field worker, a female nurse, or an aging male academic with a moral opposition to the world of drug use. Providing such information about the positioning of the researcher is not meant to be a way of identifying potential bias or error in the research, but to allow the researcher (and the reader) to consider and evaluate the potential impact of the assumptions and practices behind the research and its interpretation. Providing an explicit discussion of the assumptions that arise from such researcher positioning in the presentation will begin to allow this, although this level of reflexivity is only one step that may be taken. The reflexive researcher can go much further, and consider other types of reflexivity, such as those outlined in Box 7.1.

The influence of the researcher on the research may be made more obvious if we turn from a consideration of issues surrounding the *practices* of research – design, data collection and analysis – and consider instead the *products* of research – the published papers that document this research activity and its outcomes. These papers are, after all, how we know and communicate about research, how we know what has been done and what has been found. These articles are texts, and like all texts, have authors – the researchers. Taking this view – of research as a body of authored texts – makes the author a highly salient consideration. Texts are shaped, directed and presented by their authors, admittedly under the accepted conventions and social practices of research publications that are legitimated for (and by) them within the field. The research practices, justifications, findings, conclusions and arguments are all authored by the researcher. As Usher (1997) has argued, all social science research is ultimately textual, and involves writing the world, not uncovering it. If research is a social practice, and one that is textually mediated, then an examination of how we as authors construct our texts is more than a possibility; it becomes a highly salient and important part of our practice. This type of reflexivity is identified as textual or hermeneutic reflexivity in Box 7.1.

Once we take the view that disciplinary 'knowledge' is textual and authored, then a range of possibilities for reflexive accounting are exposed. Usher (1997) provides a persuasive discussion of these, each examining a different aspect of the author's relationship to the text and the relevant aspects of reflexivity. The first of these is the *con-text* (what comes *with* the text). This is the 'situated autobiography of the researcher' (Usher 1997: 36), marked by gender, class, ethnicity and so on. As noted above, the researcher's positioning can influence the shape and direction of the research practices and also, importantly for our purpose here, the ways in which the outcomes of the research are represented. However, we need to be aware that:

> these are not biases which can be eliminated by first admitting them and then placing ourselves under methodological control. These are 'biases', ineliminably part of us which can be recognised but cannot be willed away. They are the marks of the trajectory of our desires and emotional investments in the research act (Usher 1997: 36).

A second type is the *pre-text* (what comes *before* the text), and is related to the linguistic meanings, textual strategies, discourses and rhetorical devices used to construct the written presentation. Such practices shape the claims that are made and the conventions within which texts are written, and thus research texts are very rarely presented in the form of poetry or drama. Occasionally, researchers will seek to produce texts that are deliberately outside disciplinary conventions, and the challenge and disruption that these bring to the field can be especially revealing of current practices and traditions. Lather and Smithies (1997) provide a particularly creative and compelling example with a text about HIV/AIDS that 'troubles' the conventions of representation (as well as the angels) in very instructive ways.

A further level of textual reflexivity concerns the *sub-text* (what lies *beneath* the text). Here, we are concerned with assumptions that lie beneath the research – how the research traditions and paradigms that were used have shaped the outcomes and are influential in the production of the text. This level is also concerned with the relation between the researcher and the researched and how that relationship enabled the text. In health psychology research, this can be a particularly troubling issue for the healthy researcher working with the ill person (Radley and Billig 1996). As Usher argues, these issues are essentially involved in considerations of power:

> A reflexive questioning of the sub-text enables us to better interrogate the implications of our practice within discourses of power and how it becomes part of dominant and oppressive discourses through a...taken-for-granted acceptance of the neutrality of research, its pragmatic usefulness and its emancipatory potential – and how as writers and readers of such texts we become part of such discourses despite our best intentions (1997: 37).

Although the text is our focus of interest here, this type of reflexivity inflects other reflexivities identified in Box 7.1, in particular those focussed on epistemological and meta-theoretical concerns. As noted earlier, the attempt to classify reflexivities into types does not produce a tidy, exhaustive and independent categorisation, but merely a heuristic classification of interrelated reflexivities.

The final level of textual reflexivity is *inter-text* (what lies *between* texts). Research texts inevitably refer to other texts. This is usually, but not necessarily, achieved through direct citations to other texts within the text. Through such citation and reference to other texts, our texts are warranted and located. Further, through such representations, prior texts may be reinterpreted and repositioned, and future texts are rendered possible. For example, if we want to write a paper about the medicalisation of food in contemporary society, we would presumably draw on previous publications about the medicalisation thesis (for example, Conrad 1992) to construct the argument. It is in this sense that the notions of intertextuality can be critically examined, and a reflexive account of the text enabled. This is to recognise that texts may be invoked and used without the consent or presence of their authors, and that texts have a life of their own which may be well beyond the author's intentions. Also, as Usher reminds us, all texts are produced within historically and socially situated constraints and are subject to relations of power. Therefore, we should not loose sight of the fact that 'researchers are never fully the "authors" of their texts' (Usher 1997: 38), a point which can be salutary for us to reflect on as we seek to represent our research to others.

Although I have not pursued it here, all of these textual considerations can just as readily be applied to, or taken up by, the reader of the text; they are not restricted to the author. In fact, Usher makes no strong distinction between the two in discussing these issues. A focus on the reader and on potentially competing readings of the text could lead us into a consideration of textual deconstruction, but this is beyond our primary focus here. Rather, we are concerned to consider issues of how the author is positioned in the (texts of) research, and to raise awareness of the complexity and character of that involvement in the production of research (texts).

In summary, different forms of reflexive activity are possible and available to us as researchers. They are all interrelated, and attending to any type will inevitably open consideration of other types. Giving consideration to (any or all of) these can influence our research practices in a variety of ways: it can sensitise us to the assumptions behind our practices and improve our practice; it can give rise to concerns about the way we conduct our research (ethical issues); and to the ways our research is positioned and used (a critical approach). I turn to these issues next.

Being Ethical

Many of the judgements we make about our research practices involve us in making ethical decisions – decisions about what would be morally right and wrong to do. Can we involve participants in our research without informing them of what is involved, what they will be asked to do, and what we will do with the information they give us? Can we deceive them about the purposes of our research? Does it matter if they experience some upset or distress as a result of their participation? Can we promise them that they will be anonymous if they participate? These judgements take us beyond the practicalities of how we will conduct the research and into the realm of moral and ethical judgements about how we *should* conduct our research. Opening the door to reflexive practice necessarily leads us into ethics. Conversely, the consideration of ethical issues in our research can promote and enhance reflexive research practice, as ethical issues necessarily involve researchers in making decisions about methodological practices. Knowing about ethics is not enough; ethics must inform our research practices.

Ethical issues, such as informed consent, the minimisation of harm, the uses of data, and confidentiality and anonymity for participants, are involved in all research practice. However, once we move into interpretative qualitative research, and take a position on the value-laden nature of research, accepting that research is influenced by the values, assumptions and practices of the researcher, ethical concerns can take on a different edge.

For example, can we promise our participants anonymity in this form of research? The common practice of data collection, face-to-face interviews, means that our participants are known to us. Further, they often share with us detailed, engaging, and intimate aspects of their lives, and we become involved in their life-worlds to some degree. Hence, it may be impracticable to promise anonymity, although we frequently try to achieve this in the reports of our research. However, in these reports, we commonly seek to include quotations from our participants' accounts. This may be done for a variety of reasons, depending on the assumptions of the research (as always); to anchor the interpretation in the data, to illustrate the discourses utilised, to exemplify the negotiated nature of the talk, and so on. In presenting quotations from a participant's account, researchers often identify participants with pseudonyms to protect their anonymity. In particular projects, this may be problematic. For example, some of our participants, particularly in life history and biographical research, may request to be identified as they want to have their contributions acknowledged. This may seem unproblematic until we realise that identifying one participant may identify the site of the research and may thereby work to expose the identity of others in the research. If our project is concerned with the construction of embodiment by people promoting anorexia as a 'normal' lifestyle (pro-anorexia) in Internet forums, are we able to give quotations at all, considering how powerful Internet search engines are today and the way society operates to oppose and restrict pro-anorexics? If our project is concerned with drug use and our participants give accounts that document illegal activities, are we free to quote this material, even if anonymised in some way? If we were to mask their material by using pseudonyms, are we sure that their identities could not be determined by building up a composite picture from details given across multiple quotations? So, the broad guiding principle that participants should be anonymous is inadequate for some particular types of research activity, and we need to consider these issues carefully within the specific context of our research.

Issues surrounding the use of data give rise to other ethical concerns. Many qualitative researchers argue that one role for their research is to provide a voice for participants, and particularly for the under-researched, marginalised and oppressed in our societies. How can we ensure that this 'voice' is represented in our interpretation? Whose voice is it ultimately – the researcher's or the participants' voice? Will all participants have the same voice? Can our representations speak with multiple voices? We have already seen that the return of transcripts to participants can be problematic, depending on the purposes and underlying assumptions for doing so. Returning the interpretation to participants raises equally problematic issues. Will participants be asked to comment only on those parts of the report that are directly relevant to themselves, or on the entire interpretation? Will they be asked to do this individually, with conflicting comments between participants to be refereed by the researcher? Or will they be asked to do this as group, and how will that process be managed? Will the participants have the resources for ensuring that their voice is adequately heard, and will they be interested to participate if the goal is to produce a peer-reviewed article in a psychology journal? Interrelated with this are issues about the ownership of data and the uses to which it may be put. These issues are usually negotiated as part of the informed consent process, but in (non-reflexive) practice they are often likely to have been passed over quickly and resolved in the researcher's interest.

Consider, for example, a project where we have recorded and transcribed individual interviews with homeless people about their access to health care. Issues of data ownership, use and representation must be considered and decisions taken. Were we given this data (participants' stories of finding and failing to find access to care) to interpret as best we can? Do the participants expect that the outcomes of the research will make a difference to their lives, or to the lives of people like them? Did they merely give the data to the researcher to be used for a thesis or a research publication in an academic journal, or for a report to a health authority that could possibly enable better access, or for a report in a magazine that is read by homeless people so they can be better informed and empowered? Each of these implies a different audience and, most likely, a different representation of the data. Does the researcher have consent to do any or all of these, and through what process of negotiation with the participants? Unless we have worked through these issues carefully, and reflexively, we can be in danger of assuming the taken-for-granted positions as researchers offered to us by our profession, and of losing sight of the interests of our participants (see Rhodes 2000). As always, these issues can only be resolved in the context of a particular project. If the source of our data was publicly available, as in the records of a criminal trial or the submissions to a public enquiry into medical malpractice, then issues of consent and negotiation with participants will not be salient. However, issues around the right to access and use such records, and concerns about who benefits from, or is disadvantaged by, the representation will remain salient.

Professional bodies and institutional ethical review committees have developed codes of ethics that can guide us in regard to the principles of ethical practice. However, it should be clear by now that these always remain as *guidelines* to practice, rather than *prescriptions* for practice. Although ethical guidelines are extremely helpful, ethical concerns always require judgement, and almost always involve a balancing of considerations of cost and benefit in relation to the research practices. As noted previously, these decisions must always be made in context, taking account of the specifics of the particular research project, and being reflexive about research practices operates to enhance this decision-making.

We have focussed here primarily on methodological issues and practices in research that raise ethical issues and require researcher decision-making. However, it is difficult to consider ethical concerns only at that level, and we have

also raised issues with a more critical edge that arise out of the ethical considerations of research. Clearly, we can also be reflexive about ethics at a 'deeper'
level, and consider how such things as the development of ethical guidelines
and the practices of ethical review committees can shape our research practices.
Brown (1997) offers a detailed analysis of ethics from this perspective, arguing
how the codes of ethics developed within psychology primarily serve the interests
of the psychological profession, and do not really address issues of power, discrimination or oppression.

Being Critical

Turning our gaze back on ourselves as researchers, and being reflexive about
the assumptions and decisions surrounding our research practices, inevitably
raises questions about the value of our research and the moral worth of our
practices. Once we accept that the researcher is embedded in the research, the
notion of the detached researcher uncovering knowledge is immediately rendered untenable. Rather, as involved researchers, we must take responsibility
for our interpretations, and consider how they may be used. Could the way we
have interpreted and represented the experiences of homeless people seeking
health care be used to continue the stigmatisation of these people? Could our
interpretation of the meanings of exercise and healthy diet be used to blame
people of lower socio-economic standing for their 'failure' to follow 'educated'
practice? Is it possible that our representation of how mothers seek to care for
their ill children could sustain a notion of women as unreliable employees?
However, this critical perspective does not arise because we are engaged in
interpretative qualitative research. As Kidder and Fine (1997: 35) have noted:

> Qualitative methods and critical psychology are not co-terminous. Qualitative work
> does not automatically yield critical analyses and critical analyses do not require
> Qualitative methods. But they fit well together.

They certainly fit well together, but I would argue that they become
co-terminous if we adopt a reflexive approach to our research. Opening the door
to reflexivity inevitably leads to considerations of criticality. Being reflexively
aware requires us to contemplate how we engage and relate to our participants,
and to consider the ways in which the outcomes of our research may be represented and taken up. The representations we produce from our research are
never value-free or neutral, and always have social and political consequences.
Hence, it is incumbent on us as researchers to try and be aware of how these
consequences might operate. We must be reflexively conscious of how we tell
the stories of our research and what social practices these stories might resist
or sustain. In this sense, reflexivity is intimately bound up with taking a critical
approach to our research practices. Being reflexive means recognising and
attending to the possibilities of how power and influence, oppression and

discrimination are operative within our research practices. Who benefits from our research, what is enabled as a consequence of it, and how does it resist (or worse, support) oppressive practices?

Reflexivity Revisited

Throughout this chapter, I have been promoting reflexivity as a highly positive activity for researchers. It is this, but it is also open to critique. One criticism often directed at reflexive practice is that it has no limit. In other words, we can reflect on our research practices and then reflect on our reflections about those practices, potentially *ad infinitum*. In a practical sense, this may not be a strong criticism, but theoretically it carries more weight as the relative epistemological value of constructed interpretations is debated (see Macbeth 2001). Pels (2000), however, offers a cogent argument for suggesting that reflective activity should cease 'one step up'.

Another point of potential concern about reflexivity relates to its own representation and function in the texts of research that we write. As Rhodes (2000) has argued, reflexive writing should not be used to obscure the work needed to adequately represent the research outcomes or to limit the voice given to participants' perspective. Worse, it should not appear as '... forms of textual reflexivity that result in egocentric musings, self-promoting confessionals, and "more reflexive than thou" testimonials' (Rhodes 2000: 522). Reflexivity needs to be more than a laying bare of oneself, and should be connected fully into the context of the research. However, we also need to be conscious of the power of the author, and to remain constantly aware of the assumptions we are making about ourselves as researchers and writers (and readers) of research.

Also, I have identified various types of reflexivity that are possible (Box 7.1), and shown how many of these are effectively interconnected. However, we need to ask if it is necessary, or even possible, for the researcher to engage with all types of reflexivity within any specific project. Choosing what to engage with and to be reflexive about can be problematic, especially as engaging in a consideration of one type of reflexive activity can raise issues about other aspects of reflexivity. Further, reporting reflexive considerations requires more space in reports and promotes alternative ways of representing research, and publication sources tend to discourage these practices. For these reasons it can be difficult to locate good examples of reflective practice in research reports within health psychology.

Conclusion

We are a long way from the positivist stance of a detached, impartial researcher uncovering 'real' knowledge, whose values and assumptions have no impact on the research practices. Instead, we are giving explicit recognition to a very different alternative, that of a researcher who is intimately involved in the research process, and whose assumptions, values, decisions and interpretations shape the research practices and influence the research representations. This view, however, goes beyond the researcher to explicitly recognise research as the social practice that it is. As we have seen, a reflexive consideration of research practice opens the position and role of the researcher to critical scrutiny, but it goes further than this, raising more general considerations of the research endeavour, especially in relation to the epistemology, ethics and criticality of our research.

This discussion of reflexivity and ethics has raised more questions than it has answered. This was both deliberate and inevitable as the very notion of reflexivity is about turning back on oneself and questioning. As we saw, reflexive questioning is not limited to any single aspect of research practice, but ranges from issues associated with the researcher's personal stance through to the use of the research outcomes and beyond, to examine and criticise the whole research endeavour. Once we begin to adopt a questioning approach to research, there are no limits to its extent. In this way, as we have seen, values, assumptions, ethics and practice are all bound up together in any research undertaking; each interpenetrates the other. Reflexivity provides a means that allows us to engage with these issues and determine a coherent stance in relation to them. In doing so, our research is inevitably enhanced and our engagement as critical psychologists heightened.

Key Points

- A desire to ask and answer different types of research questions in health psychology has led to dissatisfaction with a positivist approach to research and a turn to qualitative interpretative methodologies.
- Taking up a qualitative approach positions researchers differently in relation to their research, and acknowledges how their assumptions, values and decisions shape the research and its outcomes.
- The attempt to identify and explicate the role of values, assumptions and decisions in research is termed reflexivity.
- There are various types of reflexivity, although most are highly interconnected.
- It is difficult to locate detailed examples of reflexive research in the research texts produced within health psychology.
- Explicit consideration of reflexivity in research operates to improve research quality, and also the consideration of related issues such as ethical concerns and critical approaches to research practice.
- Undertaking reflexivity is valuable for research, but the practice can be critiqued on the grounds of infinite regress and for the potential to privilege the voice of the interpreter over the interpretation.

Assignment Questions

1. Consider a piece of research that you have conducted yourself and write a reflexive statement from the position of the researcher, covering:
   (a) personal reflexivity
   (b) epistemological reflexivity.
2. Identify a qualitative article in a peer-reviewed health psychology journal and write a reflexive statement from the position of the researcher conducting that research, covering:
   (a) epistemological reflexivity
   (b) meta-theoretical reflexivity.
   (You may need to make some assumptions about the researcher's intentions to develop an adequate response here.)
3. Identify a qualitative article from a peer-reviewed health psychology journal that is different from the one used above, and write a reflexive statement from the position of the reader; that is, a textually oriented reflexive statement.
4. Identify a further qualitative article and think about the implications of changing the research methodology to address the same topic. Write an account of how the researcher's assumptions and interpretations would change as a result of using the changed methodology.
5. Choose another chapter from this book, and discuss the author's positioning in that text.

📖 Further Readings

Steier, F. (ed.)(1991) *Research and Reflexivity*, London: Sage.

Most books on qualitative research provide some commentary on reflexivity, but this one provides a more detailed consideration of the topic.

Lynch, M. (2000)'Against reflexivity as an academic virtue and source of privileged knowledge', *Theory, Culture & Society*, 17, 26–54.
Macbeth, D. (2001) 'On "reflexivity" in qualitative research: two readings, and a third', *Qualitative Inquiry*, 7, 35–68.
Pels, D. (2000) 'Reflexivity: one step up', *Theory, Culture & Society*, 17, 1–25.
Woolgar, S. (ed.)(1988) *Knowledge and Reflexivity: New Frontiers in the Sociology of Knowledge*, London: Sage.

These readings extend your reading beyond the role of reflexivity in research practice into a discussion of the theoretical and philosophical issues surrounding reflexivities of various kinds.

Stam, H. (2000) 'Theorising health and illness: functionalism, subjectivity and reflexivity', *Journal of Health Psychology*, 5, 273–283.

This article provides a general commentary on reflexivity in relation to theorising in health psychology.

Cieurzo, C. and Keitel, M.A. (1999) 'Ethics in qualitative research', in M. Kopala and L.A. Suzuki (eds), *Using Qualitative Methods in Psychology* (pp. 63–75), Thousand Oaks, CA: Sage.

This chapter provides a more detailed treatment of ethics in qualitative research.

Brown, L. S. (1997) 'Ethics in psychology: Cui bono?' in D. Fox and I. Prilleltensky (eds), *Critical Psychology: An Introduction* (pp. 51–67), London: Sage.

This chapter provides a more critical commentary on ethical principles in psychology.

CHAPTER 8

Qualitative Research as Social Transformation

Uwe Flick

Summary

After distinguishing a basically observational approach to social transformation from a more active one that is intended to stimulate transformations, this chapter outlines the relevance of qualitative research for critical health psychology. First, a definition is given of qualitative research. Then some theoretical assumptions of different forms of qualitative research are presented. Following this, some basic designs in qualitative research are outlined and compared and some examples for qualitative research methods are discussed. The focus is on qualitative methods using narratives (illness narratives, the narrative interview and the episodic interview) and on ethnography. In closing, the question of indication of qualitative research (or specific designs and methods) and the problem of how to define and assess the quality of qualitative research are discussed.

Introduction

In a recent overview, Marks (2002a: 16) has compared different approaches to health psychology – clinical, public, community and critical health psychology. For critical health psychology, he states: "It is the critical, sceptical approach that questions the values, underlying assumptions and power relations of academic study and social organisation more generally." Concerning methodology, Marks does not make a specific choice, but sees "critical analysis combined with any of the methods used in the other three approaches". Nevertheless, qualitative research attracts a special attention in the broader discourse of critical health psychology. A reason for this may be that it has a specific relation to social transformations. Different types of links between qualitative research and social transformation can be distinguished.

First, qualitative research can observe processes of social transformation and provide more detailed, more context sensitive, or more appropriate descriptions of social transformations. This is because it is sensitive for describing

transformations from the point of view of those who are subject to such transformations and for analysing the consequences of such transformations in the
area of health and illness; consequences that are linked to illness experiences as
well as to the causation of or influences of certain illnesses. An example of
such a transformation is what Beck (1992) has termed "individualisation".
This concept describes a process of increasing change from fixed positions in
a society towards new positions in which a great part of one's life has to be
planned and is subject to decisions by the individual. To be healthy and to
maintain one's own health in the context of this social transformation has a lot
to do with how one plans and leads his or her own life – healthy eating, healthy
lifestyle, taking part in prevention programmes and so on. This again has a lot
to do with the meaning of health for the individual, for social groups and in
the context of professional practices. These meanings themselves are in a process
of change.

Second, qualitative research (and researchers) can be involved in social
transformation more than quantitative or experimental research normally is.
Qualitative research can be seen as a way of transforming a science like psychology (see Tolman and Brydon-Miller 1997 and the contributions to a special
issue on this topic: Brydon-Miller and Tolman 1997a). Qualitative – or interpretive, participatory or action research – is often linked to a new understanding
of the researcher in the research process: researchers are more involved in the
research and in relations to the field under study as well as to the participants
in the field or in the study. They are more reflexive (see Chapter 8) about the
field and their own role and experience in it. Qualitative research also tends to
have a different understanding of those who participate in the research.
Unlike experimental research, in this case, participants are seen as people able
to express their viewpoints (in an interview), to give their activities a meaning
and to act consciously. Research is often carried out in a way that intends to
transform the subjects and fields under study. For example, asking ill persons to
give the researcher a narrative account of their illness and of how it has developed
can make them more aware of their illness and of the logic and structure of
their lives in the process of recounting. This can be an intended transformation
on the level of the participant and of his or her relations to the social field.

Third, qualitative research is often engaged in a critical and transformative
perspective on the subject under study. However, drawing on Habermas (1971),
we see that this is not necessarily the case. Habermas distinguishes both positivist
and interpretative approaches from critical research. This distinction is less
tied to using one or the other form of science (positivist or interpretative) but
to the interest linked to research. The first and the second forms of research
are interested in producing nomological knowledge: "Nomological knowledge
means that individual cases are put under more general regulative laws"
(Ricoeur 1991: 162), whereas: "A critical social science 'is concerned with going
beyond this goal (producing nomological knowledge – UF) to determine
when theoretical statements grasp invariant regularities of social action as such
and when they express ideologically frozen relations of dependence that can in

principle be transformed'" (Habermas 1971: 310). As these formulations show, the use of qualitative research is not necessarily critical, nor is it necessarily concerned with transformations. It can be a means to carry out research in a critical health psychology perspective. But if the research is interested in social transformation and carried out from a critical perspective, the use of qualitative research will make it easier to reach these goals. A greater sensitivity of qualitative research to participants' perspectives, to the details of social processes and to social change in general are conditions that explain why this type of research makes it easier to pursue such goals successfully.

The main thesis of this chapter is that qualitative research in health psychology can contribute to making a critical perspective work empirically; that it can also contribute to social change or at least to a better understanding of social change and social transformation. However, qualitative research does not *per se* achieve these aims. It depends on which methods are used to address social transformation as an empirical problem and beyond. It also depends on how far the researcher knows why he or she uses one or the other qualitative research method or strategy and on how far he or she is ready to face the question of the quality of qualitative research.

To substantiate this thesis, first a short outline of what qualitative research is will be given in this chapter. The basic designs of qualitative research will be compared. Then some methods will be briefly presented that address questions of social change and transformation from different angles: using narratives in research addresses processes of change and transformation from a retrospective angle, whereas the approach of ethnography allows the researcher to take part in such processes as they occur. For each of them – designs, narratives and ethnography – the questions of sensitivity for and impact on social transformation will be asked. In the end, some challenges and perspectives will be discussed. The first addresses the question of how to decide when qualitative research is appropriate and what sort of qualitative approach or method to use. This is termed the *indication* of qualitative research. The second is the – still not exhaustively answered – question of quality in qualitative research: What is quality in this context and how can we define and assess quality in qualitative research?

What is Qualitative Research

Qualitative research is one of the current trends in social science in general. Hardly any handbook is published today without a chapter on qualitative research methods (in rehabilitation, nursing science or public health, for instance). Interest in qualitative research has been growing in the social sciences (for example, Denzin and Lincoln 2000), in psychology, in general (for example, Willig 2001), and in health psychology, in particular (for example, Murray and Chamberlain 1999a). This interest has led to an increasing number of journals and textbooks that cover a wide variety of approaches and methods. It will be beyond the scope of this chapter to cover all the methods labelled as "qualitative" (see for example Flick 2002; Flick *et al.* 2003 for more comprehensive overviews). However, qualitative research is particularly relevant to a critical health psychology perspective. One reason is that qualitative research is seen as a way of giving voice to people in the health field – professionals, consumers, users, victims of health institutions.[1] Another reason is that qualitative research allows a closer look at practices, institutions, realities in the making – how are therapy or treatment practices constructed in dialogues and in institutional routines, and what is the reality of having a specific illness that is constructed in such practices? The third reason is that the closer look of qualitative research allows going beneath the surface of the distribution of social or health-related phenomena. Epidemiological studies reveal how often a specific diagnosis can be found in the population and if there are social groups that are affected more often by this diagnosis than others. A qualitative approach is needed to understand what this diagnosis means for the individual or what it means for a family to live with a member with this diagnosis.

If research in health psychology wants to get close to these meanings and their making, qualitative research is often seen as the appropriate way. In critical health psychology, qualitative research is part of the methodological programme that qualifies the alternative empirical views on health and illness as critical. In the main, the focus of qualitative research has been on the analysis of biographies, of everyday and institutional communications, of organisations and of more open fields. A major part of qualitative research is also linked to social transformations – of the field of empirical research as well of the fields under study. The first link is that qualitative research has been rediscovered and re-emphasised since the 1960s as a critical programme against standardised, positivist, quantitative and theoretically inflexible research in fields such as sociology and health studies (e.g. the seminal works of Goffman 1961; Cicourel 1964; Glaser and Strauss 1965, 1967). Qualitative research in health psychology focuses on social transformation at different levels: changes in everyday knowledge of health and illness, changes in discourses about both changing practices in this field and changes in the media concerning these topics.

Definition and Relevance of Qualitative Research for Critical Health Psychology

Qualitative research develops and uses methods that are suitable to study social and psychological processes in fields like health and illness (and other fields) in a way that takes into account micro-perspectives in order to analyse phenomena on micro-, meso-, and macro-levels. Methods need to be prepared and implemented in a systematic and transparent way. Qualitative researchers should be able to define and satisfy indicators to distinguish good from bad research.

Theoretical Backgrounds of Qualitative Research

Although there are various research programmes that have been developed against different theoretical backgrounds, some basic assumptions can be seen as constitutive for qualitative research. Qualitative approaches to health and illness start from several basic assumptions in dealing with their issues and in putting research questions into concrete terms. First, social reality is not seen as anything "just given" or taken for granted in an objective and independent way. Rather, social reality is the result of common processes of producing it and of ascribing meanings to objects, experiences and events. The members of a social setting are actively involved in such processes of meaning making and social constructions of social objects and images. Second, social reality is not seen as static but as having a process character. Social reality is seen as reflexive, which means it is influenced by the reflections of the members sharing this reality, which work back on the shaping of realities. Third, "objective" conditions become relevant through their subjective meaning for the life world of those who are concerned by these conditions. For example, poverty can be seen as an objective condition of living measured by a certain regular income. It becomes relevant for the single person or family through the subjective meaning of what it is for them to be poor. This does not mean that such conditions can be negated or ignored, but the ways of coping with them are strongly influenced by subjective meanings ascribed to them. Finally, the communicative character of social reality makes the reconstruction of constructions of social reality a starting point of research. From this point of view, it makes sense to ask people about what it means for them to be healthy or how their dealing with health has developed or changed during their personal history (see Box 8.1 for these basic assumptions). These assumptions outline a very general research programme, in which the use of qualitative methods is embedded.

Box 8.1 Basic assumptions in the theory of qualitative research

1. Social reality as common production and ascription of meanings.
2. The process character and reflexivity of social reality.
3. "Objective" conditions of living become relevant through subjective meaning for the life world.
4. The communicative character of social reality makes the reconstruction of constructions of social reality the starting point of research.

Basic Designs of Qualitative Research

In qualitative research, five main basic designs are used for analysing research questions. These designs can be classified along two axes (see Fig. 8.1; see also Flick 2003a). Case studies focus on the single case – a biography, a family, an institution, a specific field. They provide very detailed descriptions of the field and for this, the perspectives of several members of a family, for example, are included. Sometimes research projects are run as a series of case studies, which are analysed one after the other. The alternative is to plan a study right from the beginning from a comparative perspective: a series of biographical interviews is conducted and the aim of comparison is kept in mind when the questions for the interview are formulated and when the interviews are planned. The interpretation of the data is pursued with a comparative perspective as well and the answers to certain questions are compared for all participants in the study. This is the first axis: case study versus comparative study.

The second axis is the temporal perspective that a study may take. Often, qualitative research provides snapshots: descriptions of a state or a process at a given moment. For example, the practices in an institution are documented by participant observation, or a therapy dialogue is tape-recorded and analysed by using conversation analysis. Then only those events are accessible that are mentioned in the situation. An alternative is to do a longitudinal study, in which data collections are repeated over time or the same interpretation is conducted with data from different times. The researcher comes back to the field after a certain period and completes his or her interviews or observations again. This is a rather demanding design and seldom found in qualitative research. More often, we find that retrospective studies take a perspective over time by looking back on a development or process. This is the case in biographical studies where a process of development is recounted or analysed from the perspective of today. The presentation and evaluation of former events may be influenced by the subject's actual perspective. But this design is easier to apply and therefore used as a substitute for longitudinal studies. These two axes are combined in concrete research projects, for example, a longitudinal comparative study or snapshot-case study.

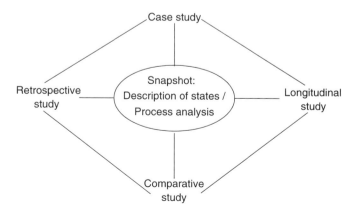

Figure 8.1   Basic designs in qualitative research

Sensitivity and Impact on Social Transformation

If qualitative research is interested in observing social transformation, it will produce a fuller account if a longer perspective is taken. Retrospective studies are more sensitive to transformations than snapshots. Longitudinal studies are most sensitive for analysing change and transformation, as they give the researcher the chance to do his or her study in parallel to the process relevant for the research. On the other hand, transformations can better be studied as *social* transformation if several cases are analysed and compared. Therefore, snapshots in case studies are the least sensitive for social transformation and longitudinal comparative studies are the most sensitive.

If qualitative research is intended to stimulate social transformation or to have an impact on it, these goals can be better achieved the closer the researcher gets involved in the field under study. An extended case study with prolonged field contacts with many members in an institution can inaugurate change in the field more easily and with more effect than, for example, single interviews about biographical processes with each member. However, following Habermas (1971), whether or not social transformations are supported or not is more a question of the intention of the researcher than of a methodological choice (of a specific design, for example).

Qualitative Methods in the Study of Social Transformation

To give a full account of the variety of qualitative research methods[2] would be beyond the limits of this chapter. Therefore, in the following section, two approaches will be presented, which are relevant for research in the context of social transformation in paradigmatic ways. In a retrospective design, narratives allow us to reconstruct social transformations from the perspective of the participant/narrator looking back from the preliminary endpoint of the transformation. Narratives will be considered here as an example of the use of verbal data.

Ethnography makes the researcher himself or herself a participant in the process of social transformation under study. It comes close to a longitudinal design due to the repeated field contacts. It goes beyond the focus of a single participant and addresses social processes from the perspective of social interaction. Ethnography will represent here the use of observation and visual data. Narratives will be discussed in more detail since this approach is more strongly rooted in psychology than is ethnography.

Reconstructing Social Transformation: Research Using Narratives

Narratives (for example, Murray 2000b, 2002, this volume) can be used in qualitative research in two ways. The first way is to record and analyse the stories that people tell in everyday or institutional contexts. Since the publication of such books as *The Illness Narratives* by Kleinman (1988) and *The Wounded Storyteller* by Frank (1995), many case histories of individual illness experiences have been collected and published. Contrary to other forms of biographical research working with narratives, in the research on illness narratives a specific instrument for collecting data is not developed to stimulate narratives. The methodological approach is limited to analysing narratives. The aim is "giving voice" – to give the patient and the story of his or her illness a chance to create a meaning of his or her illness against medical approaches and to cope with it. However, as Atkinson (1997) criticises, using this approach the patient is presented as the hero of his personal narrative while the social context in which the patient lives and in which he or she tells his or her story is neglected. The narrator is positioned in a social vacuum with his or her narrative since social influences and conditions are not sufficiently taken into account (1997: 339). More elaborated methods on how to elicit and analyse narratives in a more systematic way can be a way out of this problematic. Thus, the second way of using narratives is to employ a specific method for stimulating narratives related to the area under study.

The Narrative Interview

In biographical research in Germany, the narrative interview (Riemann and Schütze 1987, see also Flick 2002, Ch. 9) is used. Here, the interview basically consists of one narrative or story. At the beginning of such an interview, a "generative narrative question" (Riemann and Schütze 1987: 353) is asked, which refers to the topic of the study and is intended to stimulate the interviewee's main narrative. For example, "I want to ask you to tell me how the story of your life occurred. The best way to do this would be for you to start from your birth, with the little child that you once were and then to recount all that has happened, one after the other, until today. You can take your time in doing this, also for details, because for me everything is of interest that is important to you" (Hermanns 1995: 182). If the interviewee begins a narrative after this question, it is crucial for the quality of the data that this narrative is not interrupted or obstructed by the interviewer. Questions (for example, "Who is this about?"), directive interventions (for example, "Could this problem not have been managed in a different way, by . . . ?") or evaluations should be strictly avoided. Instead, the interviewer, as a listener, must support and encourage the narrator to continue his or her narrative until its end. The end of the story is indicated by a "coda", for example: "I think I've taken you through my whole life" (Riemann and Schütze 1987: 353). The latter is followed by the stage of narrative enquiry in which "narrative stumps" that were not exhaustively detailed before are completed. The last stage of the interview is the "balancing phase" in which non-narrative questions can be asked by the interviewer.

In this approach, narratives again are privileged against other forms of presentation in the interview. For example, the first step of analysing the data is to separate narrative and non-narrative parts of the interview and then to concentrate on the narrative parts. The social context is taken into account here more than in the case of Kleinman and Frank, as it is assumed that social circumstances and transformations are represented in individual biographies and narratives. These are analysed for the ways social transformations (for example the reunification of Germany in the 1990s) are reflected in individual biographies (for example in the loss of the social identities in the people of the former socialist state of East Germany). General patterns in such experiences are worked out by minimal and maximal contrasting of cases which is applied as a comparative technique. First, the most similar cases are compared (minimal contrast) and then the most different cases (maximal contrasts). In the end, a theory of the typical life courses or biographies in the field is formulated.

The Episodic Interview

The episodic interview (see Flick 2000, 2002) was developed against the background of a distinction in the psychology of memory and of knowledge. Here a distinction is made between semantic knowledge, which is more general and based on concepts and relations among them, and episodic knowledge, which is based on memories of concrete situations linked to concrete circumstances. The first part of knowledge is approached with focused questions – for example for subjective definitions of the issue under study. The second part is approached by narrative questions – invitations to recount specific situations, for example of the first encounter with the issue under study. In studies interested in health concepts and their change over time, the first sort of question is made concrete in a question on the subjective definition of health (for example "What does health mean to you? What do you link with that word?"). The second sort of question is made concrete in the invitation to recount situations in which changes occurred ("Do you have the impression that your idea of health has changed in your professional life? Please tell me about a situation that makes this clear for me"). In response to these questions narratives of episodes and, sometimes even more interesting, "repisodes" (or repeated episodes, see Neisser 1981) are presented. Applications have shown that in the episodic interview not only narratives of situations or repisodes are presented, but also other sorts of data: examples that are abstracted from concrete situations, and metaphors including clichés and stereotypes; subjective definitions (for example, of health) explicitly asked for and linked to them: argumentative-theoretical statements, for example, explanations of concepts and their relations. The episodic interview enables one to confront the more general concepts (for example, concerning health) of the interviewee with the narratives that he or she presents about the day-to-day practices concerning health. Therefore, the narratives are seen as one sort of data, and answers as another. Both have their potential and their limits.

Sensitivity and Impact on Social Transformation

Narrative methods are more sensitive to social transformations than other methods for producing verbal data. This is because they address processes (of change or development) in the life history that is recounted in the narrative interview, in the illness narrative in the case of Kleinman's research, and in the situations of change in the episodic interview. If qualitative research is interested in observing social transformation, the sensitivity of these methods is on different levels. Illness narratives focus on the transformation of the social situation of the individual due to an illness experience, but remain rather insensitive to processes of *social* transformation in a larger perspective. The narrative interview sees the narrator not only as the hero of his or her narrative, but also as someone whose life and history is strongly influenced by social circumstances. The single narrative is placed in the more general social transformation that is in the focus of the interview. The contrastive interpretation addresses such wider contexts of social transformations beyond the single case and its own logic. The episodic interview addresses social transformation through the combination of general concepts and statements and specific episodes and narratives. It allows analysing, for example, the changes in a health system from the perspective of the consumer.[3]

If qualitative research is intended to stimulate social transformation, narrative approaches can have an impact on this process. The act of telling the story of one's illness, of one's life or of episodes of one's illness, life or practices over time will make the participant more aware of what happens in his or her life and turns the attention to implicit knowledge and processes on the side of the participants in a study. This awareness can be a starting point for a transformation, but the narrative interview is difficult to use for integrating the research and the researcher in the process of social transformation. A systematic and comparative analysis of narratives and life histories is rather time consuming. Therefore, it is difficult to use the results for an immediate feedback into an ongoing process of social transformation. In the framework developed by Marks (2002a: 16), narrative approaches are a way to empirically "question the values underlying assumptions and power relations" over time and through the perspective of one or several participants in transformative processes.

Social Transformation in the Making: Ethnography

Since the early 1980s, an increase in ethnographic research can be noted. It has to a certain extent replaced studies that have been conducted employing participant observation. Ethnography is defined as follows: "The ethnographer participates, overtly or covertly, in people's daily lives for an extended period of time, watching what happens, listening to what is said, asking questions; in fact collecting whatever data are available to throw light on the issues with which he or she is concerned" (Hammersley and Atkinson 1983: 2).

Box 8.2   Features of ethnographic research

1. A strong emphasis on exploring the nature of a particular social phenomenon, rather than setting out to test hypotheses about them.
2. A tendency to work primarily with "unstructured" data, that is, data that have not been coded at the point of data collection in terms of a closed set of analytic categories.
3. Investigation of a small number of cases, perhaps just one case, in detail.
4. Analysis of data that involves explicit interpretation of the meanings and functions of human actions, the product of which mainly takes the form of verbal descriptions and explanations, with quantification and statistical analysis playing a subordinate role at most.

On the level of knowledge production, it aims less at understanding social events or processes based on *reports about* these events (for example, in an interview). Instead, the goal is to understand *from the inside* the social processes involved in making these events by participating in the development of the processes. This research is characterised by extended participation (instead of one-time interviews or observations) and by the flexible use of different methods (observation including more or less formalised interviews or analyses of documents). Of central interest since the middle of the 1980s is the part played by writing about the observed events. More generally, this interest highlights the relation between presentation and what is presented. Ethnography can also be seen as a more general attitude or approach. Atkinson and Hammersley (1998: 110–111) note several substantial features of ethnographic research that are summarised in Box 8.2

More central than explicit methods of data collection are other parts of ethnographic research. It is most important for the researcher to be able to find his or her way into the field, to build up and maintain relationships. A central methodological principle is the extended participation of the researcher, which means "that the social researcher, and the research act itself, are part and parcel of the social world under investigation" (Hammersley and Atkinson 1983: 234). A second principle is the flexible use of research techniques. Thus, more or less formal interviews, the analysis of documents, observations, interventions, etc. can be part of ethnography. A strong emphasis is on the process of writing as a way of presenting findings and of constructing data and descriptions at the same time.

Sensitivity and Impact on Social Transformation

Ethnography is the qualitative research approach that brings the researcher the closest and in more regular contact with the field under study. However, the access is often limited to current activities during the time of participation and observation in the field. If the aim is to observe social transformations linked to longer periods of change and development, these are more difficult to catch in ethnography. Therefore, many ethnographic studies use interviews as well to extend the focus of research beyond the actual situation. If the intention is to stimulate social transformation through qualitative research, ethnography can have a stronger impact due to the relative closeness to the field and due to the extended presence and involvement of the research and researcher in it. Again this impact on social transformation depends more on the intention of the researcher than on the use of a specific method. Returning to the framework of Marks (2002a: 16), ethnography is a method to "question underlying assumptions and power relations of...social organisation" on the level of institutional and everyday routines from a process perspective.

Challenges and Perspectives: Indication and Quality of Qualitative Research

Brydon-Miller and Tolman (1997b: 805) see "three pressing concerns" for the use of qualitative methods in processes of transformation: the question of validity, the issue of ownership and the "question of the morality of psychological research...'What makes research good?'" The issue of ownership – how do we respect the information that we use about the lives of our participants if we do narrative research in order to develop a scientific theory for example – is not exclusively linked to qualitative research. This is less the problem of using qualitative instead of quantitative research. It is more the question of whether research is conducted in the setting of participatory action research or not (see Chapter 11) and of the attitude the researcher has towards the field and people under study. At the present state of development, this means that there are at least two points to be further clarified inside qualitative research. The first is how to decide, which method should be selected, and the second is how to define and assess the quality of qualitative research.

Indication

In empirical research in general, textbooks of methodology hardly give any help on the decision of when to select a specific method for a study. Most books treat the single method or research design separately and describe their features and problems. In most cases, they do not provide a comparative presentation of the different methodological alternatives or starting points for how to select a specific method (and not a different one) for a research issue. Thus, one (not the only) need for qualitative research is to further clarify the question of indication. In medicine or psychotherapy, the appropriateness of a certain treatment for specific problems and groups of people is checked. This process is labelled

Table 8.1 Indication of qualitative research methods
(taken from Flick 2002: 272)

Psychotherapy and medicine			Qualitative research		
Which disease, Symptoms, Diagnosis, Population	indicate	Which treatment Or therapy?	Which issue, population, research question, knowledge of issue and population	indicate	Which method Or methods
1. When is a particular method appropriate and indicated? 2. How to make a rational decision for or against certain methods?					

as indication. The answer to this question is whether or not a specific treatment is appropriate (indicated) for a specific problem in a specific case. If this is transferred to qualitative research, the relevant questions are: When are certain qualitative methods appropriate – for which issue, for which research question, for which group of people (population) or fields to be studied and so on? When are quantitative methods or a combination of both indicated? (Table 8.1).

This leads to the search for points of orientation to answer such questions. The checklist in Box 8.3 includes orienting questions that should be helpful in deciding which research design and/or method to select for a concrete study.

First, the researcher should sort out his or her intention for the research concerning transformations: Does he or she intend to observe or to stimulate transformations? Does he or she pursue a specific – critical or transformation oriented – interest, that goes beyond the production of scientific knowledge. The next step is to clarify the theoretical background and interests of the study: Discovery of new knowledge or starting from existing knowledge, that he or she intends to develop further? What is the empirical entity that is in the focus: Individuals, social interactions or institutions? What sort of generalisation shall be reached and what are the available resources? Answering these questions and those on the checklist can help the researcher decide for or against a specific qualitative method or between qualitative and quantitative research (see Flick 2002, Ch. 22 for more details). If researchers are interested in stimulating a transformation with their research, they should also decide which ways of feedback of the results into the field under study are appropriate and how to assess the impact of the research on the field and the participants.

Quality of Qualitative Research

The issue of how to define and assess the quality of qualitative research in general or for certain areas is becoming more and more relevant. This is demonstrated

---

Box 8.3 Checklist for selecting a qualitative research method

1. What is the intention of my research – to observe or to stimulate social transformation?
2. What do I know about the issue and field of my study or how detailed is my knowledge already?
3. How developed is the theoretical or empirical knowledge in the literature about the issue and the field?
4. Am I more interested in generally exploring the field and the issue of my study?
5. What is the theoretical background of my study and which methods fit this background?
6. What is it that I want to get close to in my study – personal experiences of (a group of) certain people or social processes in the making? Or am I more interested in reconstructing the underlying structures of my issue?
7. Do I start with a very focused research question right away or do I start from a rather unfocused approach in order to develop the more focused questions underway in the process of my project?
8. What is the aggregate I want to study – personal experiences, interactions or situations or bigger entities like organisations or discourse?
9. Is it more the single case (for example, of a personal illness experience or of a certain institution) I am interested in or the comparison of various cases?
10. What are the resources (time, money, work force, skills ...) available to run my study?
11. What are the characteristics of the field I want to study and of the people in it? What can you request of them and what not?
12. What is the claim to generalisation of my study?
13. How do I intend to feed back the results of my study?
14. How does this fit the interest of transformation linked to my study?
15. How do I assess the impact of my results on the field under study?

---

by the increasing number of publications dedicated to this issue (for example, Seale 1999; Yardley 2000; Flick 2002, Chs. 18 and 22 for overviews). On the one hand, a need for qualitative research to find an answer for questions of quality is seen. On the other hand, what the answer should look like is subject to debate: Should the answer formulate criteria that bring along benchmarks for distinguishing good from less good research? Then the first question is, which criteria are appropriate for this purpose? and the second, whether these criteria should be applied to qualitative research as a whole or for specific areas and approaches in qualitative research. If these criteria are formulated – shall they be appropriate to a grounded theory study in the same way as to a discourse analytic study or ethnography? Or has the question of quality in qualitative research to be asked fundamentally differentby – beyond criteria? Then the question is, what could and should take the place of criteria in assessing the quality of qualitative research?

Sometimes it is suggested to apply the traditional criteria of reliability, validity and objectivity to qualitative research as well or to modify them for this field. Kirk and Miller (1986) have dealt with reliability and validity in this way. It becomes clear, that the reliability of data and methods in the traditional sense – as the stability of data and results in repeated collections – is inappropriate for assessing qualitative data. The identical repetition of a narrative in a repeated narrative interview is rather an indicator for a consciously constructed version than for the reliability of what was narrated. Validity is discussed for qualitative research as well as "a question of whether the researcher sees what he or she thinks he or she sees" (Kirk and Miller 1986: 21). Traditionally, internal validity is raised or guaranteed by excluding variables other than those included in the hypotheses have influenced what was observed. Internal validity shall be increased by a far-reaching control of the context condition of the investigation. This again is achieved by a far-reaching standardisation of the situations of data collection and interpretation. The necessary degree of standardisation is not compatible with most of the usual qualitative methods but undermines their actual strengths. In a similar way, it can be demonstrated for other forms of validity as to why they cannot be applied immediately to qualitative research.

The third criterion in the quantitative canon is objectivity. Few attempts have been made to apply this criterion to qualitative research. An example is a paper by Madill *et al.* (2000). The authors, however, equate objectivity of qualitative analyses with the question as to whether two researchers arrive at the same results in analysing a specific set of qualitative data. Objectivity is seen as "the 'consistency of meaning', through triangulating the findings of independent researchers" (p. 17). All in all we find claims that qualitative research has to face the questions linked to concepts of reliability and validity (Morse 1999) or objectivity. In practice, we rather find modifications or a reformulation of the concepts.

For example, a strategy for the validation of interview data is to ask for the interviewee's consent to data or interpretations. This is discussed as member check or communicative validation. Also, it is suggested to analyse the situation of the interview for any signs of strategic communication in it, that would be an indicator for false information given in the answers or narratives. Reliability of qualitative data is increased by clear instructions on how to document verbal statements in protocols or transcripts.

As an alternative to using traditional criteria or to reformulating them, new criteria or strategies are applied. Triangulation (see Flick 1992, 2003b) means to use different methods (or different data sets) in one study in order to check the quality of the data each method has produced or to widen the scope of the data.

The more general problem is whether it is useful for qualitative research to link the question of good or bad research to criteria at all. The quality of qualitative research depends more on the formulation of a good research question, of the sensitivity for the field under study and of a creative use of the data that were collected. These qualities are difficult to frame in criteria and benchmarks to separate good from bad research. Therefore, it is more fruitful to look at how well the decision for or against specific methods was reflected and how well the different steps of the qualitative research process (sampling, collecting and analysing data) fit together.

These questions concerning the quality of research applies to qualitative research in general. If the researcher is not only observing transformation but involved in a process of social transformation, the issue of the quality of qualitative research also includes aspects of doing justice to the participants and of sharing the results with them. In this case, the quality of qualitative research is not only a methodological problem but also a "moral problem" and a "question of ownership" as Brydon-Miller and Tolman (1997b: 805) put it.

Conclusion

Social transformation can be the issue under study for qualitative research or an intended outcome. Not every design and every method are equally sensitive to or have the same impact on social transformations. Therefore, it is necessary to clarify the question before using a specific method to study or even to inaugurate social transformation through qualitative research. Narrative methods can be a very fruitful way to study social transformation but there are different methodological alternatives with strengths and weaknesses. Ethnography allows the study of social processes in the making. The question of quality is important for qualitative research. We can distinguish approaches focusing on (traditional, reformulated or new) criteria from those looking for an answer for the quality problem beyond criteria. In the context of studying or stimulating social transformation, the question of quality of qualitative research is not only a methodological but also a moral problem.

Key Points

- Qualitative research can be used to study processes of social transformation. In the context of critical health psychology, qualitative research can also be used as an intervention stimulating social transformation.
- Qualitative research is sensitive to social transformations. It takes into account the perspectives of those who are involved in processes of social transformation and questions the underlying assumptions and routines in everyday practices and institutions.

- Not every research design and/or method is equally suitable for analysing/ stimulating social transformation. Narrative methods allow the study of processes of transformation retrospectively. Ethnography draws the researcher into the processes he or she studies.
- How well transformations are covered as social transformations depends on how the collection and the analysis of the data are conducted – which narrative method is applied or how and in which research design is ethnography practised? This problem can be framed as the indication of qualitative methods and designs.
- How to assess the quality of qualitative research is a crucial, but not yet fully answered question in qualitative research – as a methodological and as a moral issue.

Assignment Questions

1. Think of a research question that you want to pursue. Discuss and compare the different research designs for their suitability to your project, covering the research question itself and the issue of social transformation in it.
2. Discuss the theoretical assumptions that make it legitimate to use qualitative research for studying a socially relevant problem like mental illness.
3. Compare the three narrative approaches you learnt about for their adequacy to your research project.
4. Identify a qualitative article from a peer-reviewed health psychology journal and write a short essay about it, in which you discuss whether it gives enough information to answer the question of indication of methods in the research reported.
5. Choose another qualitative article and reflect on how the author has dealt with the problem of quality in qualitative research in the study.

Notes

1. There is the problem that you will meet different voices in the field that may express different views but have unequal chances of being listened to. Critical health psychology is often concerned with giving voice to underprivileged people (see Murray and Chamberlain 2000), for example in feminist research.
2. Other qualitative methods include semi-structured interviews, focus groups, participant observation, discourse analysis (see Chapter 9), participatory action research (see Chapter 11) and grounded theory analysis (see Flick 2002; Flick *et al.* 2003 or Murray and Chamberlain 1999a for details).
3. See Flick (2000) for examples related to East and West Germany in the transition from two different systems into one system after the reunification or to Portugal in the transition from the dictatorship until the mid-1980s into the democracy since then.

📖 Further Readings

Flick, U. (2002) *An Introduction to Qualitative Research – Second Edition*, London, Thousand Oaks, New Dehli: Sage.

Some of the issues mentioned in this chapter are more fully discussed in this introductory text.

Flick, U., Kardorff, E. V. and Steinke, I. (eds) (2003) *Qualitative Research – Paradigms, Theories, Methods, Practice & Contexts*, London, Thousand Oaks, CA, New Dehli: Sage

This book gives an overview of a wider range of theories and methods in qualitative research.

Brydon-Miller, M. and Tolman D. L. (eds) (1997a) "Special issue 'Transforming psychology: interpretive and participatory research methods'", *Journal of Social Issues* 53, 597–810.

Issues of transformation through qualitative research are subject of this special issue.

CHAPTER 9

Discourse Analysis and Health Psychology

Carla Willig

Summary

This chapter explores the role of discourse analysis in health psychology research. The chapter opens with an introduction to discourse analytic research in psychology. It identifies two versions of the discourse analytic method: *Discursive Psychology* (DP) and *Foucauldian Discourse Analysis* (FDA) (see Willig 2001, Chapters 6 and 7 for a fuller account). Each of these is characterised and illustrated with reference to published work in health psychology. The chapter compares and contrasts the two versions of discourse analysis and assesses their relevance to health psychology research in relation to *theory development, practice/applicability* and *ethics*. The chapter concludes that the two versions of discourse analysis make different contributions to health psychology research and practice, and that researchers need to be aware of these differences when they consider the use of discourse analysis in health psychology research.

Discourse Analytic Research in Psychology

In recent years, discourse analysis has gained popularity and acceptance as a qualitative research method in psychology. Psychologists' turn to language was inspired by theories and research which had emerged within other disciplines over a period of time. From the 1950s onwards, philosophers, communications theorists, historians and sociologists became increasingly interested in language as a social performance. The assumption that language provides a set of unambiguous signs with which to label internal states and with which to describe external reality began to be challenged. Instead, language was re-conceptualised as productive; this is to say, language was seen to construct versions of social reality, and it was seen to achieve social objectives. The focus of enquiry shifted from the individual and his/her intentions to language and its productive potential. Psychologists began to take up these ideas and to develop a critique of the dominant cognitive research paradigm in social psychology (for example, Potter and Wetherell 1987; Gergen 1989). Since then, two distinct approaches to the analysis of discourse have emerged within the psychological literature. Even though these two approaches share a concern with the role of language in the construction of social and psychological realities, the two versions do address different sorts of research questions and they focus on different features of discourse.[1]

Discursive Psychology (DP)

This version of discourse analysis was introduced into British social psychology with the publication of Potter and Wetherell's *Discourse and Social Psychology: Beyond Attitudes and Behaviour* in 1987. The focus of analysis in DP is on how participants use discursive resources and with what effects. In other words, discursive psychologists pay attention to the action orientation of talk. They are concerned with the ways in which speakers manage issues of stake and interest. They identify discursive strategies such as "disclaiming" or "footing" and explore their function in a particular discursive context. For example, an interviewee may disclaim a racist social identity by saying "I am not racist but I think immigration controls should be strengthened" and then legitimate the statement by referring to a higher authority: "I agree with the Prime Minister's statement that the situation requires urgent action." Other discursive devices used to manage interest and accountability include the use of metaphors and analogies, direct quotations, extreme case formulations, graphic descriptions, consensus formulations, stake inoculation and many more (see Edwards and Potter 1992; Potter 1996, for a detailed discussion of such devices).

Doing DP is a way of reading a text. This reading is informed by a conceptualisation of language as performative. This means that the reader focuses upon the internal organisation of the discourse in order to find out what the discourse is doing. It means moving beyond an understanding of its content and to trace its action orientation. Discursive Psychology requires us to adopt an orientation to talk and text as social action, and it is this orientation which directs our analytic work (see Potter and Wetherell 1987; Billig 1997; Willig 2001, for guidance on how to carry out this type of discourse analysis).

Foucauldian Discourse Analysis

The Foucauldian version of discourse analysis was introduced into Anglo-American psychology in the late 1970s (for example, Henriques *et al.* 1984). This version of discourse analysis was influenced by post-structuralist ideas, most notably the work of Michel Foucault. The focus of this type of work is the relationship between language and subjectivity and its implications for psychological research. From a Foucauldian point of view, discourses facilitate and limit, enable and constrain what can be said, by whom, where and when (see Parker 1992). Foucauldian discourse analysts focus upon the availability of discursive resources within a culture – something like a discursive economy – and its implications for those who live within it. Here, discourses may be defined as "(…) sets of statements that construct objects and an array of subject positions" (Parker 1994: 245). These constructions, in turn, make available certain ways of seeing the world and certain ways of being in the world.

The Foucauldian version of discourse analysis is concerned with language and language use; however, its interest in language takes it beyond the immediate contexts within which language may be used by speaking subjects. Thus, unlike DP which is primarily concerned with talk and conversation, FDA asks questions about the relationship between discourse and how people think or feel (subjectivity), what they may do (practices) and the material conditions within which such experiences may take place (see Parker 1992; Kendall and Wickham 1999; Willig 2001, for guidance on how to carry out this type of discourse analysis).

Discourse Analysis in Health Psychology

Both DP and FDA are currently being used in health psychology research. Discursive work is now regularly published in well-known health psychology journals (for example, the *Journal of Health Psychology*) and presented at health psychology conferences. In this section, both versions of discourse analysis will be illustrated with reference to published journal articles reporting discourse analytic research with a health psychology focus. A paper on the discursive management of identity in talk about myalgic encephalomyelitis (ME) by Mary Holton-Salway (2001) will be reviewed in order to demonstrate the ways in which DP contributes to health psychology research. This is followed by an account of a paper by Gillies and Willig (1997) on discursive constructions of cigarette-smoking by women smokers which will serve as an illustration of the use of FDA in health psychology. The presentation of the two papers is followed by a discussion of the differences between the two approaches to discourse analytic work and their relevance to health psychology.

"Narrative Identities and the Management of Personal Accountability in Talk about ME" by Mary Horton-Salway (2001)

This paper reports a case study in order to examine "the dilemmatics of illness talk" within the context of ME, also known as chronic fatigue syndrome (CFS). The study is based on a DP analysis of an interview with a married couple (Angela and Joe) on the topic of the wife's ME. ME/CFS has been the subject of much controversy concerning its origin and preferred treatment, and its status (as a physical illness, as a psychological condition) remains contested. As a result, those diagnosed with ME/CFS become accountable for their illness and their response to it, and they have a clear stake in any conversation that they may have about their illness. As we have seen, DP is concerned with the ways in which participants manage stake in social interaction and how they make use of discursive resources in order to account for themselves and their actions. This means that talk about ME constitutes suitable material for DP work.

In her paper, Horton-Salway presents four extracts from an interview with Angela and Joe which are reproduced in Boxes 9.1 to 9.4. She demonstrates how both participants construct ME in such a way as to disclaim undesirable attributions (for example, of psychological vulnerability, of malingering). Part of the discursive work performed by the couple involves the identification of

---

Box 9.1   Extract 1 from Horton-Salway 2001: 250–251

Mary	mm and how did it (.) can you remember much about how it started ?=
Joe	=heh heh
	(.)
Angela	it started off with=
Joe	=it started off with a sore throat=
Angela	=I had a sore throat and I had the very worst headache I've ever had in my life (.) it was one evening=
Joe	=go back to where we believe it was caught at the swimming baths in (town)=
Angela	=yeah=
Joe	=we'd been going down in the evening (.) swimming once a week (.) And it was after one of our sessions =
Angela	=yeah we thought we'd picked it up =
Joe	=I went swimming one week (.) you didn't feel up to it (.) then the following week=
Angela	=*you* were alright weren't you ?=
Joe	=yeah and this ties in because it's now known that ME is caused by er (.) an enterovirus which is a prime place to pick up an enterovirus is a swimming baths (.) it's also the classic (.) used to be the classic place to catch polio in the old days (.) hot summers (.) and I think with swimming (.) kids being in the bath all through the day (.) at the end of the day the water wasn't getting through the cleansing plant quick enough (.) I suspect if you'd gone first thing in the morning it would be absolutely spot clean (.) but er I suppose by the time we got there (.) I suppose the enteroviruses were still there (.) yeah (.) just unfortunate

a definitive starting point of Angela's illness (a viral infection caught at the swimming baths) (Extract 1) which constructs Angela's illness as a recognisable instance of organic disease comparable to polio.

In Extract 2, Angela and Joe provide vivid details of the progression of Angela's illness (for example, Angela's struggle to do the laundry, Joe's return from work to find Angela in bed, the contributions of both their parents to

---

Box 9.2   Extract 2 from Horton-Salway 2001: 251–252

Joe	one of the problems which caused (.) we suspect which *pushed* the ME (1.0) was ((coughs)) she had a friend in the village (.) the same friend who's now got a grand-daughter with a funny name (.) and *she* came round to see Angela (.) I think your mother had gone back (.) or your mother had gone back because she'd begun to become *very* slightly better but she was still ill when she arrived (.) but Janet came round and said 'oh you wanna get out you wanna fight it y'know' =
Angela	= 'push yourself (.) [you push yours]elf you'll be al[right']
Joe	[push yourself]
	[and]
	she did=
Angela	=and I did (.) and I got worse and worse and worse after that=
Joe	=and I'll always remember the time I came home from work (.) the kids were out (.) the house (.) when I opened the back door the house was *dead* silent y'know (.) and I knew she was back in bed again and that was really the thing that pushed her [into]
Angela	[push]ed it over the top=
Joe	= *my* Mum came back again (.) she thought Angela was ill (.) she came back for three weeks initially I – I initially was off work for two weeks anyway (.) that was special leave to look after her (.) so there was two weeks and then another three (.) both parents (.) that brings it to nine weeks=
Angela	well *this* can't [go on forever can it ? (.) so in] the end everybody had
Joe	[and then she pushed her herself]
Angela	gone back (.) Joe was at work (.) cause I've got two children there's a lot of washing isn't there ? I used to crawl round the floor and hang over the sink and washing machine trying to do a bit of washing (.) and of course now we *know* this is the last thing you must ever *do* is to push yourself when you first go down with ME (.) and I was doing *all* the wrong things (.) and I think that's why I've never ever recovered

---

Box 9.3   Extract 3 from Horton-Salway 2001: 253–254

Angela   I think my mother was around at one of these times when *that*
          was mentioned too (.) *my* mother said 'I know my daughter'
          (.) I can always remember my mother saying that (.) 'I *know* my
          daughter' (.) because I was always *so* active heh heh hyperactive
          in some respects actually (.) because my Mum used to say
          to me 'for goodness sake Angela sit down' (.) this was before
          I went down with ME (.) I never wanted to sit down (.)
          I wanted to be on the go all the while (.) I was happy that way
          (.) but er (.) things change (.) you're forced to sit down =
Joe   = to his credit (.) the consultant never *did* ever voice that
          thought =
Angela   = no (.) he didn't believe that

Angela's care). Horton-Salway draws attention to the way in which the provision of fine detail serves to establish the account's facticity and to counter any potential challenges to its accuracy or authenticity. In addition, Extract 2 is also read as a defence against a possible claim that Angela's illness could be self-serving or self-induced. This is accomplished by a construction of Angela as a fighter whose condition deteriorated as a result of following inappropriate advice from a friend, thus aligning Angela's personal story with the classic narrative of how ME usually takes hold.

Extract 3 (Box 9.3) provides another example of how Angela and Joe use rhetorical strategies in order to warrant their claims regarding Angela's illness status and identity as sufferer from a genuine, if controversial, medical condition. This time they use Angela's mother's voice as corroborative evidence by citing her comments regarding Angela's active and robust disposition prior to the onset of her ME.

The final extract (Box 9.4) constitutes another example of how Angela and Joe ward off possible accusations of malingering by working up an active, energetic self for Angela prior to her ME. This is accomplished by contrasting the active, outdoor-and exercise-oriented lifestyle of the couple prior to Angela's illness with the sedentary way of life they have had to adopt as a result of the ME. It is implied that becoming ill constitutes a loss for Angela, rather than a gain, thus undermining any psychological illness attributions. Morton-Salway's analysis of the interview extracts focuses on what she refers to as the "interactive business" that is being performed by them. She draws attention to the fact that her "(...) analysis of Angela and Joes's narrative identifies discursive devices that are commonly used by participants in mundane, everyday talk to accomplish [such] factuality and authenticity" (p. 252). In this particular case, participants make use of these devices in order to counter competing, and less

---

Box 9.4   Extract 4 from Horton-Salway 2001: 255

Joe	mm (.) it has had (.) 'cause it's altered my way of life really (.) I feel at times frustrated y'know (.) after all this time (.) frustrated (.) I suppose you could say 'yes we could go out and have a walk' but er (.) you feel there's things to be done perhaps (.) but you get out of the habit of doing that [anyway]
Angela	[because] we did it together you see (.) we always used to go [fell-walking [and hik]ing cycling heh heh heh heh heh=
Joe	[cyclists]
MHS	=outdoor people=
Angela	=yeah (.) swimming (.) physical things 'cause I know some couples aren't in to that sort of thing (.) they're quite happy to stop at home and sit (.) aren't they=
MHS	=yes=
Angela	=well we were never like that (.) but we've been forced to be like that in a way (.) to be sedentary instead of active

---

desirable, explanations for Angela's illness, and to disclaim undesirable identities which such explanations may construct. Thus, from a DP point of view, talk about ME/CFS constitutes yet another social context within which speakers use a range of discursive resources in order to construct a particular version of reality (in this case, one in which ME is an organic illness which befalls people who have nothing to gain from being ill) and thus to manage their stake in the interaction (in this case, by disclaiming undesirable attributions of malingering and psychological vulnerability).

"'You Get the Nicotine and That in Your Blood' – Constructions of Addiction and Control in Women's Accounts of Cigarette Smoking" by Val Gillies and Carla Willig (1997)

This paper presents a discursive analysis of four semi-structured interviews with women smokers. The aim of the analysis was to "explore how the women position themselves within discourses of smoking and with what consequences" (p. 288). From a FDA perspective, the discursive positions which speakers take up are associated with practices. As a result, discourse analysis of talk about smoking may tell us something about how the discursive construction of smoking is bound up with the practice of smoking. Thus, the aim of the study was to examine the role of discourse in the maintenance of women's behavioural practice. Analysis of the interviews demonstrated that all participants framed their accounts within a discourse of addiction. This discourse constructs cigarette smoking as the consequence of physiological addiction and/or psychological dependence, and it positions the smoker as the victim of these processes. A positioning as nicotine addict compromises the speaker's agency by suggesting that it is the chemical properties of cigarette smoke which are responsible for the addict's actions. Similarly, a construction of smoking as the product of psychological dependence positions the smoker as helpless and out of control, thus absolving her from full responsibility for her actions.

The authors point out that three participants also deployed constructions of control and self-regulation in their accounts. These were deployed when participants reflected on their ability to moderate their cigarette consumption when the (social) situation required it. This suggests that these participants had access to alternative, and conflicting, constructions of cigarette smoking (as compulsion vs as choice) and subject positions offered by them (as victim/addict vs as agent/in control). Gillies and Willig propose a dual conceptualisation of positioning, whereby speakers can be seen to both actively position themselves in discourse whilst also being constrained by available discursive positions in a more passive sense. They argue that, in this way, discursive constructions of cigarette smoking may actually exert a powerful influence over the way in which participants behave and experience the world. More specifically, it is suggested that a construction of cigarette smoking as "addiction" is disempowering because "[T]he more convinced an individual is of his/her addiction, the less likely he/she is to give up" (p. 298).

However, the alternative construction of smoking as subject to control and self-regulation can also be limiting in that it fosters a dualistic perception of the body as a separate entity in need of regulation and repression by the controlling self. The authors conclude by recommending the promotion of "a more affirmative construction [of the body which] would emphasise pleasure, strength and vitality" (p. 299).

Differences Between Discursive Psychology and Foucauldian Discourse Analysis

As the two illustrations demonstrate, DP and FDA are designed to answer different sorts of research questions. Discursive Psychology projects typically ask "How do participants use language in order to manage stake in social interactions?", whilst FDA is used to find out "What characterises the discursive worlds people inhabit and what are their implications for possible ways-of-being ?". The two versions also emphasise different aspects of human agency. Even though Discursive Psychology is concerned with language and its performative aspects (rather than with the speaking subject and his/her intentions), its focus on action orientation presupposes a conceptualisation of the speaker as an active agent who uses discursive strategies in order to manage stake in social interactions. By contrast, FDA draws attention to the power of discourse to construct its objects, including the human subject itself. The availability of subject positions constrains what can be said, done and felt by individuals.

Finally, DP questions the value of the category "experience" itself. Instead, it conceptualises it (along with others such as "subjectivity" and "identity") as a discursive move whereby speakers may refer to their "experiences" in order to validate their claims (for example, "I know this is hard because I've been there!"). Here, "experience" is a discursive construction, to be deployed as and when required. By contrast, FDA does attempt to theorise "experience" (and "subjectivity"). According to this approach, discursive constructions and practices are implicated in the ways in which we experience ourselves (for example, as "addicted" or as "in/out of control"). As a result, an exploration of the availability of subject positions in discourse has implications for possibilities of selfhood and subjective experience.

To summarise, DP and FDA differ in the way in which they conceptualise and work with notions of agency, experience and subjectivity. What may be the implications of these differences for the use of discourse analysis in health psychology? This question is addressed in the next section in relation to theory, practice and ethics in health psychology.

Relevance of the Two Versions of Discourse Analysis to Health Psychology

Health psychology is concerned with the ways in which social and psychological factors impact upon and/or mediate people's experience of their physicality, including states such as "ill health" and "wellness". Health psychology may be described as an applied discipline, in that much of the research conducted within health psychology is motivated by a desire to generate insights which have the potential to improve quality of life and/or health outcomes. For example, health psychologists want to find out why people smoke in order to help people quit, or they may want to gain a better understanding of what it is like to live with a chronic illness in order to identify ways in which those who are chronically ill may be supported. In the remainder of this section, I explore the contributions that discourse analytic research may make to the project of health psychology. I address this question in relation to theory, practice and ethics in health psychology, and I aim to compare and contrast the ways in which DP and FDA may make their contribution.

Theory

Earlier in this chapter it was suggested that DP and FDA address different research questions. Whilst DP is concerned with the ways in which participants use language in order to manage stake in social interactions, FDA aims to characterise the discursive worlds people inhabit and to trace their implications for human experience and action. These concerns informed the focus and the choice of analytic method of the two papers reviewed on pp. 157–162 of this chapter. As a result, the two papers make different contributions to theory development in health psychology. Holton-Salway's (2001) paper identified a range of discursive devices used by her participants in their attempt to accomplish factuality and authenticity in their account of ME. The author acknowledges that these devices "(...) are commonly used by participants in mundane and everyday talk to accomplish such factuality and authenticity" (p. 252). Thus, whilst the subject matter of the study was a couple's account of their experience of ME, the theoretical concern driving the study was the performative nature of language which was explored through the couple's attempt to manage the dilemmatics of illness talk. The findings of the study support, and add to, the identification of discursive devices which people use to manage stake and accountability and which have been explored by discursive psychologists in relation to a range of discursive contexts such as talk about prejudice, bullying, social work, the economy and many more (see Edwards and Potter 1992; Potter 1996 for an overview). Theoretically, therefore, the study contributes to the consolidation of DP rather than to the development of health psychology.[2]

More generally, DP's concern with the action orientation of talk means that the focus of enquiry is upon how people construct meaning in context, and this means that, theoretically, it cannot (and does not intend to) tell us anything about people's motivation, emotional investments, feelings or embodiment. An exclusive focus upon the rhetorical dimension of social interaction does not allow us to theorise physicality and experience. By contrast, the Foucauldian version of discourse analysis attempts to link discourse with practice and experience. Gillies and Willig (1997) used positioning theory in order to think about the ways in which their participants may be experiencing themselves in relation to their smoking (such as, as addicts, as struggling to establish control over their bodies) and how this, in turn, may serve to maintain the practice itself. Thus, theoretically, the study constituted an attempt to provide an account of how it is that individuals continue to smoke despite their knowledge of the health risks. As such, it offers a theoretical formulation which constitutes an alternative to psychological theories of health behaviour such as social cognition models or social learning theory. By linking discourse with subjectivity, FDA is able to engage with the concerns of health psychology as it attempts to theorise both experience (for example, embodiment) as well as practice (for example, risk-taking).

Practice

Both approaches to discourse analysis generate research which is potentially applicable within a health care context. Discursive Psychology's fine-grained analysis of how participants make use of discursive resources can help us gain a better understanding of the dynamics of doctor–patient communication. DP draws attention to the fact that a speaker's contribution to a conversation is a social performance and that it forms part of an action sequence. This means that a patient's description of her symptoms or a doctor's formulation of the treatment regime tells us something about what the patient and the doctor are doing with their talk within the context of the consultation. A patient may deploy rhetorical devices in order to disclaim an undesirable identity (as demonstrated by Holton-Salway's study) whilst a doctor may construct the patient's illness in such as way as to disclaim responsibility for the outcome of the treatment. DP research looks beyond the surface content of what is being said in a conversation, and is therefore (potentially) capable of generating a clearer understanding of why, and how, communication between patients and health care professionals may, or may not, be successful in meeting its objectives. Research of this type, with clear implications for practice, has been carried out by David Silverman within the context of HIV-related counselling sessions (Silverman 1997).

FDA, with its emphasis on subject positions within discourse and the practices that are bound up with such positions, is potentially applicable within the area of health promotion. An understanding of the discourses which construct meaning around activities such as smoking, unsafe sex, dieting or attending medical check-ups can help us make sense of (our own and other people's) behaviour. It can help us understand why people may engage in practices which appear not to be in their own best interest or which involve taking very high risks. Since discourse and practice reinforce one another, it is to be expected that people act in ways which support the subject position they have adopted in discourse (for example, as an addict) even if this constitutes a risk to their physical health. It follows that any attempt to change behaviour in the absence of a critical engagement with the discourses which support such behaviour is unlikely to succeed. Research using FDA can inform health promotion practice by identifying the limitations and the opportunities inherent within health-related discourses and the subject positions which they contain. Health promotion interventions may then attempt to challenge and/or to transform those discursive constructions which are bound up with practices which constitute a risk to health. Willig (1998) has formulated recommendations for sex education based on FDA (see also Willig 1999, for a full discussion of the applicability of discourse analytic research).

Ethics

Discourse analytic research in health psychology frequently works with transcripts of semi-structured interviews with people who have a personal stake in the health-related topic about which they are being interviewed. They may be people who are living with a chronic illness, those who are considering whether or not to take an important diagnostic test, or those who are concerned about potential health risks in their lives. These people agree to be interviewed and to tell their story to an interviewer who shows an interest in their experiences.

In line with the ethical guidelines which are widely accepted within the psychological research community, discourse analytic researchers obtain informed consent from participants before the interview, they inform participants of their right to withdraw from the research at any point and they guarantee confidentiality regarding any information about participants acquired during the research process. Semi-structured interviewing involves the use of open-ended questions which allow the interviewee to talk about their experiences in a way that reflects their own concerns rather than those of the interviewer. Discourse analytic researchers vary in the extent to which they offer their own views or opinions within the context of the interview.

However, the preferred style of interviewing seems to be facilitative rather than challenging. This suggests that participants are likely to experience the interview situation as supportive and non-judgemental, an opportunity to talk to someone who is interested in their side of the story. Do participants realise that in the analysis of the text they have generated, their words are not taken "at face value" and does this matter? How would (or do) participants feel when they read the discourse analytic interpretation of the accounts they produced in the interview situation? Should discourse analysts be concerned about the ways in which their analyses construct interviewees and what effects such constructions may have on participants in research? I believe that these are important questions.

Early work in DP tended to explore the ways in which phenomena such as prejudice or racism, inequalities or discrimination were talked into being and the rhetorical strategies speakers would deploy in order to legitimise their claims and assertions. Suitable texts for analysis were drawn from interviews with people who had formed opinions about current affairs or policy matters (for example, Potter and Wetherell's (1987) interviews with white, middle-class New Zealanders about Polynesian immigration) or politicians' discourse in the form of speeches or media interviews (for example, Potter and Edwards 1990). These texts, therefore, did not represent accounts of people's personal struggles or stories of suffering. More recently, a DP perspective has been applied to just such material. It could be argued that whilst a pre-occupation with the strategic use of discursive resources is entirely appropriate when analysing the political discourse of (relatively) powerful speakers, it is not suitable when it comes to personal accounts of suffering. It may not be ethically justifiable to interview an increasing number of individuals about their experiences with ill health, and to encourage them to reflect on the various ways in which their illness has been affecting them and their loved ones, when our analysis of this material is going to focus on the speakers' use of rhetorical strategies in their performance of interactive business (for example, to save face, to disclaim, to blame, to defend, etc.).

There is a sense in which the DP perspective silences speakers because it undermines the status of their illness narrative as a form of self-expression. In other words, by "[treating] the narration of subjective experience and the construction of identity as situated productions that work to accomplish interactive business" (Holton-Salway 2001: 249), DP denies speakers the right to author their account. Whilst it can generate powerful critiques of political discourse as it is used by (relatively) powerful speakers, it may not be ethically justifiable to apply this perspective to first-person accounts of distressing experiences.[3] Do these ethical concerns apply equally to FDA? In my view, FDA is more compatible with a compassionate approach to stories of suffering because it accepts, and thus validates, the experiential dimension of the account. However, FDA does limit the speaker's agency and authorship because it proposes that subjects are positioned by, and in, discourse which means that the individual's experience is constructed through discourse, and although such an experience may feel entirely unique and subjective to the individual, it is, in fact, the product of discursive resources available in the culture surrounding the individual. FDA proposes that the individual subject is quite literally constructed through discourse and its analytic focus is upon the discursive resources which make certain selves (and not others) possible. Again, the individual and his/her experiences are not at the centre of the enquiry (see also Crossley 2000: 86, for a critique of social constructionist readings of narratives and their neglect of the "subjective, reflexive, moral and existential aspect" of personal experiences).

Conclusion

DP and FDA are concerned with the role of language in the construction of social and psychological realities; however, they engage with this concern in different ways. DP approaches participants' accounts of their experiences as social productions which tell us something about their use of discursive resources in order to perform interactive business. FDA explores participants' use of discourse in order to find out how they construct their own subjectivity and experience and how these constructions are then lived through their associated practices. Thus, whilst both versions of discourse analysis are interested in the use of language in the construction of meaning, their theoretical concerns are rather different. In this chapter, I have argued that this has implications for the use of these methods in health psychology. If we aim to carry out research in order to find out why people act in ways which compromise their health, how they experience health and illness or how they feel about their bodies, that is, if we aim to carry out research which allows us to theorise experience and practice, then DP is not an appropriate method. However, if our aim is to obtain a better understanding of the dynamics of interpersonal communication within a health care setting, then DP provides us with a sound theoretical and methodological basis for our research.

I proposed that whilst only FDA addresses the theoretical concerns that, in my view, characterise health psychology, both DP and FDA generate insights which are potentially applicable within a health care context. Finally, I expressed my concerns about the ethical implications of the use of semi-structured interviews in order to obtain accounts of suffering if these are then subjected to DP analysis. I argued that by treating such accounts as social performance rather than as self-expression, DP denies participants their right to author their account, that is, it silences them in a way that is not compatible with my vision of a health psychology which promotes empowerment and respect for its research participants. I believe that a full engagement with the ethics of working with illness narratives is required if we are going to be using DP in health psychology research.

To conclude, in my view, discourse analytic research in health psychology needs to be based upon a careful consideration of the research question driving the research and a clear explication of its theoretical basis. In addition, reflection regarding the ethical implications of the use of the method within its particular context is also important. It is hoped that the points raised in this chapter will assist researchers in health psychology when they consider the use of discourse analytic methods.

Key Points

- DP and FDA are concerned with the role of language in the construction of social and psychological realities.
- DP approaches participants' accounts of their experiences as social productions that tell us something about their use of discursive resources in order to perform interactive business.
- FDA explores participants' use of discourse in order to find out how they construct their own subjectivity and experience and how these constructions are then lived through their associated practices.
- Both DP and FDA generate insights that are potentially applicable within a health care context.
- There are ethical issues if accounts of suffering obtained in semi-structured interviews are subjected to DP analysis.

Assignment Questions

1. Formulate one health psychology research question that calls for the use of *Discursive Psychology* and one that calls for the use of *Foucauldian Discourse Analysis*. What are the main differences between the two?
2. To what extent does your use of language impact upon your health-related behaviour?

Notes

1. Burr (1995) and Parker (1997) provide detailed discussions of the distinction between the two versions of discourse analysis. However, some discourse analysts do not welcome such a clear conceptual separation. For example, Potter and Wetherell

(1995: 81) argue that the distinction between the two versions "should not be painted too sharply" whilst Wetherell (1998) also advocates a synthesis of the two versions.

2. This is not to say, however, that these insights have no applicability within a health context, and some of the ways in which discursive psychology research may inform practice will be discussed in the next section (see Practice).

3. The emergence of the DP perspective is timely in that its concern with action orientation and stake reflects the assumptions underlying the contemporary "culture of spin" within which we find ourselves. It is no coincidence that at a time in history when few of us expect a politician's statement to reflect a genuinely held view or position and when news programmes are largely concerned with stripping away "the spin" in an attempt to lay bare the action orientation of what has been said, DP emerged to provide the theoretical and methodological basis for such important analytic work.

Further Readings

Wetherell, M. (1998) "Positioning and interpretative repertoires: conversation analysis and post-structuralism in dialogue", *Discourse and Society*, 9 (3), 387–413.

This paper is imporant because it develops a strong argument against splitting discursive perspectives and methods into two separate approaches to, or versions of, discourse analysis.

Willig, C. (ed.) (1999) *Applied Discourse Analysis: Social and Psychological Interventions*, Buckingham: Open University Press.

This book is important because it provides a systematic discussion of the various ways in which discourse analytic research may be of use within an applied context, including health promotion.

Burr, V. (1995) *An Introduction to Social Constructionism*, London: Routledge.

This is important because it offers an in-depth discussion of the main features of the epistemological arguments which underpin discourse analytic methodology.

PART IV

Health Psychology Practice

CHAPTER 10

Challenging Narratives and Social Representations of Health, Illness and Injury

Michael Murray

Summary

Narrative theory is concerned with one of the defining characteristics of being human: the ability to create stories about our everyday lives. It is through these stories that we make sense of the world, convey this sense to others, and define ourselves. In this chapter we will consider the potential narrative theory has for increasing our understanding of the experience of health, illness and injury. It will also consider social representations that are those broad shared understandings of reality specific to a particular community or society. We will reflect on how narratives are on the one hand the motor force of social representations and on the other hand how they are also anchored in underlying social representations. Finally, we will consider how to challenge unhealthy social representations through developing counter narratives.

Narrative Theory

The past 20 years has seen a growing interest in narrative theory, initially as a component of literary theory but increasingly within the social sciences. The Russian narratologist Propp (1928/1968) in his detailed analysis of folktales argued that they had a common underlying structure. Basically this structure consisted of seven fundamental spheres of action and thirty-one fixed elements. Subsequently the Canadian critic Frye (1956) argued after a very extended review of centuries of literature that there were four main narrative categories: comic, romantic, tragic and ironic. While debates regarding the adequacy of these and other forms of structuralist analysis continue within literary theory, within psychology and the social sciences there has grown the idea that narratives do not simply exist in books but are a much more pervasive feature of everyday social interaction and meaning making.

Psychologists like Sarbin (1986) and Bruner (1986, 1990) were two of the earliest enthusiasts of this approach. While Sarbin argued that narrative is a superior root metaphor than the machine for developing a discipline of psychology, Bruner argued that there are basically two ways of knowing about the world – the scientific and the narrative. In everyday life, the narrative form is the more dominant way of knowing and as such should be the concern of psychologists who are interested in how we construct everyday knowledge.

However, we not only make sense of our worlds through narrative but we also make sense of ourselves and indeed construct our identities through narrative. McAdams (1993) and Freeman (1993) among others have developed this argument. Their case is summarized in the famous quote from Sartre's (1964: 39) novel *Nausea* in which the central character Roquentin pronounces:

> a man is always a teller of tales, he lives surrounded by his stories and the stories of others, he sees everything that happens to him through them; and he tries to live his own life as if he were telling a story.

Although much of the research into narrative has been at the level of the personal or interpersonal, it is also possible to consider social or societal narratives (Murray 2000b). Thus a society or community defines itself through the stories it tells itself about its history and experiences. It is these social stories that define a community and distinguish it from other communities. Further, these social stories can both divide and connect communities depending upon how previous contact between the communities is defined. For example, the narrative history of two communities may be one of exploitation and conflict such that it is difficult for them to share and live together despite common interests and resources. As these societal narratives become more detached from their specific historical context, they can attain mythic status in a community. Sarbin (1997: 74) has argued that it is these myths that "hold societies together, bind the past, present and future, and provide the outlines for constructing moral codes that define good and evil. Myths provide the foundational subtexts for sacred stories, the moral messages of which are given ontological status, that is, they are taken for granted beyond doubt".

Narratives of Health and Illness

Narrative theory can be used to explore the everyday experience of illness. This is apparent in a number of recent studies by health psychologists. For example, Mathieson and Stam (1995) have argued that it is through narrative that women begin to create a new identity after the experience of surgery for breast cancer. Through their detailed analysis of women's cancer narratives, these two researchers identified three major concerns: disrupted feelings of fit concerning bodily and other changes in the women's life; renegotiating identity; and biographical work whereby the women attempt to negotiate with themselves and others a new coherent sense of identity.

In a subsequent study, Yaskowich and Stam (2003) extended the idea of renegotiating identity by arguing that the process of biographical identity work is particularly pervasive in support groups for these women. Through detailed analysis of the conversation in a sample of these support groups the two researchers suggested that the groups provide a "separate social space" within which the women could comfortably engage in the process of biographical work and the construction of new narrative identities.

Another example is the study of a sample of published accounts of the personal experience of breast cancer (Murray 1997). In this study I used Chandler's (1990) idea that crisis narratives have three common literary problems: finding words for the inexpressible, obtaining narrative perspective and choosing a narrative form. First, crises are often said to render one speechless – indeed it could be argued that a defining quality of the intensity of a crisis is the extent that it is "beyond words". This silence is compounded by the broader social representation of cancer as insidious (see Sontag 1978) and the extent to which the victim can be identified as morally culpable. Despite developments in medical treatment, there remains a silence about breast cancer (see Blaxter 1983). In their accounts the women often wrote about the challenge of talking about the disease publicly. In a much broader setting, this challenge has been discussed extensively in historical (e.g. Langer 1991) and more recently psychological (e.g. Kraft 2002) research on developing oral and written narrative accounts of the Holocaust atrocities.

Secondly, the formation of the narrative account also enables the narrator to obtain a certain amount of narrative distance or perspective. By creating their narrative account the women were able to obtain this narrative distance and then, as it were, move on with their lives. In his work on the difficulty of developing personal narrative accounts of the Holocaust, Kraft (2002) argues that in order to learn about a new event it is necessary to assimilate it into prior knowledge (cf. the concept of anchoring below). In the case of the Holocaust the horror is so outside the normal range of imagination that the narrator finds it difficult to assimilate it into prior knowledge and so in attempting to recount the details the narrator will sometimes slip back into re-experiencing the horrors.

Thirdly, there is the issue of narrative form. In reviewing the cancer stories I argued that the most popular form was that of the battle against the evil enemy. Admittedly, many of the women wanted to play down their role as the hero but rather won the battle with the help of science or religion (see also Murray 2003).

In a third example, Crossley (1999a,b) used narrative theory to explore how individuals with AIDS redefine themselves after they are diagnosed with the disease. She was particularly concerned with exploring the source of these stories not within the individual but within the broader culture. For example, she argued that the HIV positive individuals make use one of the three "dominant cultural 'stories'" (Crossley 1999a), namely the normalizing story, the conversion/growth story, and the loss story. In "choosing" or engaging with one of these cultural stories the individuals are led to interpret and to adapt to their illness in a different fashion. This threefold classification of narratives is very similar to the stable, progressive and regressive structure suggested by Gergen and Gergen (1986) (see also Murray 2002).

In telling stories it is important to realise that there is always an audience, real or imagined. A challenge faced by crisis or trauma narrators is the perceived reluctance of the audience to listen or the belief that the audience will not understand. In our analysis of the women's breast cancer narratives many of them reported that their family and friends did not want to listen – they wanted to get back to their everyday lives. This agrees with Yaskowich and Stam's argument that women with breast cancer attend support groups because there they will find someone who will listen and whom they believe will understand. Similarly Langer argued that many of the Holocaust survivors felt that it was useless even attempting to recount a narrative since no one could understand the horrors except a fellow survivor. As one survivor recounted:

> Because to understand us, somebody has to go through with it. Because nobody, but nobody fully understands us (p. xiv).

Researchers can deliberately attempt to break down this wall of silence and to engage with the audience. An example is the work of Ross Gray and his colleagues who have explored how women react to the diagnosis of breast cancer and men to the diagnosis of prostate cancer. In these studies the different narrative accounts of the participants were used to develop a series of plays that were then returned both to the participants and to a wider audience. Gray has considered a range of broader issues concerning the role of the researcher in the research process and how the researcher can begin to challenge widespread but disempowering narratives. The full details of the work are provided in Gray (2003) and Gray and Sinding (2002).

In reflecting on the process of writing plays about the experience of cancer, Gray and Sinding (2002) explored the tension between wanting their plays to publicly "represent" the experience of having cancer and at the same time evoke some feeling and empathy in the audience. It is not possible to simply summarize the transcripts of the narrative interviews. Rather the playwright selects certain issues and organizes them into a certain form to convey a certain story and to engage with the audience. Denzin (1997: 115) views play writing as being based upon "an evocative epistemology that performs rather than represents the world". The play does not only connect with the audience but can also engage with the broader process of what Gray and Sinding have described as "cultural critique". By this they mean, that the play begins to expose the particular demands placed upon the cancer patient by both their peers and by the medical system. The audience members can thus not only begin to sympathetically experience the actual disease but also become aware of these broader social demands. As such the play becomes an opportunity to expose and to critique broader social representations about the nature of health, illness and health care.

Social Representation Theory

In contrast to the individualistic information processing models that dominate much social cognition research in health psychology, social representation theory is based upon a socially dynamic view of human thought and action. It is concerned with understanding social knowledge or the ways of understanding the world developed and exchanged within a community or a collective. This particular theoretical approach was developed by the French social psychologist Serge Moscovici. It was derived from Durkheim's notion of collective representation that describes the over-arching assumptions of any particular society. However, whereas collective representations are static, social representations are dynamic and are derived from the ongoing exchange of social knowledge in any particular community (see Markova 1996). In an often-repeated definition Moscovici described social representations as:

> a set of concepts, statements and explanations originating in daily life in the course of inter-individual communications. They are the equivalent in our society of the myths and belief systems in traditional societies; they may even be said [to be] the contemporary version of common sense. (Moscovici 1981: 181).

Two processes are considered to be involved in the dynamic workings of social representations. On the one hand is the process of *anchoring* through which we interpret new phenomena by connecting them with more established phenomena. An example taken from some of the original work of Moscovici is the anchoring of new psychoanalytic concepts in more established religious knowledge. Thus the unconscious was anchored in the familiar Catholic concept of conscience. The other process is that of *objectification* by which we give meaning to an abstract concept by giving it concrete substance. Taking another example from psychoanalysis, the abstract concepts of id, ego and superego are objectified and assumed to be compartment-like entities in the individual mind. Again they could also be connected to religious entities such that the evil of the id can be objectified in the devil while good or the superego can be objectified in the angel.

Social representations can be said to have two roles. On the one hand they *conventionalize* new objects or events. As such, they define and protect social groups from threat. The emergence of new challenges initiates the development of new social representations that attempt to make sense of this potential threat. Moscovici (1981) argues that "the act of re-presentation transfers what is disturbing and threatening in our universe from the outside to the inside, from a remote to a nearby space" (p. 189).

The second role of social representations is that they are *prescriptive*. They not only evolve in particular societies but they also shape the workings of those communities. As Moscovici (1984) stated: "they impose themselves upon us with an irresistible force" (p. 23). It is these social representations that guide our everyday social exchanges. In this sense they can be said to have a function in that they enable the smooth working of a society.

Social representation theory is itself a dynamic framework that is enriched by connection with other theories. These connections are increasingly being explored. For example, Joffe (1996) has explored the connection with psychoanalytic theory and Colucci (1995) has explored its connection with Marxist, and more explicitly, Gramscian theory. Later in this chapter we will consider its connection with narrative theory.

There has been a steady growth of empirical research using social representation theory as a conceptual framework. This research program has adopted a wide range of methodologies ranging from the experimental (e.g. Doise *et al.* 1993) through to the ethnographic (e.g. Jodelet 1991). The focus is not on the particulars of the method but rather on its ability to unpack the various dimensions of the specific social representation (Murray and Flick 2002).

Social Representations of Health and Illness

The classic study of social representations of health and illness was that conducted by Herzlich (1973) in the 1960s. She carried out detailed interviews with a sample of French middle-class and rural workers. She concluded that health is commonly conceptualized both as an attribute of individuals and as a result of the degree of balance between self and society. The individual is considered a reservoir of health whereas society is considered the source of illness. It is through maintaining this balance or harmony between self and society that health is maintained. When balance is threatened either through wear and tear of the individual body or by negative changes in the world then illness results. In addition, Herzlich conceptualized illness in terms of an occupation, as a liberator or as a destructor. Previously (Murray 2002), I have noted how this threefold definition of illness has been reflected in several studies of lay understandings of illness (cf. Crossley 1999a).

A series of recent empirical studies have extended the original work by Herzlich. Flick (1999) compared the social representations of health among East and West German clerks and nurses. While he found support for Herzlich's basic model, he found more evidence that health was defined in terms of lifestyle. In addition, Flick compared the social representations of health among Portuguese and German women. Among Portuguese women he found that a central component of their definitions was a "lack of awareness" of health. By this he meant that these women did not seem particularly concerned about their health. He attributed this fatalistic attitude to the repressive social regime that had ruled Portugal for many years. Conversely the German women emphasized a feeling of being "forced to health". By this he meant that the women felt pressurized to be healthy and to look after their health. According to Flick this reflects a popular German media message of being responsible for your own health.

This argument was extended by some recent work we have been conducting on social representations of health and illness held by baby boomers in Canada (Murray *et al.* 2003). In this study we conducted individual interviews and group discussions with a large cross section of Canadians. In an analysis of those resident in Atlantic Canada, we found that although there was frequent reference to lifestyle in discussion of health this was particularly apparent among more middle-class and professional participants, the working-class participants were more sceptical of the importance of lifestyle. This illustrates how different constituencies in a larger society can engage with dominant representations of health in different ways depending upon their life circumstances – one in an accommodative manner and the other in a resistant manner.

A criticism sometimes leveled at social representation research is that it is concerned with describing social phenomenon and does not contribute theoretically to offering a solution to improving health. While this may have been the case in earlier formulations, increasingly researchers have begun to explore how social representation theory can also be linked to measures to improve health status.

For example, Campbell (1997) in her study of social representations of gender in the context of AIDS prevention work in South Africa used SR theory as a framework. She was particularly concerned to articulate an alternative to the traditional information-based health education programs. Her research involved detailed qualitative interviews with a sample of sex workers who lived in a mining community. She concluded that "the central representation informing people's life stories was that of themselves as helpless victims of poverty and male oppression" (p. 689). This denial of agency on the part of the women was considered a major obstacle to the development of assertiveness skills for safer sexual behaviour. Campbell concluded that peer education methods provide an opportunity to challenge this lack of agency on the part of the women and to help them build the confidence necessary to adopt safer sex practices.

Joffe (1996), in another study of social representations of AIDS in South Africa and England, also addressed this issue. She contrasted the dominant knowledge–attitude model of health promotion with that of social representation theory. The former separates thought and action and assumes a causal relationship between them. This approach tends to focus on "improving" individual thought and ignoring other social contextual processes. While the knowledge–attitude model focuses on the individual actor, the social representation approach is concerned with understanding the development and operation of broad social assumptions about reality. These social representations can be resistant to change since they have the function of maintaining a certain stability in a society. For example, Joffe notes that the social representation of AIDS that locates it in the sexual preferences of a minority group provides the dominant group with a sense of immunity. It is for this reason that Joffe concludes that issues of identity protection need to be central to AIDS campaigns.

Markova and Wilkie (1987) in their analysis of representations of AIDS illustrated the role of minority groups and the media in challenging and changing dominant social representations. They contrasted public reaction to syphilis in the 19th century with that to AIDS in the late 20th century. There were certain similarities but also important differences. In both cases the public response to the diseases was anchored in death, stigma, "improper sexual behaviour" and "just punishment". However, the content of these responses differed sharply due to the changing moral climate and the role of those afflicted. The 19th century was an era of conservative sexual morality that clashed with the diverse background of people infected with venereal disease. The official response was that in order to maintain the traditional family it was necessary to abstain from casual sex or at best take precautions. In the late 20th century the disease initially largely afflicted a minority group – the homosexuals. This group was influential in promoting a broader acceptance of different sexual practices such that the public response to the growth of AIDS was less to blame the gay community for the spread of the disease but rather to suggest that it was those, both straight and gay, who did not take precautions. This message was widely promoted in the media. Markova and Wilkie (1987: 406) concluded:

> The voices of the homosexual community and the press in the present public effort to cope with AIDS clearly show that social representations are formed, maintained and changed through an interaction of the conservative point of view of society with new ideas of individuals and minorities, disturbing those these may be.

This conclusion raises another important point developed by Moscovici (1976), which is the role of the minority in changing society. While the minority has often been viewed as ineffectual, Moscovici has argued that it can be very important in introducing social change through challenging dominant ideas. The impact of the minority is particularly influential when its argument is consistent, when it is coherent and when it is presented in a forceful manner. These features are important in attempts to challenge dominant social representations.

Linking Narratives and Social Representations of Health and Illness

Since both narrative and social representation theories are concerned with popular understandings of the world, it is not surprising that several researchers have recently begun to explore further their interconnections. Laszlo (1997) has argued that much previous empirical researchers have imposed a categorical structure on particular social representations and ignored their underlying narrative character. He referred in particular to the work of Herzlich (1973).

Recently, I extended this argument by looking in more detail at the empirical work reported by Herzlich (Murray 2002). It was apparent that material used to justify the three-dimensional model of illness she developed was composed of mini-narratives. Indeed, the very structure of the social representations of illness suggested by Herzlich was in many ways similar to classic narrative structures. Thus illness as liberation was comparable to the progressive narrative; illness as destruction was similar to the regressive social narrative while illness as an occupation was similar to the stable social narrative (Gergen and Gergen 1986).

These narrative structures can be said to provide a temporal or historical dimension to social representations. Consideration of time has often been ignored in social representation research. Flick (1995) introduced the concept of *retrospective anchoring* to connect interpretations of contemporary phenomena with previous events. Although as a society we may eagerly encounter new phenomena, these are often clothed in the language of past events that can act as a disincentive to progress. As Karl Marx (1852/1968) argued:

> The tradition of all the dead generations weighs like a nightmare on the brain of the living. And just when they seem engaged in revolutionizing themselves and things, in creating something that has never yet existed, precisely in such periods of revolutionary crisis they anxiously conjure up the spirits of the past to their service and borrow from them names, battle cries and costumes in order to present the new scene of world history in this time-honoured disguise and this borrowed language (p. 96).

For example, during periods of communal conflict the costumes worn by different communities and the frequent references to ancient rivalries by their leaders illustrate how we can continue to live in the narratives of the past. Interpretations of contemporary events are anchored in stories of past grievances that can continue to provide emotional currency.

It is through the exchange of narratives that communities develop and maintain social representations. Examples from anthropological work have previously been used to illustrate the role of stories in the development of social representations of particular diseases (see Murray 2000b). For example, in Farmer's (1994) study of the development of what he described as cultural representations of AIDS in Haiti he noted how, over time, particular stories about the disease began to circulate and carried with them certain ideas about its contagion. However, these narratives did not contain a novel explanation for AIDS but rather the explanation was clearly connected to an earlier model of tuberculosis. Farmer refers to the previous comment by Good (1977) on the evolution of popular ideas about illness in Iran. Good noted:

> As new medical terms become known in a society, they find their way into existing semantic networks. Thus while new explanatory models may be introduced, it is clear that changes in medical rationality seldom follow quickly (p. 27).

People exchange narratives in their everyday social interaction. While these narratives may be concerned about immediate events, their assumptions draw upon and confirm certain social representations. For example, in telling a story about an exchange between a man and a woman we are drawing upon broader social representations about gender relationships (see Campbell 1998). Further, the particulars of a specific story help to both anchor and objectify an event that can seem abstract. We can explore this further by considering the underlying assumptions of a series of stories about injury in the fishing industry.

Fishermen's Tales

The fisheries is one of the most dangerous of occupations in the world. Mortality statistics from many different countries confirm that people who work in this industry are at risk from a wide range of injuries. Despite this finding, it has attracted relatively little social and behavioural research. Although increasingly fishing is conducted in an industrial fashion with large ships, the vast majority of fishing throughout the world is still conducted in small boats crewed by one or a limited number of fishers. Traditionally these fishers have learned the skills of their trade from their fathers or uncles.

Newfoundland has historically had a major fishing industry. It was largely settled in the 18th and 19th centuries by fishermen from Ireland and England. In Irish, the province is named *Talamh an Eisc* or Land of the fish. For hundreds of years the most important source of income for the nation and the province was the fishery. The structure of the fisheries has changed radically over the past decade but it still remains an important component of the economy.

We conducted a study of the experience of fishing in the inshore among a selected number of fishers who resided in different communities around the island of Newfoundland (Murray and Dolomount 1994). In that study we carried out detailed interviews with the fishers and followed this up with an extensive survey. The interviews were tape-recorded, transcribed and then reviewed. Although narrative was not the formal theoretical framework for the interviews it rapidly became apparent in reviewing the transcripts that the fishers used the interviews to recount lots of tales about the experience of fishing. This was facilitated by the adoption of a broad life-course perspective in the structure of the interview in which the interviewer asked the fishers to recall particulars of how they entered the fishery, their experiences of working in it, the hazards they encountered and the prospects for the future of the industry.

Each of the fishermen recalled many examples of injuries they or their colleagues had incurred ranging from minor cuts and bruises to amputations and drownings. The narrative accounts they provided had a common structure of the individual fisher doing battle with the cruel sea. The narratives connect with the "frontier myth" that Sarbin (1997) argues is central to understanding contemporary American culture. In that myth, according to Sarbin:

The plot structure is built around a superhero and the image of a harmonious community threatened by sinister forces. Institutions that might cope with evil forces are weak, corrupt or absent. An altruistic hero appears, and through the exercise of violence eliminates the evil-doers, thus re-establishing harmony in the community (p. 75).

While these narrative accounts can be analysed as things in themselves or connected to mythic stories, we can also identify the underlying dynamics of the stories through careful consideration of their structure by meshing them within the concept of social representations. Reading across these fishers' stories, we can infer two broad social representations, views shared to a varying extent by the fish harvesters but providing the framework for a common social world. The first concerns the nature of masculinity. There were several aspects to this including hard work, lack of constraints, and the excitement it provides. For example, Joe a young fisherman summed up his view of fishing:

Oh, I loves fishing. I wouldn't go at nothing else. You're your own boss . . . you can come and go whenever you feel like it. If you don't feel like going out you got nobody to answer to, clear of your family, that's all. It don't even come to mind [the risks]. It's part of your job, I don't even think about it.

The fishermen continued to tell lots of personal anecdotes about going to sea and doing battle with the elements. The advent of industrial fishing threatened this traditional role:

I mean, that's the way it was. They are a hearty breed of people, you know. Nobody wants to see that changing. The fishermen are proud that they can work and make a living from the sea, right. Once you gets aboard those bigger factory boats and bigger trawlers, you're only a worker then.

It was through these stories that the fishers told tales of adventure and hard work.

The second social representation concerned the relationship of the individual with what was perceived as an unpredictable world. While you could try to take precautions, there were many things in life that were in effect pre-ordained. As Cecil, an older fisher stated:

Dangerous, yes, but again, there's a difference. There's two kinds of dangers. There's dangers that's carelessness, and there's dangers that you just can't avoid. Sometimes you got to be in danger . . . in the fishery, a real lot of danger that you just can't avoid.

In providing their accounts of their everyday working life, the fishers are constructing what could be described as a morality tale. They lived in a capricious world where their working life was threatened by the wiles of the sea and increasingly by a neglectful government. They were responsible people but they had to survive and feed their families. Thus they went to sea as their fathers had done for generations. They took precautions but despite that the sea held many dangers that were impossible to avoid.

Challenging Social Representations and Promoting Health

Social representations are not only dynamic in that they evolve and change in everyday social interaction but they are also proscriptive in that they establish guidelines for everyday behaviour. Thus attempts to improve the health of a community must consider the character of particular social representations. An example of this is the work of Campbell (1998) in which she considered the role social representations of masculinity play in restricting the impact of sex education on South African mine workers. For these men, the equating of masculinity with risk taking was necessary for their continued work in the dangerous conditions of mining. Campbell described these social representations as adaptive in the sense that they allowed men to continue to work in extremely unsafe conditions.

An important part of the process of challenge is the role of the minority that was discussed earlier. An example of this is the so-called "coming out" story that has been recently associated with public declarations of sexual preferences. Down through history an important component of how a minority group has challenged established wisdom and begun to develop support for a new perspective was through the process of "giving witness". By doing this, the committed articulated their alternative perspectives, often by publicly declaring their stories of conversion. St Augustine provides an archetypal conversion story. In the health arena, the role of key figures publicly declaring their rejection of established wisdom plays an important role in changing social representations.

Another potential strategy for challenging social representations is to involve the community in developing particular new narratives. An example of the application of such an approach to improving health and safety is provided by some recent work on farm safety developed by Tim Struttman and his colleagues in Kentucky (e.g. Struttman *et al.* 2001). Like the fisheries, farming is a very dangerous occupation. It is also male-dominated and despite the growth of large farms, still involves a considerable number of farmers working alone. Attempts to convince these small farmers to adopt various safe practices have not always met with success. These education efforts have often adopted a didactic information-based approach.

In this study, small farmers and their wives were introduced to a series of safety messages through drama and storytelling. The strategy used to develop the plays was very similar to that used by Ross Gray and his colleagues and described earlier. Stories of injury and farm life were collected from the farmers themselves and then welded into short plays that both conveyed the risk of certain actions and also provided an opportunity for the farmers to collectively consider alternative safer practices. In doing so the farmers were provided with an opportunity to challenge the more standard social representation of the risky male and of the fatalistic attitude to life that is widespread in this community. Initial evaluation of this form of intervention is promising. Currently, plans are underway to connect both of these approaches in the development of a safety program for fish harvesters.

In developing these new local stories we can also begin the task of challenging the broader myths that shape the structure of our societies and help to perpetuate social injustice. One supposed characteristic of late modernity is the collapse of metanarratives – those grand stories that have served to legitimize the inequities in modern society. In their collection entitled *Counter Narratives*, Henry Giroux and his colleagues have argued that there is an urgent need to intervene to develop counter narratives that can enhance the strength of the oppressed and challenge the power of the establishment (Giroux *et al.* 1996). These counter narratives, according to Peters and Lankshear (1996: 2) "serve the strategic political function of splintering and disturbing grand stories which gain their legitimacy from foundational myths concerning the origins and development of an unbroken history of the West based on the evolutionary ideal of progress". This means confronting the fatalism that pervades much contemporary political engagement and exposing the hidden assumptions within oppressive social representations. It also means beginning to develop an alternative social narrative that offers the prospect of both greater health and social justice.

Conclusion

Developing a critical health psychology requires connecting ideas with practice to enhance health. The linkage of ideas from narrative and social representation theory provides a starting point for such an endeavour but it needs to be linked to a perspective of social change or transformation. This perspective can be both at the local and at the broader level. More details of how to work with communities to promote health and social change are considered in subsequent chapters.

Keypoints

- Laypeople gain an understanding of the experience of health and illness through constructing narrative accounts.
- People define and redefine themselves and others through these narrative accounts.
- The public circulation of these narrative accounts contributes to the maintenance of certain social representations of health and illness.
- Narrative accounts draw upon certain social representations of health and illness.
- Drama and other forms of performance provide an opportunity to challenge established social representations.

Assignment Questions

1. What are the key defining characteristics of narrative and social representation theories and how can they best be connected to better understand health and illness?
2. Discuss the development of a program based upon narrative and social representation theories to improve the health of a community.

📖 Further Readings

Bruner, J. (1990) *Acts of Meaning*, Cambridge, MA: Harvard University Press.

A compact introduction to the argument that there are two forms of thinking – the paradigmatic and the narrative.

Herzlich, C. (1973) *Health and Illness: A Social Psychological Analysis*, London: Academic.

This remains a classic account of the social representations of health and illness that has provided inspiration to countless researchers.

Murray, M. and Flick, U. (eds) (2002) "Symposium: social representations of health and illness", *Social Science Information*, 44, 555–673.

A collection of articles that illustrate current developments in the application of social representation theory to lay understandings of health and illness.

Giroux, H.A., Lankshear, C., McLaren, P. and Peters, M. (1996) *Counter Narratives: Cultural Studies and Critical Pedagogies in Postmodern Spaces*, New York, NY: Routledge.

This collection begins to elaborate a manifesto for social change based upon developing counter narratives that engage with local communities.

CHAPTER 11

Using Participatory Action Research to Address Community Health Issues

Mary Brydon-Miller

Summary

What do students at a prestigious dance school, the people of Yellow Creek, Kentucky and women in rural Zimbabwe have in common? They have all taken an active role in research projects aimed at addressing specific health concerns facing their communities. In the case of the dance students, the health issue was body weight and shape preoccupation, a problem that can lead to bulimia and other eating disorders; in Yellow Creek it was environmental hazards; and for the women of Zimbabwe the concern was AIDS/HIV. The traditional image of the physician as the omniscient, concerned healer-of-all-ills is giving way to notions of health care as a long-term partnership emphasizing wellness and the management of chronic illness. But health research has, to a large extent, remained fixated on a belief in the exclusive power of experts to generate accurate and useful knowledge regarding medicine and health care.

This chapter will explore the ways in which participatory action research has been used as an alternative to traditional research in the areas of health and wellness. After defining participatory action research and briefly considering the theoretical and historical backgrounds of this practice, an examination of the variety of ways in which such research might be carried out will be provided. A discussion of specific studies that have used this approach in the area of health care will follow focusing on the examples noted above. We all have the power to take an active role in our own health care and in promoting wellness in our communities. Participatory action research provides a way for individuals to take part in the process of generating knowledge and advocating positive social change in order to promote more effective health care practices as well as a more equitable distribution of health care services, both in the developed world and around the globe.

Definition and a Brief History of Participatory Action Research

Participatory action research combines aspects of popular education, community-based research, and social action. As Figure 11.1 suggests (Brydon-Miller 2001a) participatory action research is a collaborative process in which the researcher works with community members to identify an area of concern to that community, generate knowledge about the issue, and plan and carry out actions meant to address the issue in some substantive way. Traditionally, participatory action research has focused on working with groups that have been

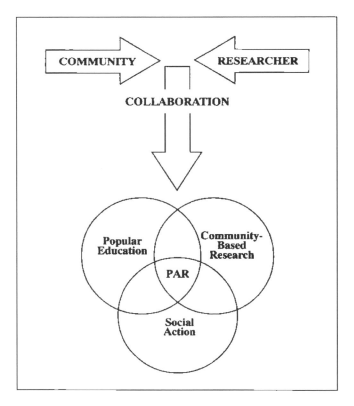

Figure 11.1 Participatory action research process. Reprinted with permission from Tolman, D. and Brydon-Miller, M. (2001) *From Subjects to Subjectives: a Handbook of Interpretive and Participatory Methods*, New York, NY: New York University Press

economically or politically marginalized or oppressed (Hall 1981). This reflects the roots of this practice within the developing world as well as its expressed commitment to working for positive social change. By emphasizing work within marginalized communities, participatory action research seeks to address the underlying causes of inequality while at the same time focusing on finding solutions to specific community concerns. Participatory action research is an iterative process, often beginning with community dialogue, it can then move to a phase in which some form of data are generated, leading to action, and from there back to dialogue. This action/reflection cycle allows participants to learn from their action and to then translate that learning into ever more sophisticated and effective forms of social action.

Beginning in the early 1970s researchers in Tanzania, Colombia and India began to recognize and discuss the ability of ordinary people to take part in the process of knowledge generation (see Fals Borda 2001 for a more detailed historical review). These early efforts emphasized the importance of developing strategies that would allow people to take part in making decisions that affected their lives in significant ways. In Europe, North America and Australasia as well, researchers were challenging the notion that knowledge must be objective and value free. Instead they suggested that scientists must be passionately committed to the struggle for social change and that a part of this commitment involved finding ways in which the principles of democracy and citizen action might become a part of the research process. The work of the Highlander Research and Education Center in New Market, Tennessee (Lewis 2001) and the International Council for Adult Education in Toronto and the Institute of Development Studies at the University of Sussex (Hall 2001) as well as ongoing efforts by Reardon *et al.* (1993) in East St Louis provide examples of participatory action research focusing on a variety of communities and concerns. Through countless projects and collaborations, these centres and others like them have established their commitment to adult literacy and education, economic development and grassroots organizing, and to improving the health and well-being of individuals, families and their communities across the country and around the world.

For many participatory action researchers the work of Brazilian educator and activist Freire (1970/1993) has been particularly influential in providing both an ethical foundation as well as practical examples of how to go about conducting such research. His notion of conscientization, the process of developing a critical understanding of the social, political, and economic forces which shape experience, underlies much of our work as participatory action researchers. In addition, his method of using the rich and nuanced knowledge already extant in communities as the source of his pedagogy and his insistence on understanding ourselves as co-learners establishes relationships with community members as equal partners in the research process. As Freire once observed, "Those promoting participatory action research believe that people have a universal right to participate in the production of knowledge which is a disciplined process of personal and social transformation" (1997: xi).

Theoretical Foundations of Participatory Action Research

Participatory action research, with its focus on social justice and its rejection of assumptions that research can or should be either objective or value neutral, was made possible by the critique of positivism provided by critical theory. Critical theorists, such as Habermas (1971), suggested that knowledge can take many forms and that no form of knowledge exists outside of the social, political, and economic contexts within which it was generated. The kind of technical expertise generally associated with science is one valid and important form of knowledge, but it is not the only way to understand ourselves and our world. We also know the world through our interactions and our relationships with others; this interpretive form of knowing has been the basis for much qualitative research.

Finally, and of most relevance to participatory action researchers, we know the world through our actions and through our attempts to change the material conditions of our lives. As early as the 1940s Lewin (1951), a well-known social psychologist, was suggesting much the same thing. When people come together to identify issues that concern them, when they gather information and discuss what they have learned, when they then take action based on this knowledge and reflect on that action in order to assess its effect and to determine their next steps they are generating what Habermas would call critical knowledge, a form of knowledge that supports the emancipatory interests of human beings. It is the generation of such critical knowledge that is the goal of participatory action research.

More recent participatory action researchers have looked to other theoretical frameworks, in particular feminist theory, to inform their work. As Maguire (2001) has noted, not only does feminist theory remind us of the critical role of gender in shaping social interactions and structures, it has also suggested that as researchers we must be aware of issues of oppression of all kinds and must continually challenge ourselves to find more effective ways to allow individuals and groups that have traditionally been silenced and often misrepresented by researchers the opportunity to speak and to advocate on their own behalf. More recent theoretical frameworks such as postcolonial and critical race theories which focus on issues of power, agency and representation offer new perspectives on the work of participatory action researchers (Bell 2001; Brydon-Miller 2001b; Williams and Brydon-Miller 2004).

Participatory Action Research Methods

Participatory action researchers use a variety of methods, including both qualitative and quantitative approaches, in order to generate knowledge about important social issues. These methods are adapted for use in community settings and emphasize data gathering that will be useful and usable to all of those participating in the process. The sophisticated statistical analyses and costly computer modelling that are the hallmarks of much current medical and epidemiological research are replaced with methods that are both comprehensible and affordable. Innovative methods drawing on art, theatre, storytelling and music have also been developed for use in community settings.

Quantitative Approaches to Participatory Action Research

The Yellow Creek project described in some detail later in this chapter is one example of the use of quantitative methods in participatory action research (Merrifield 1993). Another excellent example is the community-based survey conducted by workers at the East Side Village Health Worker Partnership of Detroit, Michigan, along with researchers from the University of Michigan (Schulz *et al.* 1998). This survey of 700 inner-city households focused on looking at the relationship between psychosocial and environmental stressors in women's lives and specific health outcomes for the women and their children. The survey was developed by a steering committee made up of representatives of local community-based organizations such as citizen action groups and community development organizations, staff from local health departments, and academic partners. Residents of the target neighbourhood were hired as interviewers because it was believed that they would be more effective in encouraging participation, better able to understand the issues facing respondents and to provide at least temporary employment opportunities in an area facing serious economic problems. Results of the survey have been disseminated to the community in a variety of ways in order to ensure that local residents have the opportunity to participate in the process of reviewing the data collected and developing action priorities based on this information. As the authors note, the process was both time-consuming and labour-intensive. It takes time to develop relationships of trust in communities that have little reason to assume that authorities will follow through on promises or act in the best interests of those without financial or political resources. It takes time to educate community participants about the research process and to work together to develop effective data gathering methods. On the other hand,

> processes that involve community members in framing the research questions, collecting and interpreting data, and determining the uses of the information in community change efforts, can both contribute to the scientific literature and to the social resources available to residents of disenfranchised communities (p. 22)

Qualitative Approaches to Participatory Action Research

Qualitative methods such as open-ended interviews, focus groups and ethnography have also been used as the basis for generating data in participatory action research projects. Using a method they refer to as "participant-focused research" or PFR, Flaskerud and Anderson (1999) describe one example of the use of ethnographic methods in working with adolescents in a juvenile detention facility. Initial ethnographic data were generated through the use of participant observation, individual interviews and group discussions. These data were then reflected back to the adolescents who were able to confirm the ideas presented and the preliminary interpretations of the researcher. The results of this process were then used to develop content for health classes focused on issues identified by the youth themselves. This resulted in sessions dealing with topics from the treatment of acne and strategies for effective muscle-building to the prevention of sexually transmitted disease. At the same time, the adolescents participating in the study expressed an interest in using their experience in order to help other teens to avoid the same problems that had led them to detention. Finally, the results of this research are being used to develop a risk reduction curriculum involving adolescents in all phases of planning, implementation and evaluation of the project.

Arts-based Approaches to Participatory Action Research

In an effort to maximize community involvement, participatory action researchers have developed a variety of innovative arts-based methods as well. As Budd Hall (2001: 174) recently observed:

> outside the more formal structures of the academy, knowledge is in fact created in a myriad of socially constructed and creative ways. Participatory research is among other things about the social construction of knowledge, the collective construction of knowledge. When looking for inspiration around methods of participatory research we need to take our clues from the creative and collectively constructed practices which abound in our societies and movements

These methods serve both to record critical data about specific issues and to provide a focus for community dialogue. For example, Caroline Wang *et al.* (1996) pioneered the use of photography as a data collection device in participatory action research. Photography has, almost since its inception, been used to record social disparities and to advocate on behalf of the oppressed. The images of photographers such as Jacob Riis, Lewis Hine and Dorthea Lange documented the poverty, unsafe housing and other social problems of their time in a way that still touches viewers today. But photovoice or photo novella puts the cameras in the hands of the people themselves, giving them the opportunity to tell their own stories in a way that transcends differences in education, social class and language. Wang *et al.* worked with women in rural China to document the health care needs within their communities. As the authors note, this method, "served not only as an information-gathering tool, but was also designed to create community and to empower participants to express their vision, literally and figuratively, to policymakers" (1996: 1395). This same process has been used to document the lives of refugee families in the United States (Brydon-Miller 2001b) and with rural Mayan women to examine issues such as work, health and illness, and the effects of war (Lykes 2001a,b). Lykes also describes the use of other creative arts such as storytelling, movement and dance, dramatizations, drawing, collage and mask-making in her work in Mayan communities.

Drama has been used by other participatory action researchers as a means of engaging communities in dialogue and of giving participants an opportunity to communicate their concerns to a broader audience (Lynd 1992). Using what they call "ethnodrama", Mienczakowski and Morgan (2001) have developed performances dealing with issues such as attitudes toward schizophrenia, drug and alcohol treatment, and sexual assault. Beginning with ethnographic methods similar to those described above, the researchers gather detailed accounts from consumers, health care providers and others. These accounts are then used to construct a dramatic performance in which these experiences are enacted, requiring the researchers to find a way to represent the multiple understandings and responses to complex issues and interactions. Following performances the audience is invited to discuss the material and their own experiences with the actors and other members of the creative staff. Performances are used as means of educating health care professionals about the perspectives of consumers, as well as to provide other audiences with an opportunity to gain insight into these difficult and compelling issues.

Social Action Approaches to Participatory Action Research

Perhaps the purest form of participatory action research, the approach which most directly addresses Habermas' notion of the emancipatory interests of humankind, is in the generation of knowledge through direct social action. Of course, all participatory action research by definition involves some attempt to achieve positive social change. But these actions in and of themselves can provide an important source of knowledge. Individuals with physical disabilities who successfully challenged the owners of a local mall on their failure to provide access and, in so doing, created a state Supreme Court precedent on architectural accessibility provide an example of this type of participatory action research (Brydon-Miller 1993). In another example, women in rural India, who originally organized around the issue of domestic violence following the dowry-related death of a young woman in their community, continued to work together to develop educational opportunities for girls and women and health care for their village (Auluck-Wilson 1995). And in a third case, Yeich (1996) describes how, in her work with homeless people in Lansing, Michigan, participants engaged in a variety of actions including organizing demonstrations, testifying at hearings, and working with the media. She notes that no two participatory action research projects will look the same, because communities and the issues they face all take on different and distinct dimensions. However, she goes on to observe that, "The only guideline that is universal to all organizing projects is the need to encourage the leadership and decision making of group members. This is the heart of grassroots organizing. It is PR's unrelenting focus on this principle that makes it a useful approach" (p. 120).

Applications of Theory and Methods of Participatory Action Research

The three examples referred to in the opening of this chapter serve as good models for the variety of health issues that participatory action researchers have addressed, as well as providing a sense of the range of methods that are available to researchers using this approach. We will examine each of these studies in some depth and consider the implications of this work for future research in the field of health psychology.

Dance Students Confront Issues with Body Weight and Shape Preoccupation

Piran (2001) used her long-term involvement with a co-educational, residential dance school as the basis for her participatory action research project. Asked to work with students and staff at the school to address concerns regarding body weight and shape preoccupation, Piran involved the students in focus group discussions that allowed them to explore together their attitudes towards their bodies and the forces that influence this relationship. In discussing these concerns, the students became aware of the pressures they encountered within the school environment, and within society as a whole, which provoked body weight and shape preoccupation and in some cases led to more serious problems with anorexia, bulimia and other eating disorders. Piran's ten-year relationship with the school allowed her to witness dramatic changes in the culture within the school as she describes in her account of one of the focus group meetings. In this meeting a group of first-year high school students, some new to the programme, some veterans, were discussing attitudes toward body image when one of the new students made a comment about "fat chicks". This led some of the veteran students to challenge her use of such derogatory terminology and to consider what characteristics were really central to being a talented dancer. As one student observed, "You can express your feelings no matter what your actual weight is. We have a right to be who we are. I don't want to change my body" (p. 232).

In addition to achieving a more mature and nuanced understanding of the way in which their bodies were being objectified and used to control their behaviour, the young women also engaged in a number of actions which altered school policies and procedures in fundamental ways. For example, they challenged their male partners who complained about the weight of the female students as a way of excusing their own inability to perform adequately in a pas-de-deux class. In this way they were able to convince the school to institute safety training for male dancers before they began these classes and to convince their male partners that both parties must take responsibility in such situations.

In one particularly telling incident, Piran describes an "emergency" focus group meeting called by the girls themselves after they had been teasing one of the other female students for being a "butch". As they discussed their behaviour they came to realize that they had been jealous of the young woman's athleticism and physical power. When one of the girls suggested that "girls can't have too much power", they were struck by the implications of their own prejudices and determined to apologize as a group to the student they had teased.

Piran's work points to the importance of establishing a long-term commitment to the community with which you are working. Participatory action research requires that the researcher establish a genuine rapport with the people involved in the project, that she have respect for these individuals and their ability to take an active and informed role in creating change. This recognition of the power of community participants then allows for a shift in control of the project to take place, from the academic researcher to members of the community itself, as Piran's work demonstrates. It is this shift which makes it possible for such collaborations to achieve fundamental change in the way in which individuals and institutions understand and address issues which concern them and provides them with the skills and resources necessary to maintain these changes over time.

Appalachian Activists Study Water Pollution and Health

Since it was founded in the early 1930s, the Highlander Researcher and Education Center in New Market Tennessee has provided the opportunity for citizen's groups of all kinds to come together and to gain the knowledge and skills necessary to effect social change in their communities. Highlander played a pivotal role in early labour organizing and the civil rights movement, led efforts on land reform, and was the site of much of the early participatory action research to take place in the United States (Lewis 2001).

One area of particular interest at Highlander has been environmental health. Merrifield (1993) describes the efforts of one group of activists from Yellow Creek, Kentucky, who were concerned about the possible effects of chromium and other toxins that had polluted the local drinking water. With support from students and faculty from Vanderbilt University, this group conducted a health survey of nearly three hundred households along the creek. The results of this survey showed increased levels of kidney and gastrointestinal problems as well as an elevated risk of miscarriage. Not only was the process successful in identifying specific health problems, but as Merrifield notes, the survey gave them a reason and an incentive to call at every household along the fourteen-mile length of the creek, and sit down and discuss with them the problems they were experiencing. Without the survey they might not have found the time and energy to do this. Second, it broadened and strengthened the leadership within the group. The prime activists in the health survey were women who became better informed and more vocal and confident through their work with the survey. And finally, the process of doing the survey enabled the group to draw on and mobilize new outside resources (p. 78).

One of the goals of participatory action research, reflected in the experience of the Yellow Creek community, is to develop the capacity of citizens to understand and develop solutions to their own problems rather than relying on outside experts to do this on their behalf. One shortcoming of this project, according to Merrifield, was in the reliance on others, in this case students from Vanderbilt University, to analyse the data generated in the survey which took time and shifted ownership of the process away from the community itself. Even so, this project demonstrates that community groups can use quantitative methods in order to generate data that will be taken seriously by authorities. This often requires some support by those trained in such methods which can lead to tensions such as Merrifield describes around issues of ownership and use of the data. Nonetheless it can be a powerful tool for community groups, especially when they are dealing with situations such as this in which the case is most compellingly made by the use of quantitative data. Negotiating effective relationships between community groups and those with the requisite technical skill requires an open dialogue regarding issues of ownership, control and representation.

Merrifield describes another project supported by Highlander staff in which citizens stopped a local landfill from operating after it was discovered that hazardous materials had been improperly disposed of at the site. Here local activists learned to identify which chemicals had been transported to the site, and to research the possible health effects of exposure to these substances. Merrifield describes what happened when the group finally had the opportunity to meet with an official from the health department.

> In a standard technique, he reeled off a list of chemicals with long names which had been found in the samples from the well, then hastened to assure the citizens that these chemicals were harmless. They pulled out their copy of a chemical directory which we had given them, looked up the names of the chemicals, and challenged the inspector. "This book says this chemical may cause liver damage, that one affects the central nervous system." The inspector left speedily, and the citizens, while disturbed by the nature of the information they had found, felt empowered to have been able to challenge an "expert" on his own ground (pp. 80–81).

Merrifield does not suggest that scientific knowledge is invalid, but rather that science must be accessible and accountable to ordinary people. Such examples demonstrate that this is indeed possible and that such efforts can have a profound effect on the individuals involved and on the communities in which they and their families live. They also make clear the ability of community participants to acquire a sophisticated and nuanced understanding of complex issues and to use this knowledge to further their own agenda for social change. Finally, these projects and others like them demonstrate the power of community-building to provide ordinary people with the information and resources necessary to address issues once thought to be the purview of experts alone.

Using Participatory Diagramming to Understand AIDS Transmission in Zimbabwe

Perhaps the health issue most frequently addressed by participatory action researchers has been the area of AIDS education and prevention. As studies in the United States (Stevens and Hall 1998; Anderson *et al.* 2001), Canada (Lindsey and Stajduhar 1998; Roy and Cain 2001), Scotland (Huby 1997), Ghana (Mill 2001), Thailand (Jirapaet 2000), and Indonesia (Moeliono *et al.* 1998) indicate, the use of participatory methods among practitioners in this area has been widespread. The final example to be described here deals with the use of what the author calls "participatory diagramming" to facilitate discussion of safer sexual practices among women in rural Zimbabwe. Noting the difficulty these women sometimes encounter in engaging in open discussion of current sexual practices, Kesby (2000) demonstrates how the use of diagramming can provide a more effective means of identifying key behaviours and interactions in the development of practices less likely to result in the transmission of HIV/AIDS.

The project was based on the work of two focus groups of ten women each, one drawn from participants already active in a local HIV/AIDS peer education group, the other group drawn from a farming community and made up of friends and relations of a key informant with whom the author had worked in the past. The groups met two or three times for several hours of intensive discussion. Using inexpensive and readily available materials such as index cards, string and stones, the women were asked to consider a number of issues related to HIV/AIDS transmission and sexual decision-making. In a laudable effort to "avoid abuse of the term 'participatory'", the author describes the study as an example of what Cornwall and Jewkes (1995) would term "shallow" participation, "in the sense that the principal researcher maintained control over the research agenda and process." (Kesby 2000: 1726). That notwithstanding, the study is an excellent example of the way in which innovative methods readily available to community members can be used to generate knowledge and to guide planning for both individual and collective action.

The themes raised in the focus groups included the women's basic understanding of HIV and AIDS, the context of sexual decision making, and the identification of future goals for sexual health. Specific questions related to each theme were used to generate discussion with participants being asked to write down key words on cards and then arrange the cards into diagrams indicating the way in which the various ideas related to one another. Thus "risk of catching AIDS" was related to other issues such as "dislike of condoms", "ignorance" and "STDs" on one group's chart and to "having too many partners", "married women have no option to use condoms" and "lack of information" on the other group's. These terms are then related to other ideas to form complex flow charts which illustrate the many factors influencing aspects of HIV/AIDS infection. The author is explicit in stating that "analysis cannot be based on (idealised) western models of sexual behaviour", further noting that "condemnation of contemporary men's multiple partnering and liaisons with commercial sex workers risks ignoring the historical development of these practices and their roots in colonial male labour migrancy and the dehumanising conditions of all-male hostels" (p. 1724), the legacy of Zimbabwe's colonial past. On the other hand, as he goes on to suggest, "cultural sensitivity does not imply that existing behaviour is beyond challenge", especially not when the consequences of the behaviour have had such devastating effects on individuals, their families and communities. Finding this balance between cultural sensitivity and a respect for the historical, political and economic forces that shape behaviour on the one hand, and a commitment to promoting positive social change on the other, is a major challenge to participatory action researchers working outside of their own cultural and social contexts and requires continued vigilance, self-reflection and dialogue with community members.

This final example demonstrates the potential for creative methods to begin to address the seemingly intractable problems facing poor communities around the world and the importance of exploring alternative means of generating community understanding and control of issues. Research methods must be adapted to address the needs of local communities and to take advantage of the existing skills and resources of local peoples. Finally, it points to the importance of addressing both the immediate needs of communities, while at the same time engaging in a collaborative exploration of the broader social and economic inequalities which create and maintain these problems.

Continuing Challenges in Conducting Participatory Action Research

"In practice, participatory research rarely follows the smooth pathway implied by theoretical writing" (Cornwall and Jewkes 1995: 1672). First of all there are the everyday challenges of working with a group of people who bring to the project their own differences of opinion, their own ways of interacting with one another, not to mention the constant demands on their time and energy that make devoting additional effort to community problem-solving so difficult. Most often the participatory action researcher is an outsider, someone who is at least initially unfamiliar with the various stakeholders in the community, making it all too easy to get sidetracked by the demands of the loudest or most organized factions within a community. Many communities have had experience with outside researchers before, and most often these experiences have not been positive. The researcher may have been happy with the results, more publications and grant money, but what did the community gain through their involvement?

Chataway (2001) discusses her experiences working in the Native community of Kahnawake with particular candour. Factionalism within the community, combined with a suspicion of outsiders well justified by past history, created tension around the research process. Chataway notes one session in which a local leader with whom she had met and talked extensively stood up in the public meeting and said, "You white people think you can just come in here for half an hour, take what you want, and leave" (p. 249). The author describes her own anger and indignation on hearing this accusation levelled at her after months of work within the community. I faced a similar experience myself when, after more than two years of working within the disabled community, a fellow participant and friend read a draft of my work and accused me of taking advantage of the community to further my own interests (Brydon-Miller 1993).

These community responses, though perhaps not justified, are certainly understandable. It takes time to build trust, and often years of commitment before you begin to see any substantive change in the lives of the people with whom you are working. And there are sometimes setbacks as these examples suggest. In a sense we researchers have brought this distrust upon ourselves by our use of deception, our lack of real commitment to local issues, and our focus on our own careers over the pressing needs of the communities we claim to serve. The only remedy to this lack of trust is to renew our own commitment to working with community members in an egalitarian and open fashion in order to earn the trust we and other researchers have abused and lost in the past.

This brings up another dilemma that faces the participatory action researcher. When are you done? As Northway (2000: 33) suggests, it is important for researchers "to work closely with their co-researchers to ensure that there is a common understanding of the extent of commitment that everyone is prepared to give and the level of commitment desired by others". In Northway's research this negotiation was made particularly challenging because her co-researchers were individuals with learning disabilities for whom the process and opportunity for participation were new and for whom such relationships were particularly important. But in any case in which researchers enter into a community, encourage people to become involved, establish friendships and relationships of trust and mutual reliance, the process of completing the project must be approached with particular care.

In attempting to address some of the ethical issues that plague traditional research, participatory action researchers encounter a new set of challenges. No matter how committed the participatory action researcher might be to working with members of the community in an open and egalitarian manner, the realities of differences in power and privilege cannot be simply erased or set aside. Who speaks on behalf of the community? Whose interpretation of events is heard and whose silenced? Well-meaning academics may assume that they understand the issues facing the individuals and communities with whom they work, and believe that they can serve as effective advocates for these groups, but this presumption simply maintains the existing hierarchies which have silenced poor and oppressed communities in the past. At the same time, it is important to recognize the broader political and economic forces that work to maintain such inequalities. (For a discussion of some of the theoretical and practical aspects of this issue see Williams and Brydon-Miller 2004.) These differences in power and authority are exacerbated in areas such as health care in which practitioners have traditionally been treated with unquestioning respect and in which people believe they have no expertise or relevant experience on which to base their actions (Mason and Boutilier 1996; Hagey 1997; Stuart 1998). But as the examples discussed in this chapter have, I hope, made clear, it is in just such arenas that participatory action research can make the most difference in people's lives. The challenge for the participatory action researcher, then, is to remain mindful of the ever-present influences of power and privilege and to endeavour to bring these dynamics into dialogue with community members in an open and honest manner. In addition, researchers must use whatever power and authority they do possess to further the interests of the community and to see that their voices are heard.

Conclusion: A Call to Action

Participatory action research is always time-consuming, often frustrating and confusing, and sometimes not much seems to get accomplished. Nonetheless, after almost 20 years, I cannot imagine working in any other way. Why? Because I find it to be the research practice most consistent with my own values and belief system. I believe that people have the right to participate in the decisions that influence their lives and the lives of their families and communities. I respect people and their knowledge of their own experience and concerns. I enjoy spending time with people and coming to know them as individuals. I am practical. I like to solve problems, real problems and witness change taking place. And I like to have fun, it is not worth doing if you are not having fun. Does this describe you as well?

What health-related issues are of most concern to you and to members of your community? How can you take an active role in addressing these issues? This discussion of participatory action research provides examples (and I hope some inspiration) to those of you who would like to take and find ways of making a difference. I encourage you to find and read some of the studies discussed here. Contact organizations in your community that deal with problems you feel are important. Spend time volunteering. Offer your expertise and labour to support their efforts. Talk with your friends and other volunteers about the work you are doing. Try to understand why the problems you are dealing with have developed and what is keeping them from being solved. And let me know what you are doing. I would love to hear from you about your work and about how you have taken this discussion of participatory action research and adapted it to the issues of most concern to you and your own community. You have the power and the knowledge to make a real difference in the problems you see around you, you only have to make a commitment to working with others in order for change to happen.

Key Points

- People have the right to participate in decisions that affect their lives and the lives of their families and communities. This is especially imperative when basic issues of health and wellness are at stake.
- Participatory action research combines popular education, community-based research, and action for social change.
- Participatory action research focuses on working to promote social justice within communities that have been marginalized or exploited.

Assignment Questions

1. Describe an experience related to health or illness in which you felt that decisions were being made without your input or involvement. Compare this to a situation in which you felt in control of the process. What made these two situations different? How important is it to you to feel involved in such health-related decisions?
2. What are the most serious health care issues currently facing your community? How might a participatory action researcher go about addressing these concerns?

📖 Further Readings

Brydon-Miller, M. (2001a) "Education, research, and action: theory and methods of participatory action research", in D. Tolman and M. Brydon-Miller (eds), *From Subjects to Subjectivities: A Handbook of Interpretive and Participatory Methods* (pp. 76–89), New York: New York University Press.

This chapter provides an overview of the theory and practice of participatory action research. Other chapters in this volume describe specific examples of participatory action research projects that might also be of interest.

Cornwall, A. and Jewkes, R. (1995) "What is participatory research?", *Social Science and Medicine*, 41(12), pp. 1667–1676.

This article examines participatory action research within the context of health research. The authors present a number of models of participatory action research and compare participatory and conventional research processes. They also consider how differences in power influence the process of participatory action research.

Kesby, M. (2000) "Participatory diagramming as a means to improve communication about sex in rural Zimbabwe: a pilot study", *Social Science and Medicine*, 50, pp. 1723–1741.

The article describes an innovative approach to participatory action research using inexpensive and locally available resources to conduct a study of HIV/AIDS prevention in Zimbabwe.

Maguire, P. (2001) "Uneven ground: feminisms and action research", in P. Reason and H. Bradbury (eds), *Handbook of Action Research: Participative Inquiry and Practice* (pp. 59–69), London: Sage Publications.

This chapter, by one of the most respected authors in the field, discusses the relationship between feminist theory and action research providing a key theoretical framework to those interested in engaging in action research.

Merrifield, J. (1993) "Putting scientists in their place: participatory research in environmental and occupational health", in P. Park, M. Brydon-Miller, Budd Hall and T. Jackson (eds), *Voices of Change: Participatory Research in the United States and Canada* (pp. 65–84), Westport, CT: Bergin and Garvey.

The use of quantitative data in conducting community-based health research is described in this chapter which provides specific examples of environmental health research studies using an action research approach.

Piran, N. (2001) "Re-inhabiting the body from the inside out: girls transform their school environment", in D. Tolman and M. Brydon-Miller (eds), *From Subjects to Subjectivities: a Handbook of Interpretive and Participatory Methods* (pp. 218–238), New York: New York University Press.

This chapter describes the use of action research to address issues of body image and weight preoccupation in a dance school setting. It is an especially clear and insightful example of how action researchers can develop an on-going relationship with members of a particular community.

Reason, P. and Bradbury, H. (eds) (2001) "Handbook of Action Research: Participative Inquiry and Practice", London: Sage Publications.

This volume offers a comprehensive introduction to the theory and practice of action research with chapters by internationally known authors representing a wide variety of disciplines and perspectives.

CHAPTER 12

Health Psychology and Community Action

Catherine Campbell

Summary

What contribution can community action make to promoting health-enhancing behaviours? What are the social psychological processes underlying the impact of collective action on health? In this chapter these questions are framed by an interest in health promotion amongst marginalised social groupings, which often suffer the poorest health (Leon and Walt 2000; Chapter 4). The discussion is located against the backdrop of the global HIV/AIDS epidemic that flourishes in contexts of poverty and gender inequalities.

Introduction

HIV/AIDS has caused indescribable suffering to tens of millions of people. The possibilities of effective vaccines, and affordable and accessible drug treatments, continue to lie beyond the reach of the vast majority of those affected by the epidemic. Most of these are located within those social groups that suffer the greatest lack of economic power and political influence. This has been put forward as one of the reasons why national and global responses to the epidemic have tended to be so lukewarm in proportion to the magnitude of the epidemic, and so often been characterised by various forms of ignorance, denial and silence (Barnett and Whiteside 2002).

One key dimension of this denial has been the ongoing tendency to characterise HIV/AIDS as a biomedical and behavioural problem, in ways that draw attention away from the epidemic's roots in local, national and global systems of injustice and inequality. It has recently been suggested that health psychology has been complicit in this process of denial and silencing. This is through the role that health psychologists have played in persistently directing attention towards the individual level of analysis in explaining health-related behaviours such as unsafe sex (Waldo and Coates 2000). They have been accused of generating over-optimistic expectations that individualistic conceptualisations of behaviour, and associated individual-level health promotion approaches, have the potential to impact on complex sexual behaviours – which are in fact determined by a much wider range of factors than individual-level phenomena. In so doing, health psychology has been part of a wider process of masking the contribution of economic, political and symbolic social inequalities to patterns of ill health, both globally and within particular countries (Campbell 2003).

Within the field of critical health promotion there is a growing emphasis on the importance of moving away from individualistic explanations of ill-health and health promotion, in favour of collective action approaches. Such approaches seek to provide contexts in which groups of people can work together not only to change their behaviour, but equally importantly to work towards the development of community and social contexts which support and enable health-enhancing behaviour change. This chapter begins with a brief review of contrasting approaches to health promotion as a backdrop to its key focus, namely the potential of participatory collective action to promote health-enhancing behaviour change in marginalised communities. Through this focus, this chapter seeks to contribute to the ongoing challenge of developing critical theory and practice within applied health psychology.

Contrasting Approaches to Health Promotion

Health psychologists have traditionally sought to explain health-related behaviours using the constructs of individual-level social psychology, usually within the "social cognition" tradition (Norman *et al*. 2000). Behaviour is explained in terms of the individual's subjective perceptions of her social environment, using concepts such as individual attitudes, intentions or perceived behavioural control. Against the background of such theoretical frameworks, health promotion programmes have sought to promote behaviour change at the individual level, through a variety of different approaches. One of these is the Information-provision approach (Box 12.1). This involves providing people with information about the causes of health risks, and how to avoid them, through channels such as school lessons, counselling by health professionals, the mass media, leaflets or posters (Bennett and Murphy 1997; Rutter and Quine 2002). Such approaches are didactic in nature, involving the transmission of information from an outside expert to a passive target audience. They are based on the assumption that people engage in unhealthy behaviour due to ignorance. Once they are in possession of correct information they will allegedly change their behaviour, since individuals are viewed as rational decision-makers, whose cognitions inform their actions (Fishbein and Middlestadt 1989).

However, one study after another has shown that people often smoke or eat junk food or have unprotected sex despite sound knowledge of the dangers of their actions: information about health risks is often a very weak determinant of health-relevant behaviours. Given the limitations of information-based

Box 12.1   The three most commonly used strategies of health promotion are:

1. *Information-provision approaches*: These seek to change the behaviour of individuals through increasing their knowledge of health risks, as well as their sense of personal vulnerability. They use traditional didactic methods, where an active expert "teaches" a passive target audience.

2. *Self-empowerment approaches*: These seek to change the behaviour of individuals through providing them with information, enhancing their personal motivation to change, and providing them with relevant new behavioural skills. They use participatory methods in small group settings, such as role-plays and assertiveness training courses.

3. *Community-development approaches*: These seek to promote healthy behaviour through collective action to create community contexts that enable and support behaviour change. Ideally they use a combination of methods such as consciousness-raising, community-strengthening, coalition-building and economic empowerment initiatives.

approaches, a second group of health promoters argue that in addition to providing people with *information*, it is necessary to increase individuals' *motivation* to perform healthy behaviours, as well as training them in the appropriate *behavioural skills*. The so-called self-empowerment approaches seek to address all three dimensions, aiming to empower individuals to make rational health choices through various strategies to increase their motivation and control over their physical, social and internal environments (Marks *et al.* 1999). Such approaches are based on the assumption that every individual has the power to act in ways that protect his or her health, and that the role of health promoters is to help people identify that power, and teach them how to use it. Self-empowerment approaches might work with young people to empower them to resist peer pressure to smoke or drink to excess by developing their psychological resources to "say no" – through methods such as assertiveness training or social skills training. In relation to sexual health, such approaches may involve working with target groupings to rehearse communication scripts or interaction sequences involved in condom purchase or in sexual negotiation with a condom-averse partner.

However people often engage in unhealthy behaviours despite being motivated not to do so. Furthermore, the skills that people develop in self-empowerment role-plays may not generalise to real-life settings. The best information-provision or self-empowerment approaches are unlikely to change the behaviour of more than one in four people, generally the more affluent and educated members of a social group (Gillies 1998). This is because health-related behaviours are determined not only by conscious rational choice on the basis of sound information about health risks, and the extent to which people are motivated or skilled to perform them; they are also determined by the extent to which community and societal contexts enable and support the performance of such behaviours. In unequal societies, where material, social and psychological resources are unequally distributed, individuals do not always have the power to put healthy choices into practice (Seedat 2001).

This presents health workers with the challenge of developing policies and interventions that aim not only to provide people with information, motivation and behavioural skills at the individual level, but also to promote the development of social and community contexts that enable and support the performance of health-enhancing behaviours. In this regard, the concepts of grassroots participation and the related concepts of community mobilisation and local representation have emerged as key conceptual tools in the *practice* of health promotion. Practitioners are starting to shift their attention away from individual-level strategies in favour of community development approaches (Beeker *et al.* 1998; Bracht 1999). These concepts, which advocate the collective action of local community members in the interests of creating health-enabling environments, form the cornerstones of public health programmes with marginalised groupings all over the world. However, academic *researchers* have failed to keep up with these developments in public health practice. Our intellectual understandings of the mechanisms whereby community-level processes impact on the likelihood of health-enhancing behaviour change are still in their infancy. One of the goals of this chapter will be to outline elements of a "social psychology of participation" (Campbell and Jovchelovitch 2000). This highlights some of the mechanisms whereby collective action impacts on peoples' health. This framework will be illustrated with a case study of a community-led HIV-prevention programme amongst commercial sex workers in South Africa.

Participation as a Means of Addressing Health Inequalities

Three forms of grassroots participation are said to impact on health. First, there is growing recognition of the need to involve local community groups in strategic and operational decisions about health service design and delivery. This is deemed crucial for addressing issues such as differential access, cultural differences, racism, and communication difficulties which are often believed to undermine the level of health service provision received by marginalised groups in various countries and contexts (Department of Health 1999; Leon and Walt 2000). Second, it is argued that local community groups should participate in health promotional programmes – since people are far more likely to change their behaviour if they see that liked and trusted peers are changing theirs (Campbell and MacPhail 2002).

Third, there is an argument that recognises the more indirect but equally important influence of local community/neighbourhood conditions on health, with many studies emphasising that people are more likely to be healthy in socially cohesive communities (Blaxter 2000). For this reason, health promoters are increasingly seeking to involve themselves in general "community strengthening" programmes that seek to create "health-enabling communities" characterised by trust, mutual support and high levels of local involvement in local community projects of mutual interest. Such programmes seek to provide opportunities for local people to meet, and to develop informal friendships around leisure activities or common interests, or to work together in more organised networks in pursuit of mutually beneficial goals (Saegert *et al.* 2001). Such initiatives may, for example, promote the development of local community centres, mother-and-toddler groups, retired peoples' clubs, or interest groups such as Neighbourhood Watch associations or local environmental groupings. Whilst such activities are not directly related to health, it is believed that they promote supportive and caring contexts that reduce health-damaging stress and maximise the likelihood of health-enhancing behaviour (Campbell 2000b).

Peer education is an approach that attempts to promote the second form of participation: namely the involvement of local people in programmes designed to improve the health of their peers. Peer education is one of the most commonly used strategies of health promotion throughout the world, particularly with young people and hard-to-reach groups (UN AIDS 1999). In the HIV arena, for example, peer education involves training members of groups who live and work in situations that place them at high risk of HIV-infection to disseminate information about sexual health risks, and to distribute condoms. Peer educators are given basic knowledge about sexual health, as well as training in participatory health educational skills, such as dramas and role-plays. Peer education is based on the assumption that people are most likely to change their behaviour through collective action to change peer norms. As such, it offers an improvement on self-empowerment approaches outlined above, insofar as it shifts the locus of behaviour change from the individual to the peer group, acknowledging that sexuality is shaped and constrained by collectively negotiated peer identities, rather than simply by individual-level information, motivation and behavioural skills.

Whilst peer education programmes have had some success in some countries and contexts, this is not always the case. Shifting the level of analysis from the individual to the peer group level is often not enough. The peer groupings that are often the most vulnerable to poor sexual health (such as women or young people) are also those that have the least power to change environmental factors that undermine their sexual health. As a result, some peer education programmes are located within the context of a broader community development approach, with much emphasis given to strategies such as "women's empowerment" or "community strengthening".

Such approaches seek to promote the third form of participation outlined above: through seeking to build strong local networks, and the resulting social cohesion, which are indirectly rather than directly promoting of health. Such activities may include team-building and organisational skills amongst groups who have not had the experience of working co-operatively within organised settings to meet mutually beneficial goals. They may also include the development of leadership skills amongst groups of women, who might never have had the opportunities to exercise leadership in strongly male-dominated communities. Such programmes often also seek to promote women's economic empowerment programmes, to reduce women's economic dependence on men who might refuse to use condoms (Tawil *et al.* 1995).

Towards a Social Psychology of Participation

What are the mechanisms underlying the impact of participatory approaches such as community-led peer education on health? Participatory health approaches, such as peer education, succeed or fail to the extent that they facilitate three inter-linked processes: the re-negotiation of peer identities; the empowerment of participants; and the development of health-enabling community contexts (Box 12.2). The concept of power is central to each of these three processes (Campbell and Jovchelovitch 2000; Campbell 2003).

Social Identities

Our social identities consist of those aspects of our self-definitions that arise from our memberships of particular social groups (for example, age-linked peer groups, or occupational groups such as sex workers) or from our positioning within networks of power relationships shaped by factors such as gender, ethnicity or socio-economic position (Kelly and Breinlinger 1996). Different identities or positionings are associated with different behavioural possibilities

---

Box 12.2   Participatory peer education is a form of collective action that promotes health to the extent that it:

- creates opportunities for *the re-negotiation of social identities*, given that health-related behaviours are determined as much by peer norms as by individual decisions;
- promotes the *empowerment* of participants, including the development of *critical consciousness* of the social obstacles to behaviour change;
- results in the development of both *bonding social capital* (trusting collaborative horizontal relationships within peer groups) and *bridging social capital* (vertical bridges between marginalised peer groups and groups with greater access to political and economic influence and resources).

Each of these processes are integrally shaped and constrained by the social distribution of power, which may serve either to enable and/or to constrain the possibility of change.

or constraints. Rather than being static, permanent or given, social identities are constantly constructed and reconstructed from one moment to the next. This process of construction takes place within social contexts that enable or constrain the degree of agency that people have to construct identities or to behave in ways that meet their needs or represent their interests.

In contrast to traditional views that health-related behaviours are determined by individual rational choice, the social identity literature emphasises how health-related behaviours are shaped and constrained by collectively negotiated social identities (Stockdale 1995). Thus, for example, using a condom, or visiting a traditional healer, are acts structured by social identities, rather than simply by individual decisions.

Social identities play a key role in the processes whereby unequal power relations (such as relations between men and women) are reproduced or transformed (Leonard 1984). Identities are constructed and reconstructed within a range of structural and symbolic constraints that often place limits on the extent to which people are able to construct images of themselves that adequately reflect their potentialities and interests. Thus for example, female identities are often constructed in ways that predispose women to collude with men in sexual relations that do not necessarily meet their needs and interests (Holland 1998). These may include situations where young women feel pressured into having sex, or agree to participate in sexual relationships that prioritise male pleasure over female pleasure and well-being. Ideally, peer educational settings should provide a context within which a group of people may come together – and through the processes of debate and dialogue – re-negotiate their collective identities that challenge the ways in which traditional gender relations place their sexual health at risk. In such a situation, social identities become potent tools for social change. As we shall discuss in more detail below, successful participation in collective community projects provides one important arena for the reconstruction of social identities in health-enhancing ways.

Empowerment and Critical Consciousness

The re-negotiation of collective identities within peer education settings needs to take place in conjunction with the development of peoples' confidence and ability to act on collective decisions in favour of health-enhancing behaviour. Powerlessness or a "lack of control over destiny" severely undermines the health of people in chronically marginalised or demanding situations (Wallerstein 1992). People who have little control over important aspects of their lives are unlikely to believe they can control their health. Some writers have emphasised the *psychological* role that empowerment plays in promoting the health-enhancing behaviours. This is a superficial notion of empowerment, assuming that people can be empowered as individuals through the development of individual skills. Others argue that psychological empowerment cannot take place without real political and economic empowerment.

Many debates about empowerment focus on the *emotional* or *motivational* dimensions of empowerment, conceptualising it in terms of a subjective sense of confidence. Freire's (1973 1993) conceptualisation of empowerment adds a more *cognitive* or *intellectual* dimension to our understandings of empowerment, focusing on people's intellectual analyses of their circumstances. He argues that a vital precondition for positive behaviour change by marginalised social groups is the development of "critical consciousness". This involves the development of a group of people's intellectual understanding of (i) the way in which social conditions have fostered their situations of disadvantage in ways that undermine their health, (ii) the development of beliefs that existing sexual norms can be changed, and (iii) the construction of visions of alternative ways of being. In the context of HIV prevention in southern Africa, this might involve the development of some kind of self-conscious intellectual understanding, by participants in HIV-prevention programmes, of the way in which factors such as poverty and gender shape the poor sexual health experienced by local people. Such intellectual understandings would ideally go hand in hand with people collectively working to challenge or resist some of the ways in which adverse social circumstances place their health at risk.

Thus, for example, a successful peer education programme might provide a group of men with the opportunity to discuss the way in which the achievement of masculine identities was limited by poverty and unemployment, and how men often compensate for this by adopting an overly macho and controlling attitude to women in sexual relationships. From a Freirean perspective, such understandings would form the starting point from which men could collectively work towards redefining their masculine identities in ways that were less endangering of their sexual health.

Social Capital

It has been argued that people are most likely to undergo health-enhancing behaviour change, and less likely to suffer from health-damaging stress, if they live in communities characterised by high levels of social capital (Baum 1999). Such "health-enabling community contexts" are believed to enable and support the re-negotiation of social identities and the development of empowerment and critical consciousness outlined above. Social capital is defined in terms of participation in local networks and organisations (Putnam 2000). These may include informal networks of friends and neighbours; voluntary associations linked with hobbies, leisure and personal development, or community activist groupings concerned with matters of local interest. Such participation is associated with increased levels of trust, reciprocal help and support and a positive local community identity. High levels of local participation are associated with high levels of "collective efficacy" or "perceived citizen power". This is a characteristic of communities where people feel that their needs and views are respected and valued, and where they have channels to participate in making decisions in the context of the family, school and neighbourhood.

An important determinant of the success of participatory health promotional interventions – such as peer education – is the extent to which they mobilise or create social capital. Ideally peer education programmes mobilise existing sources of social capital, by drawing on existing community networks. Ideally, they also create new social capital in the form of strong and valued peer education networks. Such networks impact on health directly through their efforts to promote healthy behaviours. They also impact on health indirectly through creating generalised social cohesion and trust that not only increases the likelihood of positive health behaviours but also reduces health-damaging stress.

The "Double-Edged" Nature of Power

As outlined above, identities are constructed and reconstructed within a range of material and symbolic constraints which often place limits on the extent to which people are able to construct images of themselves and their claimed group memberships that fully reflect their potentialities and interests. However, at particular historical moments, often through participation in collective projects and networks, members of socially excluded groupings may indeed come together to construct identities that challenge their marginalised status. In some circumstances, participation may take the form of participation in networks of collective action that serve either directly or indirectly to improve peoples' material life circumstances, or raise the levels of social recognition they receive from other groups. Within such a context, social identities and participation have the potential to serve as important mechanisms for social change (Campbell and Jovchelovitch 2000).

However, social capital is not equally distributed in any community (Bourdieu 1986). People who are marginalised by virtue of poverty, or gender, or social stigma may have reduced opportunities for positive and empowering participation in local community life. It is vitally important that policies that advocate participation as a means of addressing health inequalities are not blind to obstacles to such participation by socially excluded groups (Burkey 1996; Nelson and Wright 1995). Different social groups hold different levels of power to construct life projects to meet their needs and interests. Community development approaches treat a thin line between the processes of enablement (grassroots community agency) and constraint (structural obstacles resulting from unequal power relations, or resistance to social change by powerful groups). As will be discussed in the case study below, it is often at the very moment that local community development programmes open up the tantalising possibility of the empowerment of local people to take control of their sexual health that they simultaneously come up against a series of institutional barriers to such change.

Jovchelovitch (1996) points to the "double-edged" nature of power. Power can be a negative force, something that constrains people and holds them back. But it can also be "a space of possible action, where social subjects strive to exert their effects". Power, in the latter sense, "is deeply intertwined with participation, it refers to being capable of: to be able to produce an effect, to construct a reality, to institute a meaning". Whenever a community participates in activities and initiatives that enhance their interests, it actualises the power it holds to participate in shaping its way of life. The concept of power is relevant to the distinction that is made between bridging and bonding social capital below.

A distinction is commonly made between two forms of social capital, which provide a useful way of conceptualising the types of local community relationships that might contribute to the development of a health-enabling community (Putnam 2000). The first of these is *bonding* social capital, which refers to exclusive, inward-looking social capital located within homogenous groups ("within-group" social capital). Such social capital bonds similar people together in strong horizontal peer groups characterised by trust, reciprocal help and support, and a positive common identity. Such relationships result in the benefits and resources that accrue from close trusting relations with similar others. The second is called *bridging* social capital, and refers to links that occur between diverse social groups. This links together diverse groups with varying levels of access to material and symbolic power ("between-group" social capital). Bridging social capital brings people in contact with the resources and benefits that accrue from having a wide and varied range of social contacts. It is associated with trusting and supportive relationships amongst groups whose world views, interests and access to resources might be very different, but who have some sort of overlapping mutual interest. Thus, for example, bridging social capital might bring together representatives of youth peer groups, local employers, local civic groupings and government health and education representatives, all of whom have a mutual interest in promoting healthy sexual behaviour amongst young people.

The importance of bridging social capital is based on the assumption that "the whole is greater than the sum of the parts". Many health-related behaviours have complex multi-causal roots, and are too multi-faceted to be changed by any single constituency (for example, health departments, or marginalised peer groups). For this reason, it is essential that peer education programmes build alliances with the widest possible range of relevant constituencies so that a wide range of actors pool their resources and their creativity in working to promote healthy behaviour. Bridging social capital ensures that traditionally isolated and disadvantaged groups (for example, young people, or sex workers) are put in touch with vertical networks of political and economic influence and expertise that will assist them in maximising their efforts to address particular problems.

This bonding/bridging distinction is vital for clarifying those forms of participation and collaboration most likely to further the goals of community-led health promotion. It is through the development of bonding social capital that a group of people take the first step towards developing a critical consciousness of the material and symbolic obstacles to their health and well-being, and begin to develop both the insight and the confidence to address these obstacles. However, it is vital that community development projects promote the development of two forms of bridging social capital. The first is the development of bridges between small peer education groups and more powerful groups – in their local geographical area – who may have the power and resources to assist them in their quest to develop more health-enabling community contexts. The second form of bridging social capital links small local groups into networks of influence beyond the geographical location of the local community. Here, we refer to the importance of developing channels through which umbrella alliances of small local peer groups can add their voices to extra-local debates about regional and national policies and interventions that are supportive of their local efforts. According to Paulo Freire, a key dimension of successful participation includes the development of opportunities for small local groups to influence wider initiatives for positive social change beyond their immediate community contexts. He argues that the activity of participation is most likely to be successful when it enables people to simultaneously change themselves, their local communities, and the wider societies in which they live.

Case Study: Peer Education by Commercial Sex Workers in South Africa

This section reports on a three-year study of a peer education programme amongst commercial sex workers in an isolated 400-person shack settlement in a southern African gold mining community, where more than six out of ten women were HIV positive (Campbell 2000a, 2003; Campbell and Mzaidume 2001). Women lived in conditions of poverty and violence in makeshift tin structures without running water or sanitation. Most came from extremely deprived backgrounds characterised by physical or emotional abuse. Relationships between sex workers were often unsupportive and competitive in a context where women competed fiercely for a short supply of paying clients. They had little formal education and few skills in a country where unemployment stood at around 40 per cent, with no social security, and minimal employment opportunities for unskilled women. Sex workers made their living from the sale of sex and alcohol to migrant workers on a nearby gold mine. The harsh working conditions of underground mining led to strongly macho identities amongst mineworkers, associated with reluctance to using condoms in commercial encounters. Sex workers lacked both economic and psychological power to resist client's wishes, and condom use was virtually non-existent at the start of the peer education programme.

Aims of the Programme

The aims of the programme, co-ordinated by a nursing sister employed by a local NGO, were threefold. These were: to increase knowledge about sexual health risks and a sense of perceived vulnerability to HIV infection; to encourage people to seek out early diagnosis and appropriate treatment of other sexually transmitted infections, which increase vulnerability to HIV; and to encourage the use of condoms, and make them freely available. The programme aimed to achieve these goals through the processes outlined above. The first of these was to provide opportunities for the re-negotiation of the social and sexual identities that made it unlikely that sex workers would assert their health interests in the fact of client reluctance. This would involve examining the way in which both their identities as women, in a male-dominated society, and as workers in a highly stigmatised profession undermined their confidence and their negotiating power. The programme hoped to increase a sense of empowerment amongst women through placing health-related knowledge – usually the province of outside experts – in their hands, and through providing them with the opportunities to exercise leadership of an important health initiative. The dialogical nature of the peer education approach would encourage development of a sense of critical consciousness of the social obstacles to behaviour change, and of the need for collective action to begin to challenge the ways in which these impacted negatively on their sexual health.

Finally, and most importantly, the programme sought to build not only bonding social capital within sex worker communities, but also to build bridging social capital to link sex workers to sources of power and influence beyond their marginalised local settings. This would be created in two ways. First, through putting this particular sex worker–peer educator group in touch with other similar groups in the region. Secondly, through involving a wide range of more powerful local community "stakeholders" in supporting the programme. These would include representatives of the provincial and national health departments, the largest local employer, namely the mining industry as well as a range of local civic, religious and political groupings. A central goal was to ensure that parallel peer education efforts were implemented amongst mine-worker clients. This was because clients held both psychological power (as men) and economic power (as paying customers) over sex workers. Efforts to promote behaviour change amongst sex workers would have very limited impact without simultaneous efforts to promote such behaviour change amongst men. In addition, the programme sought to reduce women's total economic dependence on clients through providing opportunities for alternative forms of income generation (such as savings clubs and small business opportunities).

Challenges of Setting up the Programme

The nursing sister employed to facilitate the programme struggled against great odds to develop a strong and united team of peer educators. The shack community was run by a group of un-elected armed men, who served as gatekeepers to the settlement, and much effort had to go into getting their permission for the project to be set up. Women had little experience of working collectively to achieve mutually beneficial goals. Much work had to go into team-building, and developing codes of conduct in the chaotic and conflict-ridden community, with high alcohol use and fighting, and low levels of trust. Despite many set-backs, the peer educator team developed into a strong and respected group of local women. They worked tirelessly to distribute condoms, and to educate their peers about the risks of STDs, using participatory methods. It was through such methods that the programme sought to promote a critical awareness of the way in which gender relations and the stigmatisation of sex work undermined women's confidence and ability to protect their health.

Disappointing Outcomes: Varying Impacts of Poverty on Peoples' Ability to Change

However, despite these efforts, the programme had little success in increasing condom use or reducing sexually transmitted diseases over a three-year period. Programme evaluators have identified a complex array of reasons for its disappointing results at each level of analysis (Campbell 2003). A detailed account is beyond the scope of a short case study, but some key points are raised here, all related in some way or another to the impact of poverty on peoples' abilities to change their life circumstances. The programme had great success in uniting a small group of women in a motivated and dedicated group who met regularly, and worked tirelessly at promoting peer educational activities. They also actively involved themselves in regular meetings with similar sex worker peer education teams in the region, participating in the training of new peer educators in other regions, with teams from different local communities providing important advice for one another.

However, despite this partial success, some sex workers did not collaborate with the peer education team. In hindsight, in relation to its goal of providing contexts for the re-negotiation of social identities, the programme probably began with the unrealistic expectation that women in such a divided, competitive and highly stigmatised community would automatically constitute "peers", simply by virtue of the fact that they were all sex workers. The concept of a "peer education" presupposes the possibility that a collection of people might have enough of a sense of a common identity and mutually defined interests to learn to work together in pursuit of collaborative goals. The forces dividing the programme's intended "peers" were often greater than those uniting them. One major dividing force was the fierce competition for clients, which undermined the likelihood of women forming a united front against condom-averse clients. If a sex worker refused to have sex without a condom, the customer would simply move on from shack to shack until he found someone who agreed, and in conditions of severe poverty turning away a paying client was not always an option.

Programme goals ran strongly against the strategies that some women had developed to deal with their harsh lives. One way in which some sex workers chose to cope with the stigma and contempt associated with sex work was to conduct their profession in secret. They loudly dissociated themselves from an openly sex worker led health promotion programme as part of their ongoing struggle to maintain an image of respectability. Ironically, the programme rationale of working with women to feel more open and assertive about their work as a means of improving their confidence succeeded with some sex workers, but had the unintended consequence of alienating others. In this community, the sale of alcohol was a key economic survival strategy, and the use of alcohol was a psychological strategy for dealing with ongoing stresses. Yet, people were far less likely to use condoms when they had been drinking. Another survival strategy in a context of poverty and violence – where women had little control over their lives – was an attitude of fatalism. This fatalism discouraged some women from believing that they had any power to control their sexual health.

Attempts to generate alternative means of income generation for women – through setting up child care schemes or vegetable stalls in the local shack settlement – met with little interest. Sex workers pointed out that fellow shack residents had already exploited existing commercial opportunities to their utmost limit. They saw mainstream income generating activities as unrewarding drudgery in comparison with sex work which, for all its disadvantages, yielded financial rewards which were not only immediate, but also far in excess of what could be raised in a small business.

Lack of Collaboration by Powerful Community Stakeholders

The greatest obstacle to programme success was mineworkers' continued refusal to use condoms. Despite its ambitious goals, in reality the project, under the auspices of a small and humble non-governmental organisation, had little influence on the powerful mining industry. The latter group had little commitment to implementing peer education amongst the vast majority of mineworker clients. Mine medical doctors responsible for sexual health were unfamiliar with the social understandings of disease transmission and prevention that underlie the peer-education approach. Within this context, they dismissed peer education as "vague social science", and preferred to throw their HIV-prevention energies into biomedical STI-control programmes, which had little impact on reducing STIs amongst mineworkers over our three-year study period. Such attitudes, combined with lack of mineworker trade union commitment to participating in project management, meant that the majority of miners were not exposed to peer education, as outlined in the original project proposal. Yet, it was male miners who held both economic and psychological power in encounters with female sex workers. Much remains to be learned about the factors shaping the likelihood that powerful stakeholders will collaborate in partnerships with marginalised community groups in addressing social problems such as HIV transmission. There is a need for insights into systems incentives and accountability that might motivate powerful groupings to collaborate with marginalised communities who have little political or economic power or influence over more powerful stakeholders.

Bonding Social Capital is Not Enough

This case study has illustrated the way in which the conceptual framework outlined above served to inform the design and intervention of a community-led peer education programme in a highly marginalised and disorganised community. In short, while the programme went some way to promoting bonding social capital amongst some women within this community, as well as bonds between this group of women and similar sex worker peer educators in similar settlements in the region, its goals were crucially undermined by its lack of success in building bridging social capital and, in particular, mobilising support from more powerful local constituencies, such as the gold mining industry and its workers.

Conclusion

Participatory peer approaches are widely used to promote health in both rich and poor countries, and have succeeded in improving the sexual health of disadvantaged groups in a variety of countries and contexts. The chapter has outlined a framework for conceptualising the processes underlying the potential health-enhancing impact of collective action, with particular reference to participatory peer education. This has highlighted the processes of *social identity* construction, *empowerment and critical consciousness*, and *social capital* as conceptual tools for a "social psychology of participation", with particular emphasis on the way in which these processes are enabled and constrained by unequal *power relations*. It has illustrated the way in which this conceptual framework informed the design and evaluation of a community-led peer education programme amongst sex workers in South Africa. This is a situation where peer education failed to achieve its intended effects in reducing levels of HIV and other STDs. Critics of the programme have argued that this failure undermines the credibility of participatory peer education. Defenders of the peer education approach point out that participatory peer education has often been successful in reducing disease and promoting behaviour change in particular countries and contexts (Janz 1996; UN AIDS 1999, 2001). They also argue that it may have been unrealistic to expect results in a community as chaotic and divided as this one, where levels of HIV were already almost 70 per cent before the programme had even started. In this chapter, it is argued that it would be unfair to dismiss the peer education approach on the basis of this particular programme, given that the approach was not implemented properly. Furthermore, there are many lessons to be learned from this case study that could inform future efforts.

The main lesson relates to the importance of building bridging social capital. The brief case study provided above has sought to highlight the ways in which poverty, stigma and gender oppression undermined attempts to promote the collective identity and critical empowerment that underlie successful peer education. Within such a context, it was unlikely that marginalised sex workers would succeed in improving their sexual health without significant efforts to change the behaviour of their psychologically and economically more powerful male clients, for example. Collective action by members of marginalised social groupings is unlikely to be effective in the absence of alliances with more powerful social groupings, which have access to the economic and political power necessary for the success of programme goals.

Grassroots Participation is Not a Magic Bullet

This argument is consistent with the UN AIDS (2000) analysis of the common features of initiatives that have succeeded in reducing HIV transmission. This analysis highlights the mobilisation and participation of local communities as a necessary precondition for successful HIV prevention. However, on its own, it is not a sufficient condition. Community action is not a "magic bullet". The UN AIDS report emphasises that the potential for grassroots participation to bring about health-enhancing social change is shaped and constrained by the quality of the partnerships or alliances that local communities develop with a wide range of actors – in government, the private sector, civil society and (where appropriate) project donors. Participants and facilitators of social psychological and community-level interventions – such as peer education – need to stand side by side with a much wider range of agencies and actors if they are to have optimal benefits in reducing health inequalities, and improving the health of marginalised groups.

The UN AIDS emphasis on the role of appropriate alliances and partnerships in successful community health interventions resonates with frequently voiced critiques of many so-called community action programmes that seek only to promote local grassroots participation in community health projects. Such programmes are criticised for failing to pay adequate attention to the way in which the ability of marginalised communities to improve their health is constrained by extra-local political and economic power relations (Campbell 2000a, 2003). They have been criticised for being "reformist" insofar as they fail to challenge the political and economic inequalities that often prevent marginalised people from improving their health. They have also been charged with "victim-blaming" through suggesting that politically and economically disempowered groupings are capable of taking control of their health in contexts where contextual factors militate against this possibility (Seedat 2001). In social capital discourse, such approaches fall short through their overemphasis on the development of bonding social capital, and their corresponding failure to take account of the key role that bridging social capital needs to play in supporting and enabling the success of participatory community development approaches to health promotion. The sex worker programme outlined above illustrates the strength of this critique.

Towards a More Critical Health Psychology

This chapter has pointed to some of the social psychological processes underlying the impact of collective action on health, through a discussion of community-led peer education. How does this work contribute to health psychology? As stated above, mainstream health psychology has tended to favour individual-level conceptualisations of health behaviour, with social cognition models playing an influential role in thinking and research in this area. These models have had some success in predicting the behaviour of individuals in carefully controlled experimental studies. They tend to be less useful in designing interventions, however, for two reasons. First, they focus almost exclusively on the proximal determinants of behaviour (such as attitudes, intentions, perceived norms or individual action plans), with little attention to the way in which these proximal factors are influenced by social context. Yet, social context plays a key role in enabling and supporting health-enhancing behaviour change, particularly in marginalised communities in less affluent settings – where individuals have even less cognitive control over their behaviour than their more privileged counterparts. Secondly, whilst mainstream health psychologists have played an important role in identifying *which* individual factors are related to health-related behavioural intentions, or behaviours, they do not give much indication as to how to *change* these cognitive factors.

The approach outlined above was developed within the spirit of a critical health psychology that aims to take account of the social determinants of behaviour in addition to the individual determinants. It also seeks to contribute to the development of *actionable* theories of behaviour, theorisations that have direct implications for the design of public health interventions and policies through their attention to the complex individual–society dialectic. It is this dialectic that lies at the heart of collective action. Ideally, approaches such as participatory peer education provide the opportunities for collectivities of individuals to collaborate in efforts to change not only themselves and each other, but also to challenge the social circumstances that have placed their health at risk.

Key Points

- Within health promotion, the information-provision and self-empowerment approaches seek to promote health-enhancing behaviour at the individual level. Such approaches provide people with information about health risks;

try to increase their motivation to engage in healthy behaviour; and train them in relevant behavioural skills (for example, condom negotiation and condom use).

- These approaches tend to change the behaviour of at the most one in four people, generally those in the most privileged social groups. They have had limited success amongst marginalised groups. This is because behaviour change is determined not only by individual factors, but also by (i) peer norms; and (ii) the extent to which community contexts enable and support the performance of health-enhancing behaviours.
- Community-development approaches – such as community-led peer education – seek increase in healthy behaviours through promoting collective action to change peer norms and build healthy communities.
- These approaches impact on health to the extent that they provide contexts for: the re-negotiation of peer identities, the empowerment of participants, the development of their critical consciousness of obstacles to their health, and the building of bonding and bridging social capital.
- Bonding social capital consists of trusting and collaborative relationships within homogenous peer groups. Bridging social capital refers to collaborative links between local peer groups and diverse groups who may have greater access to the political and economic power and influence which are necessary for the achievement of programme goals.
- A South African case study of community-led peer education by female sex workers highlights how women succeeded in building a degree of bonding social capital in extremely challenging circumstances. The programme floundered, however, because of its lack of success in building the bridging social capital that would have been necessary to change the behaviour of sex workers' male clients.
- Male clients held both psychological and economic power in sexual encounters, and without their participation in the programme, efforts by impoverished women to promote sexual health were severely undermined.
- Community action by marginalised groupings is not a "magic bullet". The success of collective action by small local groupings is unlikely to succeed without the support of appropriate collaborative partnerships. Such partnerships will often need to unite local people with diverse groupings (drawn from the private and public sectors and civil society) who have the power to assist them in working towards the development of health-enabling contexts.

Assignment Questions

1. Compare and contrast three approaches to health promotion (information provision; self-empowerment; community-development). Contrast and critically evaluate the assumptions that each approach makes about the processes underlying behaviour change.
2. What constitutes a health-enabling community context?

3. Identify a particular behaviour-related health problem facing people in your local community. Outline some of the factors that would need to be taken into account in designing a campaign to promote behaviour change.

📖 Further Readings

Baum, F. (1999) *The New Public Health: An Australian Perspective*, Melbourne: Oxford University Press.

A comprehensive multi-disciplinary overview of contemporary public health theory and practice. Part 6: "Health choices: individuals, behaviour and communities" is particularly useful for psychologists, but needs to be located within the context of the whole book.

Campbell, C. (2003) *Letting Them Die: Why HIV Prevention Programmes Often Fail*, Oxford: James Currey. Bloomington, IN: Indiana University Press.

A detailed account of the social psychology of participation, with an illustrative case study of how these principles can inform the design and evaluation of community-led health-promotional interventions and policies.

Freire, P. (1970/1993) *Pedagogy of the Oppressed*, New York, NY: Continuum.

This masterpiece, written by a Brazilian educationalist, is one of the most important books ever written about the role and possibilities of collective action, combining theoretical and practical insights in a brilliant polemical synthesis. The author is not a health specialist, but the book is full of generalisable insights. Whilst the old-fashioned, revolutionary language might seem strange to a 21st-century reader, persistent readers will be amply rewarded for their efforts.

Leonard, P. (1984) *Personality and Ideology*, London: MacMillan.

Whilst this book is a little dated, it provides an excellent discussion of the processes through which social relations impact on individual experience and behaviour. Again, not specifically about health, it provides a useful theoretical framework for understanding the individual–society relationship in a way that throws light on the way in which collective action has the potential to improve health.

Marks, D., Murray, M., Evans, B. and Willig, C. (1999) *Health Psychology: Theory and Practice*, London: Sage.

Part 3 of this book, "Health promotion and disease prevention" provides a useful and accessible overview of issues currently being debated within contemporary health promotion. Chapter 15 provides a clear account of the information-provision, self-empowerment and collective-action approaches.

Conclusion: Towards a Critical Health Psychology

Michael Murray

In the introduction to this volume it was stressed that the intention was not to provide a coherent introduction to a single unified critical heath psychology. Rather the aim was to challenge certain assumptions in mainstream health psychology and to encourage the reader to consider alternative ways of doing health psychology. In this conclusion I want to review some of the issues raised in the previous chapters and to perhaps take the debate a little further.

Theorizing Health and Health Psychology

Within health psychology, some theories and methods have gained a certain prominence while others have been pushed to the margins. These dominant theories all share a common epistemological base in positivism that assumes unmediated access to an objective world out there. This world can be confidently broken up into a series of uncontested variables, and, with the power of statistics, it is possible to measure the relationship between these variables (Murray and Chamberlain 1999b). The enthusiasm with which many health psychologists have pursued the measurement of these variables has concealed the lack of attention to the social factors contributing to the definition of these variables and to the development of particular theories. Theory is not something that we put together like building blocks, but rather its very generation reflects certain assumptions about the nature of the world and of our roles in it. Unfortunately, health psychology has been slow to tackle these assumptions. As Stam (2000) has argued:

> It is unreflexive about its knowledge production, namely that of constituent players engaged in the construction of health and illness. Behind its universalism lies an individualism that characterises much of psychology; what the scientific knower knows is independent of who the knower happens to be, the knower's social position, and the use to which such knowledge is put (p. 278).

This individualism pervades contemporary psychology. It is a discipline that is premised upon the belief in the separateness of the human individual. The challenge of mainstream psychology is to identify and describe those internal

222

mechanisms that explain human behaviour. But we are not individuals but rather social beings. As relational psychology argues, the focus of our concern should not be within the individual but on the multi-faceted relationship with the other (Sampson 2003). We cannot survive without other people. To understand health and illness we need to move beyond the individual to consider our interpersonal and social qualities.

The first part of this book was designed to encourage health psychology to deliberately adopt a more self-critical stance to the generation of theoretical frameworks. The chapter by Hank Stam pursued his plea for more sustained attention to theory. Coupled with this he emphasized the need for an awareness of the intellectual, institutional and historical context within which health psychology has evolved and currently operates. One aspect of this was how biomedicine underlies traditional health psychology's understanding of health and illness. These are considered almost as discrete entities that have psychological characteristics. There is an obvious need to theorize what we mean by health and illness.

This need for theory was taken up further by both Alan Radley and Bob Kugelmann in their chapters. They argued that a central aspect of illness is that people who are ill suffer. Despite this, health psychology has ignored what it means to suffer over and beyond the restrictions on our ability to perform everyday activities. To understand suffering, health psychology needs to consider the meaning of suffering to the individual and its interpersonal character. Suffering not only affects the individual with illness but pervades that person's social relationships.

Further, suffering is not just a quality of the individual or even of the interpersonal situation, it is a much more expansive social and cultural phenomenon (Kleinman *et al.* 1997). For example, all around us is the widespread human suffering as a consequence of such tragedies as hunger, homelessness and violence. While Radley talks of the muteness of the individual sufferer we need also to consider the muteness of society's response to such social suffering. We read about these tragedies from the comfort of our homes and view them from a position of impotence on our television screens (see Kleinman and Kleinman 1991). The need is for health psychologists to begin to disrupt this indifference to social suffering through both their research and practice.

Contextualizing Health and Illness

This indifference extends to the endemic social inequalities in health that exist both within advanced industrialised countries but even more dramatically between rich and poor countries. It is well established that poverty is the major cause of disease and death in the world. As the World Health Organization (1995) stated:

> The world's most ruthless killer and the greatest cause of suffering on earth is... extreme poverty. Poverty is the main reason why babies are not vaccinated, clean

water and sanitation is not provided, and curative drugs and other treatments are unavailable and why mothers die in childbirth. Poverty is the main cause of reduced life expectancy, of handicap and disability, and of starvation. Poverty is a major contributor to mental illness, stress, suicide, family disintegration and substance.

But poverty is not a natural condition but a consequence of particular social and political arrangements. Further, poverty is not just a condition of people in developing countries but increasingly of millions in advanced industrialized societies. For example, the poverty rate in the United States is now higher than what it was in the 1970s with almost 35 million people living below the official poverty line (Mirowski and Ross 2003). David Marks emphasized in his chapter that it is an important role for health psychologists to expose the deleterious effects of poverty and social inequality on health and well-being. There is a danger that by evading this debate health psychologists will adopt an individualistic victim-blaming stance in their work.

Sometimes, individual psychologists can feel impotent in the face of such massive political issues but there is a need to find a way to participate in the debate in our everyday psychological practice. Several contributors to this volume have referred to the inspirational Brazilian scholar, Freire (1970/1993), who has contributed much in developing the outlines of a strategy to engage in such broader social debates. Freire argued that it was the task of the critical pedagogue, to which we could add the critical health psychologist, to engage in the process of developing a wider critical consciousness of the social injustices in our world and the linking of personal liberation with social transformation (see also Nelson and Prilleltensky 2003; Prilleltensky and Nelson 2004). Freire criticised what he described as the "banking" model of education whereby "education becomes an act of depositing, in which the students are the depositories and the teacher the depositor" (p. 45). The alternative he envisaged is a socially active form of education in which "knowledge emerges only through the restless, impatient, hopeful inquiry men [*sic*] pursue in the world, with the world, and with each other" (p. 46). It is through the process of praxis, the linking of theory and action, that we can collectively identify the myriad sources of social and personal oppression and develop ways of resisting and challenging them so as to build a healthier society.

Health psychology needs also to consider the contribution of feminist theory to understanding health and illness. From the early days, feminists have been involved in direct challenge to the oppressive role of traditional medical science. This struggle with medicine is far from over. As we enter the 21st century, medical science has become increasingly involved in control of the female body through developments in conception, pregnancy, childbirth and the control of menstruation (see Lock and Kaufert 1998). Sue Wilkinson illustrated in her chapter how both quantitative and qualitative research can contribute to both revealing the connection between gender and health and also contributing to the broader struggle for health especially among the oppressed and marginalized.

This includes ethnic and cultural minorities who were referred to by Mac MacLachlan in his chapter. Much cross-cultural psychology has been concerned with tabulating how one group is different or even lesser than another group. However, as MacLachlan emphasizes, culture is not something apart from us but rather we are all cultural beings engaged in everyday cultural practices. These cultural practices, healthy or unhealthy, in turn mesh with political and economic arrangements. Frequently certain practices have been identified as part of the endemic culture of a particular group when they are really the consequences of what could be described as the culture of poverty. MacLachlan in his sevenfold typology considered how the power of multinationals is condemning millions to lives of poverty and transforming us into a society of consumers rather than of participants. In the western world it is estimated that over one billion people are overweight and as many as 300 million clinically obese (WHO 2002). The search for explanations for this major health problem lies not in individual genes or psychological characteristics but in the cultural processes of modern capitalism. Health psychologists need to participate in efforts to unravel these processes.

Researching Health and Health Psychology

An awareness of culture makes us sensitive to the very cultural locatedness of our sub-discipline, its theories and research methods. Tuhwai Smith (1999: 1) has described research as "one of the dirtiest words of the indigenous world's vocabulary". It was a method used to humiliate and oppress indigenous people. As we move to develop a critical health psychology we need to consider how we can elaborate a research methodology that will not oppress but enhance the strengths of individuals and communities. The third part of the book considered this challenge further considering the underlying assumptions and implications of our research methods.

Concern with methodology has been a particular concern of psychology since its inception. However, this concern was more about the techniques of research rather than its underlying assumptions and values. Writing about the so-called crisis that faced social psychology in the 1970s Serge Moscovici had this to say:

the terms 'science' and 'scientific' are still imbued with a fetishism the abandonment of which is the sine qua non of knowledge. Social psychology will be unable to formulate dangerous truths while it adheres to this fetishism. This is its principle handicap, and this is what forces it to focus on minor problems and to remain a minor pursuit. All really successful sciences managed to produce dangerous truths for which they fought and of which they envisaged the consequences. That is why social psychology cannot attain the true idea of a science until it also becomes dangerous. (Moscovici 1972: 66)

Substituting the word "health" for "social" is a good starting point for developing a critical health psychology. Health psychology is a child of psychology and as such carries with it this same fetishism for a particular form of science, in particular experimentation and measurement. Indeed, its whole approach favours method over theory. There is an enthusiasm to collect more and more data with the belief that this will lead us to a better understanding of the world. It is what forms a large proportion of training in health psychology. It is supposedly possible to access the truth through following certain carefully formulated rules of inquiry. However, this fascination with method over theory conceals an unease about the ability of psychology to provide greater understanding of the human condition than can the layperson (see Smith 1997).

Psychology arose in the 19th century – a time of great exploration and colonization by the imperialist powers. These conquerors and explorers were extremely proud to bring home their booty that was displayed in specially built museums. Psychology continues to carry many of these characteristics in its quest to discover and display new phenomena for an inquisitive audience. But surely there is more to research in health psychology than revealing more statistical associations between more variables or even delving deeper into the phenomenological experience of suffering.

Health psychology needs to reflect on the purpose of research and to consider the connection between methods, and personal and social transformation. The chapters by Kerry Chamberlain and Uwe Flick consider some of the assumptions underlying qualitative research. Initially it was argued that this new form of research freed the research participants from the limits of the questionnaire or the psychological scale. It gave the research participants the opportunity to express their voices. But whose voice is it exactly? The participant's voice, like all voices, is not just emitted from within but is socially constructed. The language that he or she uses contains certain socially agreed meanings.

The detailed study of language by those psychologists interested in discourse has played an important role in clarifying how the very language that we use shapes the way we grasp our world. Its introduction into health psychology has provided us with an opportunity to explore how concepts of health and illness are socially constructed and reconstructed in everyday practice. However, despite these developments there is also the attendant danger that the focus on language, to the neglect of other dimensions of our humanity, is leading to the development of a very one-dimensional picture of health and illness. We are not just linguistic beings but material and cultural beings (see Murray and Campbell 2003). Carla Willig in her introduction to discourse analysis indicates the particular contribution of Foucauldian discourse analysis in this arena. Other theoretical approaches such as social representation theory also offers the prospect of deliberately connecting the study of both language and social practices within a broader context of social action.

Kerry Chamberlain and Uwe Flick in their chapters highlighted the need for health psychologists to reflect on the purpose of research. Flick argued that the desire to implement change raises many ethical and moral issues that the critical health psychologist must consider. This is a frequent challenge to those who desire to implement social change, but it is not one that should lead to any form of resignation and complacency. We are all both social and moral beings. We cannot separate ourselves from society and its many social ills and injustices.

As we move to develop a critical health psychology we need to consider how we can elaborate a research methodology that will not oppress but enhance the strengths of individuals and communities. Latin America has much to contribute to articulating a research strategy for a critical health psychology. I refer in particular to the liberation psychology of Martin-Baro (1994) that is gradually gaining an echo within health psychology in some parts of the world (e.g. Lykes 1999). This form of psychology is one that from the outset clearly takes a political stand on the side of the oppressed masses. In developing its research programme, health psychology needs to consider how it can contribute to "constructing a society where the welfare of the few is not built on the wretch-edness of the many" (p. 46). This is a mighty challenge for a critical health psychology but one on which we need to reflect.

Health Psychology and Social Action

Health psychology since its inception has adopted an applied orientation. Its aim has been to improve health. As Matarazzo (1982: 815) originally defined the discipline, it is the contribution of psychology "to the promotion and maintenance of health, the prevention and treatment of illness, and the identi-fication of etiologic and diagnostic correlates of health, illness and related dys-functiuon". However, as Marks (2002a) has stressed, the underlying assumption of this definition is the focus on individual responsibility for health and health improvement. Throughout this collection we have emphasized the broader social, cultural and political dimensions of health and illness. Thus in developing prac-tice in a critical health psychology it is necessary to adopt a broader perspective.

The most influential theories in health psychology concerned with improving health behaviour are those based upon social cognition. For example, in 2001 the British Division of Health Psychology identified the book *Predicting Health Behaviour: Research and Practice with Social Cognition Models* edited by Conner and Norman (1996) as the most influential book published by their members. The most popular of these social cognition models was the theory of reasoned action/planned behaviour that has been applied in hundreds of studies in attempts to predict a wide range of health-related behaviours. Although the social cognition models have found a certain degree of success in statistically predicting these behaviours, there has been increasing frustration at their restricted range and underlying assumptions. In particular, although they are defined as "social" cognition models, their orientation is still towards the indi-vidual actor as an information processor in a social context rather than the actor being a fully social being who constructs and is constructed by the social world (see Rise 2002). Further, as Stainton Rogers (1991: 55) has argued, they portray "thinking as a passive, mindless activity rather than an active striving after meaning, and portray people as thinking-machines rather than as aware and insightful, open to being beguiled by convincing tales and rhetoric, and investigative story-tellers". There is a need to expand our understanding of health and health improvement through engagement with more social psychological and sociological theories of change.

The final part of the book considered how health psychology can more directly position itself as an agent for promoting health through varied methods of social rather than individual change. It needs to consider the broader dimensions of health and illness that are ignored by popular social cognition models. One underlying issue is the need to work with study participants rather than attempting to impose a particular framework. This was referred to by the authors of the final three chapters but particularly by Brydon-Miller and Campbell, who considered how critical health psychologists can work with communities to promote health. Admittedly, there are limits to working within communities and ignoring the broader social and political context. The challenge for health psychologists is to explore how to connect local and community efforts to mobilize resistance to social oppression to broader national and international movements (Murray and Campbell 2003, 2004). Here critical health psychology has the opportunity of engaging with the more established tradition in community social psychology (see Montero 2002) and in the more political liberation community psychology (Watts and Serrano-Garcia 2003).

A Fable

Let us consider a fable as a means of concluding this book. Saramago (1998/ 1999) told the story of the man who beseeched the king to give him a boat. When the king asked why he wanted a boat the man replied that it was so that he could find the unknown island. The king replied that there were no unknown islands. They are all on the maps, he claimed. The man replied that only the known islands are on the maps and he wanted to find the unknown island. The king was reluctant to accede to the man's request but he became embarrassed when onlookers began to jeer at him. Finally, the king granted the man his request but he insisted that he would only give him a basic boat and that it was the man's responsibility to fit out the boat and recruit the crew. He instructed the man to go down to the harbour and the harbour master would give him a boat.

A woman who worked at the palace overheard the conversation and was attracted by this opportunity for adventure. She decided to follow the man to the harbour where she watched as the harbour master agreed to give the man a boat as instructed by the king. The boat was in very poor condition but the woman agreed to clean it up while the man went into town to recruit the crew. He returned later despondent since he had not been able to convince anybody to join him on his voyage of discovery. The potential sailors were concerned that on this old boat the sea would be dark and they might get lost. The man had told them that the sea may appear dark but that it all depends on how you look at it. While he could not give them a map, at least he could promise them some adventure.

The man insisted to the woman that he still wanted to find the unknown island. He told her that he felt that unless he was prepared to step outside himself he would never discover whom he was. That night the man and the cleaning woman slept and dreamed many dreams. The next morning they awoke and decided that despite the lack of support they had attracted for their voyage they would put to sea in search of the unknown island. But before they set out they thought they should name their boat and proudly painted on its side the name – the Unknown Island. Then, with the sun rising, they set sail in search of the unknown island.

Like all narratives there are many ways of interpreting this fable. Here it is sufficient to say that in this voyage to unknown islands, this book may not have been able to give you a fully detailed map to follow. Perhaps, it has not shown you any unknown islands but at least if it encourages you to reflect upon your own theoretical and methodological assumptions then perhaps the sea may not seem so dark and you can begin to see the outlines of those unknown islands.

📖 Further Readings

Martin-Baro, I. (1994) *Writings for a Liberation Psychology*, in A. Aron and S. Corne (eds), Cambridge, MA: Harvard University Press.

An inspirational classic collection of articles by a Jesuit priest and psychologist who was killed by a Salvadorean death squad in 1989. It includes a critique of traditional positivist psychology, and discussion on how to develop a liberation psychology that is grounded in the everyday experiences of the oppressed masses. Although drawing on the experiences of human exploitation and misery in Latin America, it has many lessons for the development of a critical health psychology in industrialised nations.

Nelson, G. and Prilleltensky, I. (2003) *Critical Psychology in Practice*, London: Palgrave.

This book further takes up strategies for critical psychology in practice.

Tuhiwai Smith, L. (1999) *Decolonizing Methodologies: Research and Indigenous Peoples*, London: Zed Books.

An important critique of traditional social research methods that seriously questions the purpose of much social research, not just with indigenous peoples but also begins to consider alternative strategies of social inquiry.

References

Acheson, D. (1998) *Independent Inquiry into Inequalities in Health*, London: The Stationery Office.

Ackroyd, P. (2000) *London: The Biography*, London: Vintage.

Addelson, K.P. (1994) *Moral Passages: Toward a Collectivist Moral Theory*, New York, NY: Routledge.

Adesso, V.J., Reddy, D.M. and Fleming, R. (eds) (1994) *Psychological Perspectives on Women's Health*, Washington, DC: Taylor & Francis.

Alarcon, R.D. and Foulks, E.F. (1995) 'Personality disorders and culture: contemporary clinical views', *Cultural Diversity & Mental Health*, 1, 3–17.

American Psychological Association (2000) 'Resolution on poverty and socioeconomic status' [http://www.apa.org/pi/urban/povres.html] .

Anderson, N.L.R., Nyamathi, A., McAvoy, J.A., Conde, F. and Casey, C. (2001) 'Perceptions about risk for HIV/AIDS among adolescents in juvenile detention', *Western Journal of Nursing Research*, 23(4), 336–359.

Aries, N. and Kennedy, L. (1990) 'The health labor force: the effects of change', in P. Conrad and R. Kern (eds), *The Sociology of Health and Illness: Critical Perspectives* (3rd edn), New York, NY: St. Martin's.

Armstrong, D. (1984) 'The patient's view', *Social Science and Medicine*, 18, 737–744.

Armstrong, D. (1987) 'Theoretical tensions in biopsychosocial medicine', *Social Science and Medicine*, 25, 1213–1218.

Arney, W.R. and Bergen, B.J. (1983) *Medicine and the Management of Living*, Chicago, IL: University of Chicago Press.

Atkinson, P. (1997) 'Narrative turn or blind alley?', *Qualitative Health Research*, 7, 325–344.

Atkinson, P. and Hammersley, M. (1998) 'Ethnography and participant observation', in N. Denzin and Y.S. Lincoln (eds), *Strategies of Qualitative Inquiry* (pp. 110–136), London: Sage.

Auluck-Wilson, C.A. (1995) 'When all the women lift', *Signs: Journal of Women in Culture and Society*, 20(4), 1029–1038.

Baider, L., Kaufman, B., Ever-Hadani, P. and De-Nour, A.K. (1996) 'Coping with additional stresses: comparative study of healthy and cancer patient new immigrants', *Social Science and Medicine*, 42(7), 1077–1084.

Bannister, E.M. (1999) 'Evolving reflexivity: negotiating meaning of women's midlife experience', *Qualitative Inquiry*, 5, 3–23.

Barker-Benfield, G.J. (1972) 'The spermatic economy: a nineteenth century view of sexuality', *Feminist Studies*, 1, 45–74.

Barker-Benfield, G.J. (1976) *The Horrors of the Half-known Life*, New York, NY: Harper & Row.

Barnett, T. and Whiteside, A. (2002) *AIDS in the 21st Century: Disease and Globalisation*, New York, NY: Palgrave MacMillan.

Batt, S. (1994) *Patient No More: the Politics of Breast Cancer*, London: Scarlet Press.

Baum, F. (1999) 'The role of social capital in health promotion: Australian perspectives', *Health Promotion Journal of Australia*, 9(3), 171–178.

Beck, U. (1992) *Risk-Society*, London: Sage.

Becker, E. (1962) *The Birth and Death of Meaning*, New York, NY: Braziller.

Becker, E. (1968) *The Structure of Evil: an Essay on the Unification of the Science of Man*, New York, NY: Braziller.

Becker, E. (1975) *Escape from Evil*, New York's Free Press.

Beeker, C., Guenther Gray, C. and Raj, A. (1998) 'Community empowerment paradigm and the primary prevention of HIV/AIDS', *Social Science and Medicine*, 46(7), 831–842.

Bell, E.E. (2001) 'Infusing race into the U.S. discourse on action research', in P. Reason and H. Bradbury (eds), *Handbook of Action Research: Participative Inquiry and Practice* (pp. 48–58), London: Sage.

Bennett, P. and Murphy, S. (1997) *Psychology and Health Promotion*, Buckingham: Open University Press.

Berry, J.W. (1990) 'Psychology of acculturation', in R. Breslin (ed.) *Applied Cross-cultural Psychology* (pp. 232–253), London: Sage.

Berry, J.W. (1997) 'Lead article: immigration, acculturation and adaptation', *Applied Psychology: An International Review*, 46, 5–68.

Berry, J.W. and Kim, U. (1988) 'Acculturation and mental health', in P. Dasen, J.W. Berry and N. Satorious (eds), *Health and Cross-cultural Psychology*, London: Sage.

Billig, M. (1997) 'Rhetorical and discursive analysis: how families talk about the royal family', in N. Hayes (ed.), *Doing Qualitative Analysis in Psychology*, Hove: Psychology Press.

Blaxter, M. (1983) 'The causes of disease: women talking', *Social Science and Medicine*, 17, 56–69.

Blaxter M. (2000) 'Medical sociology at the start of the new millennium', *Social Science & Medicine*, 51, 1139–1142.

Bollnow, O.F. (1961) 'Lived-space', *Philosophy Today*, 5, 31–39.

Boltanski, L. (1999) *Distant Suffering: Morality, Media and Politics*, translated by G. Burchell, Cambridge: Cambridge University Press.

Booth C. (1889) *Life and Labour of the People: First Series, Poverty (i) East, Central and South London*, London: Macmillan (Republished 1969).

Booth C. (1902a) *Life and Labour of the People: First Series, Poverty (ii) Streets and Population Classified*, London: Macmillan (Republished 1969).

Booth C. (1902b) *Life and Labour of the People in London. Final Volume. Notes on Social Influences and Conclusions*, London: Macmillan.

Boston Women's Health Book Collective (1971) *Our Bodies, Ourselves*, Boston, MA: The Boston Women's Health Collective, Inc.

Bourdieu, P. (1986) 'The forms of capital', in J. Richardson (ed.), *Handbook of Theory and Research for the Sociology of Education* (pp. 241–248), New York, NY: Greenwood.

Bracht, N. (1999) *Health Promotion at the Community Level 2: New Advances*, London: Sage.

Brady, M. (1995) 'Culture in treatment, culture as treatment: a critical appraisal of developments in addiction programmes for indigenous North Americans and Australians', *Social Science and Medicine*, 41, 1487–1498.

Brems, S. and Griffiths, M. (1993) 'Health women's way: learning to listen', in M. Koblinsky, J. Timyan and J. Gay (eds), *The Health of Women: a Global Perspective*, Boulder, CO: Westview Press.

Brown, L.S. (1997) 'Ethics in psychology: Cui bono?' in D. Fox and I. Prilleltensky (eds), *Critical Psychology: An Introduction* (pp. 51–67), London: Sage.

Bruner, J. (1986) *Actual Minds, Possible Worlds*, Cambridge, MA: Harvard University Press.

Bruner, J. (1990) *Acts of Meaning*, Cambridge, MA: Harvard University Press.

Brydon-Miller, M. (1993) 'Breaking down barriers: accessibility self-advocacy in the disabled community', in P. Park, M. Brydon-Miller, B. Hall and T. Jackson (eds), *Voices of Change: Participatory Research in the United States and Canada* (pp. 125–143), Westport, CT: Bergin and Garvey.

Brydon-Miller, M. (2001a) 'Education research and action: theory and methods of participatory action research', in D. Tolman and M. Brydon-Miller (eds), *From Subjects to Subjectives: A Handbook of Interpretive and Participatory Methods* (pp. 76–89), New York, NY: New York University Press.

Brydon-Miller, M. (2001b) 'A glimpse of a lighthouse: participatory action research, postcolonial theory and work in refugee communities', in M. Hopkins and N. Wellmeier (eds), *Negotiating Transnationalism: Selected Papers on Refugees and Immigrants*, Volume IX, 254–276.

Brydon-Miller, M. and Tolman D.L. (eds) (1997a) 'Special issue: transforming psychology: interpretive and participatory research methods', *Journal of Social Issues*, 53, 597–810.

Brydon-Miller, M. and Tolman D.L. (eds) (1997b) 'Engaging the process of transformation', *Journal of Social Issues*, 53, 803–810.

Bullock, H.E. and Lott, B. (2001) 'Building a research and advocacy agenda on issues of economic injustice', *Analyses of Social Issues and Public Policy*, 1, 147–162.

Burke, M. and Stevenson, H.M. (1993) 'Fiscal crisis and restructuring in Medicare: the politics and political science of health in Canada', *Health and Canadian Society*, 1, 51–80.

Burkey, S. (1996) *People First*, London/New York: Zed Books.

Burman, E. and Parker, I. (eds) (1993) *Discourse Analytic Work*, London: Routledge.

Burr, V. (1995) *An Introduction to Social Constructionism*, London: Routledge.

Bury, M. (1988) 'Meanings at risk: the experience of arthritis', in R. Anderson and M. Bury (eds), *Living with Chronic Illness*, London: Unwin Hyman.

Butler, S. and Rosenblum, B. (1994) *Cancer in Two Voices*, London: Women's Press.

Campbell, C. (1997) 'Migrancy, masculine identities and AIDS: the psycho-social context of HIV-transmission on the South African gold mines', *Social Science and Medicine*, 45, 273–281.

Campbell, C. (1998) 'Representations of gender, respectability and commercial sex in the shadow of AIDS: a South African case study', *Social Science Information*, 37, 687–708.

Campbell, C. (2000a) 'Selling sex in the time of AIDS: the psycho-social context of condom use by southern African sex workers', *Social Science and Medicine*, 50, 479–494.

Campbell, C. (2000b) 'Social capital and health: contextualising health promotion within local community networks', in S. Baron, J. Field and T. Schuller (eds), *Social Capital: Critical Perspectives* (pp. 182–196), Oxford: Oxford University Press.

Campbell, C. (2003) *Letting them Die: Why HIV/AIDS Prevention Programmes Often Fail*, Oxford: James Currey/Bloomington, IN: Indiana University Press.

Campbell, C. and Jovchelovitch, S. (2000) 'Health, community and development: towards a social psychology of participation', *Journal of Community and Applied Social Psychology*, 10, 255–270.

Campbell, C. and MacPhail, C. (2002) 'Peer education, gender and the development of critical consciousness: participatory HIV prevention by South African youth', *Social Science and Medicine*, 55(2), 331–345.

Campbell, C. and Mzaidume, Y. (2001) 'Grassroots participation in health promotional projects: peer education and HIV prevention by sex workers in South Africa', *American Journal of Public Health*, 91(12), 1978–1987.

Carr, S.C. (2002), *Social Psychology*, Chichester: Wiley.

Carr, S.C. and MacLachlan, M. (1998) 'Psychology in developing countries: reassessing its impact', *Psychology and Developing Societies*, 10(1), 1–20.

Carr, S.C., McAuliffe, E. and MacLachlan, M. (1998) *Psychology of Aid*, London: Routledge.

Carr, S.C. and Sloan, T.S. (eds) (2003), *Poverty and Psychology: From Global Perspective to Local Practice*, New York, NY: Kluwer Academic.

Casimir, G.J. and Morrison, B.J. (1993) 'Rethinking work with "multicultural populations"', *Community Mental Health Journal*, 29(6), 547–559.

Cassell, E.J. (1991) *The Nature of Suffering: and the Goals of Medicine*, New York, NY: Oxford University Press.

Cassen, R. (1994) *Does Aid Work?* Oxford: Oxford University Press.

Caton, D. (1985) 'The secularization of pain', *Anesthesiology*, 62, 493–501.

Chamberlain, K. (2000) 'Methodolatry in qualitative health research', *Journal of Health Psychology*, 5, 285–296.

Chandler, M. (1990) *A Healing Art: Regeneration Through Autobiography*, New York, NY: Garland.

Charmaz, K. (1999) 'Stories of suffering: subjective tales and research narratives', *Qualitative Health Research*, 9, 362–382.

Chataway, C. (2001) 'Negotiating the observer–observed relationship: participatory action research', in D. Tolman and M. Brydon-Miller (eds), *From Subjects to Subjectivities: a Handbook of Interpretive and Participatory Methods* (pp. 239–255), New York, NY: New York University Press.

Chrisler, J. and Hemstreet, A.H. (1995) 'The diversity of women's health needs', in J.C. Chrisler and A.H. Hemstreet (eds), *Variations on a Theme: Diversity and the Psychology of Women*, Albany, NY: State University of New York Press.

Cicourel, A.V. (1964) *Method and Measurement in Sociology*, New York, NY: Free Press.

Clorfene-Casten, L. (1996) *Breast Cancer: Poisons, Profits and Prevention*, Monroe, ME: Common Courage Press.

Cohen, A. (1974) *Two-dimensional Man: An Essay on the Anthropology of Power and Symbolism in Complex Society*, Berkeley, CA: University of California Press.

Colucci, F.P. (1995) 'Common sense, transformation, and elites', *International Gramsci Society Newsletter*, 4, 38–43.

Concern (2002) *Annual Report*, Dublin: Concern.

Conner, M. and Norman, P. (eds) (1996) *Predicting Health Behaviour: Research and Practice with Social Cognition Models*, Buckingham: Open University Press.

Conrad, P. (1992) 'Medicalisation and social control', *Annual Review of Sociology*, 18, 209–232.

Cooper, M.L., Agocha, V.B. and Powers, A.M. (1999) 'Motivations for condom use: do pregnancy prevention goals undermine disease prevention among heterosexual young adults?', *Health Psychology*, 18, 464–474.

Cooper, N., Stevenson, C. and Hale, G. (1996) The biopsychosocial model, in N. Copper, C. Stevenson and Hale G. (eds), *Integrating Perspectives on Health* (pp. 1–17), Buckingham: Open University Press.

Corea, G. (1985) *The Hidden Malpractice*, New York, NY: Harper Colophon/Harper & Row.

Crawford, R. (1980) 'Healthism and the medicalization of everyday life', *International Journal of Health Services*, 10, 365–368.

Crawford, M. and Kimmel, M. (eds) (1999) 'Special issue: innovative methods in feminist research', *Psychology of Women Quarterly*, 23, 1–2.

Crossley, M.L. (1999a) 'Stories of illness and trauma survival: liberation or repression', *Social Science & Medicine*, 48, 1685–1695.

Crossley, M.L. (1999b) 'Making sense of HIV infection: discourse and adaptation to life with a long-term HIV positive diagnosis', *Health*, 3, 95–119.

Crossley, M. (2000) *Rethinking Health Psychology*, Buckingham: Open University Press.

Crotty, M. (1998) *The Foundations of Social Research*, Melbourne: Allen & Unwin.

Csordas, T.J. (1994) 'Introduction: the body as representation and being-in-the-world', in T.J. Csordas (ed.), *Embodiment and Experience: the Existential Ground of Culture and Self* (pp. 1–24), Cambridge: Cambridge University Press.

Danziger, K. (1990) *Constructing the Subject: Historical Origins of Psychological Research*, Cambridge: Cambridge University Press.

Danziger, K. (1994) 'Does the history of psychology have a future?' *Theory & Psychology*, 4, 467–484.

Daudpota, I. (2000) 'Water shortage – A way out', *The Economist*, 26 May [http://lists.isb.sdnpk.org/pipermail/econo-list-old/2000-May/001313.html].

de Raeve, L. (1997) 'Positive thinking and moral oppression in cancer care', *European Journal of Cancer Care*, 6, 249–256.

Denny, C. (2003) 'Hypocrisy that underlies HIPC', *Guardian*, 6 January, p. 19.

Denzin, N. (1997) *Interpretive Ethnography*, Thousand Oaks, CA: Sage.

Denzin, N. and Lincoln, Y.S. (eds) (2000) *Handbook of Qualitative Research* (2nd edn), London, Thousand Oaks, New Dehli: Sage.

Department of Health (1999) *Reducing Health Inequalities: An Action Report*, London: Department of Health.

DiGiacomo, S. (1992) 'Metaphor as illness: post-modern dilemmas in the representation of body, mind and disorder', *Medical Anthropology*, 14, 109–137.

Dobson, P. (1998). *Will the circle be unbroken? Cycles of survival for indigenous Australians*. Discussion paper No. 12. Darwin: North Australia Research Unit/Australian National University.

Doise, W., Clemence, A. and Lorenzi-Cioldi, F. (1993) *The Quantitative Analysis of Social Representations*, New York, NY: Harvester Wheatsheaf.

Dorling, D., Mitchell, R., Shaw, M., Orford, S. and Davey Smith, G. (2000) 'The ghost of Christmas past: health effects of poverty in London in 1896 and 1991', *British Medical Journal*, 321, 1547–1551.

Dubow, S. (1995) *Illicit Union: Scientific Racism in Modern South Africa*, Johannesburg: Witwatersrand University Press.

Durkheim, E. (1897) *Le Suicide*, Paris (Translated by J.A. Spaulding and C. Simpson, 1952) as *Suicide: a Study of Sociology*, London: Routledge and Kegan Paul.

Edwards, D. and Potter, J. (1992) *Discursive Psychology*, London: Sage.

Ehrenreich, B. and English, D. (1973) *Complaints and Disorders: The Sexual Politics of Sickness*, Old Westbury, NY: The Feminist Press.

Ellul, J. (1965) *The Technological Society* (Translated by J. Wilkinson), New York, NY: Alfred A. Knopf.

Engel, G.L. (1977) 'The need for a new medical model: A challenge for biomedicine', *Science*, 196, 129–136.

Engels, F. (1892) *The Condition of the Working-class in England in 1844*, London: Swan Sonnenschein & Co.

Evans-Pritchard, E.E. (1951) *Social Anthropology*, London: Cohen & West.

Fals Borda, O. (2001) 'Participatory (action) research in social theory: origins and challenges', in P. Reason and H. Bradbury (eds), *Handbook of Action Research: Participative Inquiry and Practice* (pp. 27–37), London: Sage.

Farmer, P. (1994) 'AIDS talk and the constitution of cultural models', *Social Science and Medicine*, 38, 801–809.

Ferrie, J.E., Shipley, M.J., Marmot, M.G., Stansfield, S. and Davey-Smith, G. (1995) 'Health effects of anticipation of job change and non-employment: longitudinal data from the Whitehall II study', *British Medical Journal*, 311, 1264–1269.

Fishbein, M. and Middlestadt, S. (1989) 'Using the theory of reasoned action for understanding and changing AIDS-related behaviours', in V. Mays, G. Albee and S. Schneider (eds), *Primary Prevention of AIDS: Psychological Approaches* (pp. 93–110), Newbury Park, CA: Sage.

Fisher, S. (1996) 'Life stress, personal control and the risk of disease', in C. Cooper (ed.), *Handbook of Stress, Medicine and Health*, London: CRC Press.

Flaskerud, J.H. and Anderson, N. (1999) 'Disseminating the results of participant-focused research', *Journal of Transcultural Nursing*, 10(4), 340–349.

Flick, U. (1992) 'Triangulation revisited – Strategy of or alternative to validation of qualitative data', *Journal for the Theory of Social Behavior*, 22, 175–197.

Flick, U. (1995) 'Social representations', in J. Smith, R. Harre and L. van Langenhove (eds), *Rethinking Psychology* (pp. 70–96), London: Sage.

Flick, U. (1999) 'Qualitative inquiries into social representations of health', *Journal of Health Psychology*, 5, 309–318.

Flick, U. (2000) 'Episodic interviewing', in M. Bauer and G. Gaskell (eds), *Qualitative Researching with Text, Image and Sound – a Handbook* (pp. 75–92), London, Sage.

Flick, U. (2002) *An Introduction to Qualitative Research – Second Edition*, London, Thousand Oaks, CA, New Delhi: Sage.

Flick, U. (2003a) 'Design and process in qualitative research', in U. Flick, E.v. Kardorff and I. Steinke (eds), *Qualitative Research – Paradigms, Theories, Methods, Practice & Contexts*, London, Thousand Oaks, New Delhi: Sage.

Flick, U. (2003b) 'Triangulation in qualitative research', in U. Flick, E. v. Kardorff and I. Steinke (eds), *Qualitative Research – Paradigms, Theories, Methods, Practice & Contexts*, London, Thousand Oaks, New Delhi: Sage.

Flick, U., Kardorff, E.v. and Steinke, I. (eds) (2003) *Qualitative Research – Paradigms, Theories, Methods, Practice & Contexts*, London, Thousand Oaks, New Delhi: Sage.

Foucault, M. (1978) *The History of Sexuality* (Translated by R. Hurley) (Vol. 1: An introduction), New York, NY: Random House.

Fox, D.R and Prilleltensky, I. (eds) (1997) *Critical Psychology: An Introduction*, London: Sage.

Francome, C. and Marks, D.F. (1996) *Improving the Health of the Nation*, London: Middlesex University Press.

Frank, A. (1995) *The Wounded Story Teller: Body, Illness, and Ethics*, Chicago, IL: University of Chicago Press.

Frank, A.W. (1991) *At the Will of the Body: Reflections on Illness*, Boston, MA: Houghton Mifflin.

Frank, A.W. (2001) 'Can we research suffering?' *Qualitative Health Research*, 11, 353–362.

Freeman, M. (1993) *Rewriting the Self: History, Memory, Narrative*, London: Routledge.

Freire, P. (1970/1993) *Pedagogy of the Oppressed*, New York, NY: Continuum.

Freire, P. (1973/1993) *Education for Critical Consciousness*, New York, NY: Continnum.

Freire, P. (1997) 'Forward', in S.E. Smith, D.G. Williams and N.A. Johnson (eds), *Nurtured by Knowledge: Learning to Do Participatory Action Research* (pp. xi–xii), New York, NY: Apex Press.

Freud, S. (1923/1961) *Beyond the Pleasure Principle* (Translated by J. Strachey), New York, NY: Norton.

Frye, N. (1956) *Anatomy of Criticism*, Princeton,NJ: Princeton University Press.

Furnham, A. and Vincent, C. (2001) 'Cultivating health through complementary medicine', in M. MacLachlan (ed.), *Cultivating Health: Cultural Perspectives on Promoting Health*, Chichester: Wiley.

Gadamer, H.-G. (1978) *Truth and Method* (Translated by J. Weinsheimer and D.G. Marshall) (2nd revised edn), New York, NY: Continuum.

Gadamer, H.-G. (1996) *The Enigma of Health*, Stanford, CA: Stanford University Press.

Gendlin, E.T. (1978–1979) '*Befindlichkeit*: Heidegger and the philosophy of psychology', *Review of Existential Psychology and Psychiatry*, 16, 43–71.

George, S. (1988) *A Fate Worse Than Debt*, London: Pelican.

Gergen, K.J. (1989) 'Social psychology and the wrong revolution', *European Journal of Social Psychology*, 19: 463–484.

Gergen, K.J. and Gergen, M.M. (1986) 'Narrative form and the construction of psychological science', in T.R. Sarbin (ed.), *Narrative Psychology: the Storied Nature of Human Conduct* (pp. 22–44), New York, NY: Praeger.

Gibson, K. and Swartz, L. (2001) 'Psychology, social transition and organisational life in South Africa: "I can't change the past – but I can try"', *Psychoanalytic Studies*, 3, 381–392.

Giddens, A. (1999) *Runaway World: How Globalisation is Reshaping Our Lives*, London: Profile Books.

Gigerenzer, G. (1993) 'The superego, the ego, and the id in statistical reasoning', in G. Keren and C. Lewis (eds), *A Handbook for Data Analysis in the Behavioural Sciences: Methodological Issues* (pp. 311–339), Hillsdale, NJ: Erlbaum.

Gillies, P. (1998) 'The effectiveness of alliances and partnerships for health promotion', *Health Promotion International*, 13, 1–21.

Gillies, V. and Willig, C. (1997) 'You get the nicotine and that in your blood – Constructions of addiction and control in women's accounts of cigarette smoking', *Journal of Community & Applied Social Psychology*, 7, 285–301.

Giroux, H.A., Lankshear, C., McLaren, P. and Peters, M. (1996) *Counter Narratives: Cultural Studies and Critical Pedagogies in Postmodern Spaces*, New York, NY: Routledge.

Glaser, B.G. and Strauss, A.L. (1965) *Awareness of Dying*, Chicago, IL: Aldine.

Glaser, B.G. and Strauss, A.L. (1967) *The Discovery of Grounded Theory: Strategies for Qualitative Research*, New York, NY: Aldine.

Goffman, E. (1961) *Asylums: Essays on the Social Situation of Mental Patients and Other Inmates*, New York, NY: Anchor Doubleday.

Good, B. (1977) 'The heart of what's the matter: the semantics of illness in Iran', *Culture, Medicine, and Psychiatry*, 1, 25–28.

Gordon, D.F. (1995) 'Testicular cancer and masculinity', in D.J. Sabo and D.F. Gordon (eds), *Men's Health and Illness*, Thousand Oaks, CA: Sage.

Gray, R. (1998) Four Perspectives on Unconventional Therapy, *Health*, 2, 55–74.

Gray, R. (2003) *Prostate Tales: Men's Experiences with Prostate Cancer*, Harriman, TN: Men's Press.

Gray, R. and Sinding, C. (2002) *Standing Ovation: Performing Social Science Research About Cancer*, Walnut Creek, CA: AltaMira.

Greer, S., Moorey, S. and Watson, M. (1989) 'Patients' adjustment to cancer', *Journal of Psychosomatic Research*, 33, 373–377.

Guba, E.G. and Lincoln, Y.S. (1994) 'Competing paradigms in qualitative research' in N.K. Denzin and Y.S. Lincoln (eds), *Handbook of Qualitative Research*, Thousand Oaks, CA: Sage.

Gurr, T.R. (1993) *Minorities at Risk: A Global View of Ethno Political Conflicts*, Washington, DC: Institute of Peace Press.

Habermas, J. (1971) *Knowledge and Human Interest*, Boston, MA: Beacon Press.

Hafferty, F.W. (1991) *Into the Valley: Death and the Socialization of Medical Students*, New Haven, CT: Yale University Press.

Hagey, R.S. (1997) 'The use and abuse of participatory action research', *Chronic Diseases in Canada*, 18(1), 1–4.

Hall, B. (1981) 'Participatory research, popular knowledge, and power: a personal reflection', *Convergence*, 14(3), 6–17.

Hall, B. (2001) 'I wish this were a poem of practices of participatory research', in P. Reason and H. Bradbury (eds), *Handbook of Action Research: Participative Inquiry and Practice* (pp. 171–178), London: Sage.

Hammersley, M. and Atkinson, P. (1983), *Ethnography – Principles in Practice*, London: Tavistock.

Harding, S. (1993) 'Rethinking standpoint epistemology', in L. Alcoff and E. Potter (eds), *Feminist Epistemologies*, London: Routledge.

Harrison, J., Chin, J. and Ficarrotto, T. (1995) 'Warning: masculinity may be dangerous to your health', in M.S. Kimmel and M.A. Messner (eds), *Men's Lives*, Boston, MA: Allyn & Bacon.

Hay, L. (1984) *Cancer – Discovering Your Healing Power* (Tape), Santa Monica, CA: Hay House Inc.

Heidegger, M. (1962), *Being and Time* (Translated by J. Macquarrie and E. Robinson), New York, NY: Harper & Row.

Helman, C.G. (2001) *Culture, Health and Illness*, London: Arnold.

Henriques, J., Hollway, W., Urwin, C., Venn, C. and Walkerdine, V. (1984) *Changing the Subject: Psychology, Social Regulation and Subjectivity*, London: Methuen.

Henwood, K., Griffin, C. and Phoenix, A. (1998) *Standpoints and Differences: Essays in the Practice of Feminist Psychology*, London: Sage.

Heritage, J. (1984) *Garfinkel and Ethnomethodology*, Cambridge: Polity Press.

Heritage, J. and Sefi, S. (1992) 'Dilemmas of advice', in P.Drew and J. Heritage (eds), *Talk at Work*, Cambridge: Cambridge University Press.

Hermanns, H. (1995) 'Narrative interview', in U. Flick, E.v. Kardorff, H. Keupp, L.v. Rosenstiel and S. Wolff (eds), *Handbuch Qualitative Sozialforschung* (2nd edn) (pp. 182–185), München: Psychologie Verlags Union.

Hermans, H.J.M. and Kempen, H.J.G. (1998) 'Moving cultures: the perilous problems of cultural dichotomies in a globalizing society', *American Psychologist*, 53(10), 1111–1120.

Herzlich, C. (1973) *Health and Illness: A Social Psychological Analysis*, London: Academic.

Hoinacki, L. (1992) *The Health of Americans?*, Unpublished manuscript, Drafted in Bremen, Germany.

Holdstock, L. (2000) *Re-examining Psychology: Critical Perspectives and African Insights*. London: Routledge.

Holland, J. (1998) *The Male in the Head*, London: Tufnell.

Holland, J.C. and Mastrovito, R. (1980) 'Psychologic adaptation to breast cancer', *Cancer*, 46, 1045.

Horton-Salway, M. (2001) 'Narrative identities and the management of personal accountability in talk about ME', *Journal of Health Psychology*, 6(2), 247–259.

Hopkin, J. (2002) 'Development – the basics: making sense of the world', in C. Regan (ed.) *80:20, Development in an Unequal World*. Wicklow, Ireland: Bray, Co. 80:20 Educating and Acting for a Better World.

Horowitz, D. (1985) *Ethnic Groups in Conflict*, Berkeley, CA: University of California Press.

Huby, G. (1997) 'Interpreting silence, documenting experience: an anthropological approach to the study of health service users', experience with HIV/AIDS care in Lothian, Scotland', *Social Science and Medicine*, 44(8), 1149–1160.

Human Development Report (2000) *Human Rights and Human Development*, New York, NY: United Nations Development Program.

Ibanez, T. and Iniguez, L. (eds) (1997) *Critical Social Psychology*, London: Sage.

Illich, I. (1976) *Medical Nemesis: the Expropriation of Health*, New York, NY: Pantheon.

Illich, I. (1985) 'Subsistence', in K. Vaux (ed.), *Powers that Make us Human* (pp. 45–53), Urbana and Chicago, IL: University of Illinois Press.

Illich, I. (1992) *In the Mirror of the Past*, Boston: Marion Boyars.

Inglehart, R. and Baker, W.E. (2000) 'Modernization, cultural change and the persistence of traditional values', *American Sociological Review*, 65, 19–51.

James, W. (1890) *The Principles of Psychology* (Vol. 1), New York, NY: Henry Holt.

James, N. (1999) *The A-Z of Positive Thinking*, London: Hodder and Stoughton.

Janz, N. (1996) 'Evaluation of 37 AIDS prevention projects: successful approaches and barriers to program effectiveness', *Health Education Quarterly*, 23, 80–97.

Järvinen, M. (2000) 'The biographical illusion: constructing meaning in qualitative interviews', *Qualitative Inquiry*, 6, 370–391.

Jirapaet, V. (2000) 'Effects of an empowerment program on coping, quality of life, and the maternal role adaptation of Thai HIV-infected mothers', *Journal of the Association of Nurses in AIDS Care*, 11(4), 34–45.

Jodelet, D. (1991) *Madness and Social Representations: Living with the Mad in One French Community*, Berkeley, CA: University of California Press.

Joffe, H. (1996) 'The shock of the new: a psycho-dynamic extension of social representation theory', *Journal for the Theory of Social Behaviour*, 26, 197–219.

Johnson, K. (1992) 'Women's health: developing a new interdisciplinary specialty', *Journal of Women's Health*, 1, 95–99.

Jovchelovitch, S. (1996) 'Peripheral communities and the transformation of social representations: queries on power and recognition', *Social Psychological Review*, 1(1), 16–26.

Justice, B. (1998) 'Being well inside the self: a different measure of health', *Advances in Mind–Body Medicine*, 14, 61–68.

Kaufert, P.A. (1998) 'Women, resistance and the breast cancer movement', in P.A. Kaufert (ed.), *Pragmatic Women and Body Politics*, Cambridge: Cambridge University Press.

Kelly, C. and Breinlinger, S. (1996) *The Social Psychology of Collective Action: Identity, Injustice and Gender*, London: Taylor & Francis.

Kendall, G. and Wickham, G. (1999) *Using Foucault's Methods*, London: Sage.

Kidder, L.H. and Fine, M. (1997) 'Qualitative inquiry in psychology: a radical tradition', in D. Fox and I. Prilleltensky (eds), *Critical Psychology: An Introduction* (pp. 34–50), London: Sage.

Kirk, J.L. and Miller, M. (1986) *Reliability and Validity in Qualitative Research*, Beverley Hills, CA: Sage.

Kitzinger, C. (2000a) 'How to resist an idiom', *Research on Language and Social Interaction*, 33, 121–154.

Kitzinger, C. (2000b) 'Doing feminist conversation analysis', *Feminism & Psychology*, 10, 163–193.

Kleinman, A. (1980) *Patients and Healers in the Context of Culture*, Berkeley, CA: University of California Press.

Kleinman, A. (1988) *The Illness Narratives: Suffering, Healing, and the Human Condition*, Berkeley, CA: The University of California Press.

Kleinman, A., Das, V. and Lock, M.M. (eds) (1997) *Social Suffering*, Berkeley, CA: University of California Press.

Kleinman, A. and Kleinman, J. (1991) 'Suffering and its professional transformation', *Culture, Medicine and Psychiatry*, 15, 275–301.

Kopp, S. (1973) *If You Meet the Buddha on the Road, Kill Him!*, New York, NY: Sheldon.

Kraft, R.N. (2002) *Memory Perceived: Recalling the Holocaust*, Westport, CT: Praeger.

Kugelmann, R. (1992) *Stress: the Nature and History of Engineered Grief*, Westport, CT: Praeger.

Kugelmann, R. (1998) 'The psychology and management of pain: gate control as theory and symbol', in H. Stam (ed.), *The Body and Social Psychology* (pp. 182–204), London: Sage.

Kunst, A.E. and Mackenbach, J.P. (1994) 'The size of mortality differences associated with educational level in 9 industrialised countries', *American Journal of Public Health*, 84, 932–937.

Kushner, R. (1975) *Breast Cancer: A Personal History and Investigative Report*, New York, NY: Harcourt Brace.

Lacan, J. (1978) *The Four Fundamental Concepts of Psychoanalysis: The Seminar of Jacques Lacan Book XI* (Translated by A. Sheridan), New York, NY: Norton.

Lang, R. (1984) 'The dwelling door: a phenomenological exploration of transition', in C.M. Aanstoos (ed.), *West Georgia College Studies in the Social Sciences: Vol. 23. Exploring the Lived World: Readings in Phenomenological Psychology* (pp. 137–150), Carrollton, GA: West Georgia College.

Langer, L.L. (1991) *Holocaust Testimonies: The Ruins of Memory*, New Haven, CT: Yale University Press.

Lapsley, H., Nikora, L.W. and Black, R. (2000) 'Women's narratives of recovery from disabling mental health problems', in J.M. Ussher (ed.), *Women's Health: Contemporary International Perspectives*, London: BPS Blackwell Books.

Laszlo, J. (1997) 'Narrative organization of social representations', *Papers on Social Representations*, 6, 155–172.

Lather, P. and Smithies, C. (1997) *Troubling the Angels: Women Living with HIV/AIDS*, Boulder, CO: Westview Press.

Laurence, L. and Weinhouse, B. (1994) *Outrageous Practices: How Gender Bias Threatens Women's Health*, New Brunswick, NJ: Rutgers University Press.

Leary, D.E. (1987) 'Telling likely stories: the rhetoric of the new psychology', 1880–1920, *Journal of the History of the Behavioral Sciences*, 23, 315–331.

Leder, D. (1990) *The Absent Body*, Chicago, IL: University of Chicago Press.

Lee, C. (1988) *Women's Health: Psychological and Social Perspectives*, London: Sage.

Leon, D. and Walt, G. (2000) *Poverty, Inequality and Health: An International Perspective*, Oxford: Oxford University Press.

Leventhal, H. (1996) 'President's column', *The Health Psychologists*, 18(4), 1, 22.

Levinas, E. (1969) *Totality and Infinity* (Translated by A. Lingis), Pittsburgh, PA: Duquesne University Press.

Levinas, E. (1978) *Existents and Existence* (Translated by A. Lingis), Dordrecht: Kluwer Academic.

Levinas, E. (1988) 'Useless suffering' (Translated by R. Cohen), in R. Bernasconi and D. Wood (eds), *The Provocation of Levinas: Rethinking the Other* (pp. 156–167), London: Routledge.

Lewin, K. (1951) *Field Theory in Social Science: Selected Theoretical Papers*, New York, NY: Harper and Row.

Lewis, H.M. (2001) 'Participatory research and education for social change: High-lander Research and Education Center', in P. Reason and H. Bradbury (eds), *Handbook of Action Research: Participative Inquiry and Practice* (pp. 356–362), London: Sage.

Lindsey, E. and Stajduhar, K. (1998) 'From rhetoric to action: Establishing community participatory in AIDS-related research', *Canadian Journal of Nursing Research*, 30(1), 137–152.

Lock, M. and Kaufert, P.A. (eds) (1998) *Pragmatic Women and Body Politics*, Cambridge: Cambridge University Press.

Longino, H. (1993) 'Subjects, power and knowledge: description and prescription in feminist philosophies of science', in L. Alcoff and E. Potter (eds), *Feminist Epistemologies*, London: Routledge.

Lorde, A. (1980) *The Cancer Journals*, London: Sheba Feminist Publishers.

Love, S. (with Lindsey, K.) (1995) *Dr Susan Love's Breast Book* (2nd edn), Reading, MA: Addison-Wesley.

Lubek, I. and Wong, M.L. (2002) *Some Unexpected Research Consequences of a Re-engagement with the History of Social Psychology: Lewinian (1946) Action Research and the Current Cambodian HIV/AIDS Crisis* [http://www.angkorwatngo.com].

Lubek, I. and Wong, M.L. (2003) 'Sites, camera, action: contemplating the relations among theory, Lewinian "Action Research" and a community health intervention while touring the Angkor Wat Emples', in N. Stephenson, H.L. Radtke, R. Jorna and H.J. Stam (eds), *Theoretical Psychology: Critical Contributions* (pp. 248–357), Toronto: Captus Press.

Luijpen, W. and Koren, H.J. (1969) *A First Introduction to Existential Phenomenology*, Pittsburgh, PA: Duquesne University Press.

Lykes, M.B. (1999) 'Possible contributions of a psychology of liberation: whither health and human rights', *Journal of Health Psychology*, 5, 383–397.

Lykes, M.B. (2001a) 'Activist participatory research and the arts with rural Mayan women: interculturality and situated meaning making', in D. Tolman and M. Brydon-Miller (eds) *From Subjects to Subjectivities: A Handbook of Interpretive and Participatory Methods* (pp. 183–199), New York, NY: New York University Press.

Lykes, M.B. (2001b) 'Creative arts and photography in participatory action research in Guatemala', in P. Reason and H. Bradbury (eds), *Handbook of Action Research: Participative Inquiry and Practice* (pp. 363–371), London: Sage.

Lynch, M. (2000) 'Against reflexivity as an academic virtue and source of privileged knowledge', *Theory, Culture & Society*, 17, 26–54.

Lynd, M. (1992) 'Creating knowledge through theater: a case study with developmentally disabled adults', *American Sociologist*, 23(4), 100–115.

Macbeth, D. (2001) 'On "reflexivity" in qualitative research: two readings, and a third'. *Qualitative Inquiry*, 7, 35–68.

MacLachlan, M. (1997) *Culture & Health*, Chichester: John Wiley & Sons.

MacLachlan, M. (ed.) (2001) *Cultivating Health: Cultural Perspectives on Promoting Health*, Chichester: John Wiley & Sons.

MacLachlan, M. (2002) 'Die Arbeit mit Psychotrauma: Personliche, kuterelle and kontextuelle Probleme [Working with Psychotrauma: Personal, Cultural and Contextual Reflections]', in Ottomeyer, K. and Peltzer, K. (eds), *Uberleban am Abgrund: Psychotrauma & Menschenrechte* (pp. 231–244), Klagenfurt/Celovec: Drava Verlag .

MacLachlan, M. and Carr, S.C. (1994) 'Pathways to a psychology for development: reconstituting, restating, refuting, and realizing', *Psychology and Developing Societies*, 6, 119–129.

MacLachlan, M. and O'Connell, M. (eds) (2000) *Cultivating Pluralism: Psychological, Social and Cultural Perspectives on a Changing Ireland*, Dublin: Oak Tree Press.

MacLachlan, M., Smyth, C.L., Breen, F. and Madden, T. (in press) Temporal Acculturation and Mental Health in Modern Ireland. *International Journal of Social Psychiatry.*

Madill, A., Jordan, A. and Shirley, C. (2000) 'Objectivity and reliability in qualitative analysis: Realist, contextualist and radical constructionist epistemologies', *British Journal of Psychology*, 91, 1–20.

Marin, M.P.U. (1999) 'Where Development will lead to mass suicide', *The Ecologist*, 29, 42–46.

Markova, I. (1996) 'Towards an epistemology of social representations', *Journal for the Theory of Social Behaviour*, 26, 177–196.

Markova, I. and Wilkie, P. (1987) 'Representations, concepts and social change: the phenomenon of AIDS', *Journal for the Theory of Social behaviour*, 17, 389–409.

Marks, D.F. (1996) 'Health psychology in context', *Journal of Health Psychology*, 1, 7–22.

Marks, D.F. (2002a) 'Freedom, power and responsibility: contrasting approaches to health psychology', *Journal of Health Psychology*, 7, 5–19.

Marks, D.F. (2002b) 'Perspectives on evidence-based practice: Health Development Agency, Key paper' [http://194.83.94.80/hda/docs/evidence/eb2000/corehtml/persp_evid_dmarks.html].

Marks, D., Murray, M., Evans, B. and Willig, C. (1999) *Health Psychology: Theory and Practice*, London: Sage.

Marmot, M.G., Rose, G., Shipley, M. and Hamilton, P.J.S. (1978) 'Employment grade and coronary heart disease in British civil servants', *Journal of Epidemiology and Community Health*, 32, 244–249.

Marsella, A.J. (1998) 'Toward a "Global-community psychology": meeting the needs of a changing world', *American Psychologist*, 53(12), 1282–1291.

Marshall, H. and Yazdani, A. (2000) 'Young Asian women and self-harm', in J.M. Ussher (ed.), *Women's Health: Contemporary International Perspectives*, London: BPS Blackwell Books.

Martens, W.J.M., Niessen, W., Rotmans, J., Jetten, T.H. and McMichael, A.J. (1995) 'Potential impact of global climate change on malaria risk', *Environmental Health Perspectives*, 103, 458–464.

Martin-Baro, I. (1994) in A. Aron and S. Corne (eds), *Writings for a Liberation Psychology*, Cambridge, MA: Harvard University Press.

Marx, K. (1852/1968) 'The eighteenth brumaire of Louis Bonaparte', in K. Marx and F. Engels (eds), *Selected Works*, London: Lawrence and Wishart.

Mason, R. and Boutilier, M. (1996) 'The challenge of genuine power sharing in participatory research: the gap between theory and practice', *Canadian Journal of Community Mental Health*, 15(2), 145–152.

Matarazzo, J. (1980) 'Behavioral health and behavioral medicine: frontiers for a new health psychology', *American Psychologist*, 35, 807–817.

Matarazzo, J. (1982) 'Behavioral health's challenge to academic, scientific, and professional psychology', *American Psychologist*, 37, 1–14.

Mathieson, C. and Stam, H.J. (1995) 'Renegotiating identity: cancer narratives', *Sociology of Health and Illness*, 17, 283–306.

Matlin, M.W. (1993) *The Psychology of Women*, New York, NY: Harcourt Brace Jovanovich.

McAdams, D.P. (1993) *Stories We Live by: Personal Myths and the Marking of the Self*, New York, NY: Morrow.

McLaren, P. (1996) 'Liberatory politics and higher education: a Freirean perspective', in H.A. Giroux, C. Lankshear, P. McLaren and M. Peters, M. (eds), *Counter Narratives: Cultural Studies and Critical Pedagogies in Postmodern Spaces* (pp. 117–148), New York, NY: Routledge.

McLean, A. (1986) 'Family therapy workshops in the United States: potential abuses in the production of therapy in an advanced capitalist society', *Social Science and Medicine*, 12, 179–189.

Meegan, M.E., Conroy, R.M., Lengeny, S.O., Renhault, K. and Nyangole, J. (2001) 'Effect on neonatal tetanus mortality after a culturally-based health promotion programme', *The Lancet*, 358, 640–641.

Merleau-Ponty, M. (1945/1962) *Phenomenology of Perception* (Translated by C. Smith). New York, NY: Humanities Press.

Meyerowitz, B.E. (1981) 'Postmastectomy physical concerns of breast cancer patients'. Paper presented at the American Psychological Association Annual Convention, Los Angeles, CA, August.

Meyerowitz, B.E., Chaiken, S. and Clark, L.K. (1988) 'Sex roles and culture: social and personal reactions to breast cancer', in M. Fine and A. Asch (eds), *Women with Disabilities*, Philadelphia, PA: Temple University Press.

Mienczakowski, J. and Morgan, S. (2001) 'Ethnodrama: constructing participatory, experiential and compelling action research through performance', in P. Reason and H. Bradbury (eds), *Handbook of Action Research: Participative Inquiry and Practice* (pp. 219–227), London: Sage.

Mill, J.E. (2001) 'I'm not a "Basabasa" woman: an explanatory model of HIV illness in Ghanaian Women', *Clinical Nursing Research*, 10(3), 254–274.

Mills, J.A. (1998) *Control: A History of Behavioral Psychology*, New York, NY: New York University Press.

Mirowski, J. and Ross, C.E. (2003) *Education, Social Status, and Health*, Hawthorne, NY: Aldine de Gruyter.

Moeliono, L., Anggal, W. and Piercy, F. (1998) 'HIV/AIDS-risk for underserved Indonesian youth: a multi-phase participatory action-reflection-action study', *Journal of HIV/AIDS Prevention and Education for Adolescents and Children*, 2(3/4), 41–61.

Montero, M. (ed.) (2002) 'Special issue: Conceptual and epistemological aspects in community social psychology', *American Journal of Community Psychology*, 30(4), 469–584.

Morris, D. (1998) 'Illness and health in the postmodern age', *Advances in Mind–Body Medicine*, 14, 237–251.

Morse, J. (1999) 'Myth #93: Reliability and validity are not relevant for qualitative inquiry – Editorial', *Qualitative Health Research*, 9, 717–718.

Moscovici, S. (1972) 'Society and theory in social psychology', in J. Israel and H. Tajfel (eds), *The Context of Social Psychology: A Critical Assessment*, London: Academic Press.

Moscovici, S. (1976) *Social Influence and Social Change*, London: Academic Press.

Moscovici, S. (1981) 'On social representations', in J. Forgas (ed.), *Social Cognition: Perspectives on Everyday Understanding* (pp. 181–210), New York, NY: Academic Press.

Moscovici, S. (ed.) (1984) 'The phenomenon of social representations', *Social Representations: Explorations in Social Psychology* (pp. 18–77), Oxford: Polity.

Moustakas, C. (1990) *Heuristic Research: Design, Methodology, and Applications*, London: Sage.

Murray, C.J.L. and Lopez, A.D. (1996) 'Alternative visions of the future: projecting mortality and disability, 1990–2020', in C.J.L. Murray and A.D. Lopez (eds), *The Global Burden of Disease* (pp. 325–395), Geneva and Boston: World Health Organization and Harvard University Press.

Murray, M. (1997) *Narrative Health Psychology*, Visiting Scholar Series 7, Palmerston North, NZ: Massey University, Department of Psychology.

Murray, M. (ed.) (2000a) 'Reconstructing health psychology', *Journal of Health Psychology*, 5(3).

Murray, M. (2000b) 'Levels of narrative analysis in health psychology', *Journal of Health Psychology*, 5, 337–349.

Murray, M. (2002) 'Connecting narrative and social representation theory in health research', *Social Science Information*, 41, 653–673.

Murray, M. (2003) 'Narrative psychology', in J. Smith (ed.), *Qualitative Psychology: A Practical Guide to Methods* (pp. 111–131), London: Sage.

Murray, M. and Campbell, C. (2003) 'Living in a material world: reflecting on some assumptions of health psychology', *Journal of Health Psychology*, 8, 231–236.

Murray, M. and Campbell, C. (2004) 'Community health psychology: promoting analysis and action for social change', *Journal of Health Psychology*, 9(1).

Murray, M. and Chamberlain, K. (eds) (1998a) 'Qualitative research', *Journal of Health Psychology*, 3(3), whole issue.

Murray, M. and Chamberlain, K. (1998b) 'Qualitative research in health psychology: developments and directions', *Journal of Health Psychology*, 5, 291–295.

Murray, M. and Chamberlain, K. (eds) (1999a) *Qualitative Health Psychology*, London: Sage.

Murray, M. and Chamberlain, K. (1999b) 'Health psychology and qualitative research', in M. Murray and K. Chamberlain (eds), *Qualitative Health Psychology: Theories and Methods* (pp. 3–15), London: Sage.

Murray, M. and Chamberlain, K. (2000). 'Qualitative methods and women's health research', in J. Ussher (ed.), *Women's Health: Contemporary International Perspectives* (pp. 40–50), London: BPSBlackwell.

Murray, M. and Dolmount, M. (1994) *A Constant Danger*. Report submitted to the Department of Labour, Government of Newfoundland and Labrador, St. John's, NF, Canada.

Murray, M. and Flick, U. (eds) (2002) 'Symposium: social representations of health and illness', *Social Science Information*, 44, 555–673.

Murray, M., Pullman, D. and Heath Rodgers, T. (2003) 'Baby-boomers in Atlantic Canada talk about health and illness', *Journal of Health Psychology*, 8, 485–499.

Nafziger, E.Q., Stewart, F. and Varyrynen, R. (eds) (2000) *War, Hunger, and Displacement: The Origins of Humanitarian Emergencies*, Oxford: Oxford University Press.

Navarro, V. (1986) *Crisis, Health, and Medicine: A Social Critique*, New York, NY: Tavistock.

Neisser, U. (1981) 'John Dean's memory: a case study', *Cognition*, 9, 1–22.

Nelson, G. and Prilleltensky, I. (2003) *Critical Psychology in Practice*, London: Palgrave.

Nelson, N. and Wright, S. (eds) (1995) *Power and Participatory Development: Theory and Practice*, London: Intermediate Technology Publications.

Nightingale, D. and Cromby, J. (eds) (1999) *Social Constructionist Psychology: A Critical Analysis of Theory and Practice*, Buckingham: Open University Press.

Norman, P., Abraham, C. and Conner, M. (2000) *Understanding and Changing Health Behaviour: From Health Beliefs to Self-regulation*, Sydney: Harwood.

Northway, R. (2000) 'Ending participatory research?', *Journal of Learning Disabilities*, 4(1), 27–36.

Nsamenang, A.B. (1995) 'Factors influencing the development of psychology in Sub-Saharan Africa', *International Journal of Psychology*, 30(6), 729–739.

Nsamenang, A.B. and Dawes, A. (1998) 'Developmental psychology as political psychology in Sub-Saharan Africa: the challenge of Africanisation', *Applied Psychology: An International Review*, 47, 73–87.

O'Connell, M. (2001) *Changed Utterly: Ireland and the New Irish Psyche*, Dublin: Liffey Press.

O'Donnell, M., Loeffler, V., Pollock, K. and Saunders, Z. (1979) *Lesbian Health Matters!*, Santa Cruz, CA: Santa Cruz Women's Health Center.

O'Neil, W.M. (1995) 'American behaviorism: a historical and critical analysis', *Theory & Psychology*, 5, 285–306.

Ostrove, J.M., Feldman, P. and Adler, N.E. (1999) 'Relations among socio-economic status indicators and health for African-Americans and Whites', *Journal of Health Psychology*, 4, 451–463.

Palumbo, P.J. (1989) 'Cholesterol lowering for all: A closer look', *Journal of the American Medical Association*, 148, 833–847.

Parker, I. (1992) *Discourse Dynamics: Critical Analysis for Social and Individual Psychology*, London: Routledge.

Parker, I. (1994) 'Reflexive research and the grouping of Analysis: social psychology and psy-complex', *Journal of Community and Applied Social Psychology*, 4(4), 239–252.

Parker, I. (1997) Discursive psychology in D. Fox and I. Prilleltensky (eds), *Critical Psychology: An Introduction*, (pp. 284–298), London: Sage.

Parliamentary Office of Science and Technology (2002) *Access to water in developing countries*, Postnote, No. 178.

Parry, M.L. and Rosenzweig, C. (1999) 'Climate change and world food security: a new assessment', *Global Environmental Change*, S51–S67.

Peale, N.V. (1998) *The power of Positive Thinking*, London: Vermillion.

Pels, D. (2000) 'Reflexivity: one step up', *Theory, Culture & Society*, 17, 1–25.

Peltzer, K. (1995) *Psychology and Health in African Cultures: Examples of Ethnopsycho-therapeutic Practice*, Frankfurt: IKO Verlag.

Peltzer, K. (2002) 'Personality and social behaviour in Africa', *Journal of Personality and Social Behaviour*.

Pendleton, L. and Smith, A. (1986) 'Provision of breast prostheses', *Nursing Times*, 82 (4 June), 37–39.

Perrot, M. (1990) 'At home', in M. Perrot (ed.), *A History of Private Life. Vol. 4: From the Fires of Revolution to the Great War* (pp. 341–358), Cambridge, MA: Harvard University Press.

Perspectives on pain and suffering. (1998) *Advances in Mind–body Medicine*, 14, 167–203.

Peters, M. and Lankshear, C. (1996) 'Postmodern counternarratives', in H.A. Giroux, C. Lankshear, P. McLaren and M. Peters (eds). *Counter Narratives: Cultural Studies and Critical Pedagogies in Postmodern Spaces* (pp. 1–39), New York, NY: Routledge.

Piper, A.M.S. (1991) 'Impartiality, compassion and the modal imagination', *Ethics*, 101, 726–757.

Piran, N. (2001) 'Re-inhabiting the body', *Feminism & Psychology*, 11, 171–175.

Potter, J. (1996) *Representing Reality: Discourse, Rhetoric and Social Construction*, London: Sage.

Potter, J. and Edwards, D. (1990) 'Nigel Lawson's tent: discourse analysis, attribution theory and the social psychology of fact', *European Journal of Social Psychology*, 20, 24–40.

Potter, J. and Wetherell, M. (1987) *Discourse and Social Psychology: Beyond Attitudes and Behaviour*, London: Sage.

Potter, J. and Wetherell, M. (1995) Discourse analysis, in J.M. Smith, R. Harré and L. Van Langenhove (eds), *Rethinking Methods in Psychology*, (pp. 80–92), London: Sage.

Prilleltensky, I. (2001) 'Cultural assumptions, social justice and mental health: challenging the status quo', in J. Schumaker and T. Ward (eds) *Cultural Cognition and Psychopathology* (pp. 251–265), Westport, CT: Praeger.

Prilleltensky, I. and Nelson, G. (2004) *Doing Psychology Critically: Making a Difference in Diverse Settings*, London: Palgrave.

Prilleltensky, I. and Prilleltensky, I. (2003) 'Toward a critical health psychology', *Journal of Health Psychology*, 8, 197–210.

Propp, V. (1928/1968) *The Morphology of the Folktale*, Austin, TX: University of Texas Press.

Putnam, R. (2000) *Bowling Alone: The Collapse and Revival of American Community*, New York, NY: Simon Schuster.

Radley, A. (1994) *Making Sense of Illness: The Social Psychology of Health and Disease*, London: Sage.

Radley, A. (1999a) 'Abhorrence, compassion and the social response to suffering', *Health: An Interdisciplinary Journal for the Social Study of Health, Illness and Medicine*, 3, 167–187.

Radley, A. (1999b) 'The aesthetics of illness: narrative, horror and the sublime', *Sociology of Health and Illness*, 21, 778–796.

Radley, A. and Billig, M. (1996) 'Accounts of health and illness: dilemmas and representations', *Sociology of Health & Illness*, 18, 220–240.

Rankow, E.J. (1995) 'Breast and cervical cancer among lesbians', *Women's Health Issues*, 5, 123–129.

Reardon, K., Welsh, J., Kreiswith, B. and Forester, J. (1993) 'Participatory action research from the inside: community development practice in East St. Louis', *American Sociologist*, 21(4), 69–91.

Reid, P.T. (1993) 'Poor women in psychological research: shut up and shut out', *Psychology of Women Quarterly*, 17, 133–150.

Rhodes, C. (2000) 'Ghostwriting research: positioning the researcher in the interview text', *Qualitative Inquiry*, 6, 511–525.

Richardson, C.R. (1988) *Mind over Cancer*, London: W. Foulsham and Co. Ltd.

Ricoeur, P. (1991) 'Habermas', in M.J. Valdés (ed.), *A Ricoeur Reader: Reflection and Imagination* (pp. 159–181), New York, NY: Harvester Wheatsheaf.

Riemann, G. and Schütze, F. (1987) 'Trajectory as a basic theoretical concept for analyzing suffering and disorderly social processes', in D. Maines (ed.), *Social Organization and Social Process – Essays in Honour of Anselm Strauss* (pp. 333–357), New York, NY: Aldine de Gruyter.

Rise, J. (2002) 'Review of Understanding and changing health behavior: from beliefs to self-regulation', by P. Norman, C. Abraham, and M. Conner (eds), London: Harwood. *Journal of Health Psychology*, 7, 737–739.

Robinson, I. (1990) 'Personal narratives, social careers and medical courses: analysing life trajectories in autobiographies of people with multiple sclerosis', *Social Science & Medicine*, 30, 1173–1186.

Rodin, J. and Ickovics, J.R. (1990) 'Women's health: Review and research agenda as we approach the 21st century', *American Psychologist*, 45, 1018–1034.

Rodin, J. and Stone, G.C. (1987) 'Historical highlights in the emergence of the field', in G.C. Stone, S.M. Weiss, J.D. Mararazzo, N.E. Miller and J. Rodin (eds), *Health Psychology: A Discipline and a Profession* (pp. 15–26), Chicago, IL: University of Chicago Press.

Rogler, L.H., Malgady, R.G., Costantino, G. and Blumenthal, R. (1987) 'What do culturally sensitive mental health services mean? The case of Hispanics', *American Psychologist*, 42(6), 565–570.

Rose, N. (1996) *Inventing Ourselves: Psychology, Power and Personhood*, Cambridge: Cambridge University Press.

Roy, C.M. and Cain, R. (2001) 'The involvement of people living with HIV/AIDS in community-based organizations: contributions and constraints', *AIDS Care*, 13(4), 421–432.

Rutter, D. and Quine, L. (2002) *Changing Health Behaviour*, Buckingham: Open University Press.

Sabo, D. and Gordon, D.F. (eds) (1995) *Men's Health & Illness: Gender, Power and the Body*, Thousand Oaks, CA: Sage.

Sacks, H., Schegloff, E.A. and Jefferson, G. (1974) 'A simplest systematics for the organization of turn-taking for conversation', *Language*, 50, 696–735.

Saegert, S., Thompson, J. and Warren, M. (2001) *Social Capital and Poor Communities*, New York, NY: Russell Sage Foundation.

Sampson, E.E. (2003) 'Unconditional kindness to strangers: Human sociality and the foundation for an ethical psychology', *Theory and Psychology*, 13, 147–175.

Sarafino, E.P. (2001) *Health Psychology: Biopsychosocial Interactions – Fourth Edition*, Hoboken, NJ: John Wiley and Sons.

Saramago, J. (1998/1999) *The Tale of the Unknown Island*, New York, NY: Norton.

Sarbin, T.R. (1986) 'The narrative as a root metaphor for psychology', in T.R. Sarbin (ed.), *Narrative Psychology: The Storied Nature of Human Conduct* (pp. 3–21), New York, NY: Praeger.

Sarbin, T.R. (1997) 'The poetics of identity', *Theory & Psychology*, 7, 67–82.

Sartre, J.P. (1964) *Nausea*, London: Penguin.

Scarry, E. (1985) *The Body in Pain: The Making and Unmaking of the World*, New York, NY: Oxford University Press.

Schulz, A.J., Parker, E.A., Israel, B.A., Becker, A.B., Maciak, B.J. and Hollis, R. (1998) 'Conducting a participatory community-based survey for a community health intervention on Detroit's East Side', *Journal of Public Health Management and Practice*, 4(2), 10–24.

Schumaker, J.F. (2001) *The Age of Insanity: Modernity and Mental Health*, Westport, CT: Praeger.

Schwartz, G.E. (1982) 'Testing the biopsychosocial model: the ultimate challenge facing behavioral medicine', *Journal of Consulting and Clinical Psychology*, 50, 1040–1053.

Seale, C. (1999) *The Quality of Qualitative Research*, London: Sage.

Searle, W. and Ward, C. (1990) 'The prediction of psychological and sociological adjustment during cross-cultural transitions', *International Journal of Intercultural Relations*, 14, 449–464.

Seedat, M. (2001) *Community Psychology: Theory, Method and Practice, South African and Other Perspectives*, Oxford: Oxford University Press.

Sen, A. (2001) *Development as Freedom*, Oxford: Oxford University Press.

Sennett, R. (1977) *The Fall of Public Man*, Boston, MA: Farber & Farber.

Sexton, S., Lohman, L., and Hildyard, L. (1998) Faith? Help? Hope? Genetic engineering and world hunger, *Corner House Briefing No. 10*

Showalter, E. (1997) *Hystories: Hysterical Epidemics and Modern Culture*, London: Picador.

Shumaker, S.A. and Smith, T.R. (1995) 'Women and coronary heart disease', in A.L. Stanton and S.J. Gallant (eds), *The Psychology of Women's Health*, Washington, DC: APA Books.

Silverman, D. (1997) *Discourses of Counselling: HIV Counselling as Social Interaction*, London: Sage.

Simons, R.C. (1985) 'The resolution of the latah paradox', in R.C. Simons and C.C. Hughes (eds), *The Culture Bound Syndromes: Folk Illness of Psychiatric and Anthropological Interest*, Dordrecht: D. Reidel.

Simons, R.C. and Hughes, C.C. (eds) (1985) *The Culture Bound Syndromes: Folk Illness of Psychiatric and Anthropological Interest*, Dordrecht: D. Reidel.

Sloan, T. (1996) 'Psychological research methods in developing countries', in S.C. Carr and J. Schumaker (eds), *Psychology and the Developing World* (pp. 38–45), New York, NY: Praeger.

Sloan, T. S. (2002) *Two Billion People in Poverty: The Challenge to Psychologists* [http://www.criticalpsych.org/].

Smith, R. (1997) *The Norton History of the Human Sciences*, New York, NY: Norton.

Smith, J.A., Jarman, M. and Osborn, M. (1999) 'Doing interpretative phenomenological analysis', in M. Murray and K. Chamberlain (eds), *Qualitative Health Psychology* (pp. 218–240), London: Sage.

Smyth, C.L., MacLachlan, M. and Clare, A. (2003) *Cultivating Suicide?: A Cultural Perspective on Suicide in Ireland*, Dublin: Liffey Press.

Solarz, A.L. (ed.) (1999) *Lesbian Health*, Washington, DC: National Academy Press.

Solomon, S., Greenberg, J. and Pyszczynski, T. (1991) 'A terror management theory of social behavior: the psychological functions of self-esteem and cultural worldviews', *Advances in Experimental Social Psychology*, 24, 93–159.

Solomon, S., Greenberg, J. and Pyszczynski, T. (1998) 'Tales from the crypt: on the role of death in life', *Zygon*, 33, 9–43.

Somers, J. (1996) 'Debt: the new colonialism', in *75/25: Ireland in an Increasingly Unequal World*, Dublin: Dochas.

Sontag, S. (1978) *Illness as Metaphor*, London: Penguin.

Soucat, A.L.B. and Yazbeck, A.S. (2002) *HNP and the Poor: Inputs into PRSPs and World Bank Operations (Session 1)*, New York, NY: World Bank.

Spicer, J. and Chamberlain, K. (1996) 'Developing psychosocial theory in health psychology', *Journal of Health Psychology*, 1, 161–171.

Sram, I. and Ashton, J. (1998) 'Millennium report to Sir Edwin Chadwick', *British Medical Journal*, 317, 592–596.

Stainton Rogers, W. (1991) *Explaining Health and Illness: An Exploration of Diversity*, Hertfordshire: Harvester Wheatsheaf.

Stainton Rogers, W. (1996) 'Critical approaches to health psychology', *Journal of Health Psychology*, 1, 65–78.

Stam, H.J. (2000) 'Theorizing health and illness: functionalism, subjectivity and reflexivity', *Journal of Health Psychology*, 5, 273–284.

Stam, H.J. and Pasay, G.A. (1998) 'The historical case against null-hypothesis significance testing', *Behavioral and Brain Sciences*, 21, 219–220.

Stanton, A.L. (1995) 'Psychology of women's health', in A.L. Stanton and S.J. Gallant (eds), *The Psychology of Women's Health*, Washington, DC: APA Books.

Stanton, A.L. and Gallant, S.J. (eds) (1995) *The Psychology of Women's Health*, Washington, DC: APA Books.

Stern, P.N. (ed.) (1993) *Lesbian Health: What are the Issues?*, Washington, DC: Taylor & Francis.

Stevens, P.E. (1998) 'The experience of lesbians of color in healthcare encounters', *Journal of Lesbian Studies*, 2, 77–94.

Stevens, P.E. and Hall. J.M. (1998) 'Participatory action research for sustaining individual and community change: a model of HIV prevention education', *AIDS Education and Prevention*, 10(5), 387–402.

Stewart, F. (2002a) 'Horizontal inequalities as a source of conflict', in F. Hampson, and D. Malone (eds), *From Reaction to Conflict Prevention* (pp. 105–136), London: Lynne Renner.

Stewart, F. (2002b) 'Root causes of violent conflict in developing countries', *British Medical Journal*, 324, 342–345.

Stockdale, J. (1995) 'The self and media messages: match or mismatch?' in I. Markova and R. Farr (eds), *Representations of Health, Illness and Handicap* (pp. 31–48), London: Harwood.

Stone, G.C. (1980) 'Psychology and the health system', in G.C. Stone, F. Cohen and N.E. Adler (eds), *Health Psychology – A Handbook* (pp. 47–75), San Francisco, CA: Jossey-Bass.

Straus, E. (1980) 'The upright posture', *Phenomenological Psychology* (pp. 137–165), New York, NY: Garland.

Struttman, T.W., Brandt, V.A., Morgan, S.E., Piercey, L.R. and Cole, H.P. (2001) 'Equipment dealers' perceptions of a community-based rollover protective structure promotion', *Journal of Rural Health*, 17, 131–139.

Stuart, C.A. (1998) 'Care and concern: an ethical journey in participatory action research', *Canadian Journal of Counselling*, 32(4), 298–314.

Suppe, F. (1989) *The Semantic Conception of Theories and Scientific Realism*, Urbana, IL: University of Illinois Press.

Swartz, L. (1997) *Culture and Mental Health: A Southern African View*, Cape Town: Oxford University Press.

Sword, W. (1999) 'Accounting for presence of self: reflections on doing qualitative research', *Qualitative Health Research*, 9, 270–278.

Tavris, C. (1992) *The Mismeasure of Woman*, New York, NY: Touchstone/Simon & Schuster.

Tawil, O., Verster, A. and O'Reilly, K. (1995) 'Enabling approaches for HIV/AIDS promotion: can we modify the environment and minimize the risk?', *AIDS*, 9, 1299–1306.

Taylor, C. and White, S. (2000) *Practising Reflexivity in Health and Welfare: Making Knowledge*, Buckingham: Open University Press.

Taylor, S.E. (1986) *Health Psychology*, New York, NY: Random House.

Taylor, S.E. (1999) *Health Psychology*, Boston, MA: McGraw-Hill.

Tolman, D.L. and Brydon-Miller, M. (1997) 'Transforming psychology: interpretive and participatory research methods', *Journal of Social Issues*, 53, 597–603.

Toombs, S.K. (1992) *The Meaning of Illness: A Phenomenological Account of the Different Perspectives of Physician and Patient*, Dordrecht: Kluwer Academic Publishers.

Townsend, P. and Davidson, N. (1982) *Inequalities in Health: The Black Report*, London: Pelican Books.

Travis, C.B. (1988) *Women and Health Psychology: Biomedical Issues*, Hillsdale, NJ: Erlbaum.

Tuhwai Smith, L. (1999) *Decolonizing Methodologies: Research and Indigenous Peoples*, London: Zed Books.

Turner, B.S. (1986) 'Sociology as an academic trade: some reflections on center and periphery in the sociology market', *Australian and New Zealand Journal of Sociology*, 22, 272–282.

UN AIDS (1999) *Peer Education and HIV/AIDS: Concepts, Uses and Challenges*, Geneva: UN AIDS.

UN AIDS (2000) *Report on the Global HIV/AIDS Epidemic*, Geneva: UN AIDS.

UN AIDS (2001) *Innovative Approaches to HIV Prevention: Selected Case Studies*, Geneva: UN AIDS.

Unger, R. (1996) 'Using the master's tools: Epistemology and empiricism', in S. Wilkinson (ed.), *Feminist Social Psychologies*, Buckingham: Open University Press.

Unger, R. and Crawford, M. (1996) *Women and Gender: A Feminist Psychology* (2nd edn), New York, NY: McGraw-Hill.

Usher, R. (1997) 'Telling a story about research and research as story-telling: postmodern approaches to social research', in G. McKenzie, J. Powell and R. Usher (eds), *Understanding Social Research: Perspectives on Methodology and Practice* (pp. 27–41), London: Falmer Press.

van den Berg, J.H. (1972) *A Different Existence: Principles of Phenomenological Psychopathology*, Pittsburgh, PA: Duquesne University Press.

van Hooft, S. (2000) 'The suffering body', *Health: An Interdisciplinary Journal for the Social Study of Health, Illness and Medicine*, 4, 179–195.

Van Kaam, A. (1963) 'Existential psychology as a comprehensive theory of personality', *Review of Existential Psychology and Psychiatry*, 3, 11–26.

Wagstaff, A. and Yazbech, A.S. (2002) *HNP and the Poor: The Roles and Constraints of Households and Communities (Session 3)*, New York, NY: World Bank.

Waldo, C.R. and Coates, T.J. (2000) 'Multiple levels of analysis and intervention in HIV prevention science: exemplars and directions for new research', *AIDS*, 14 (Suppl. 2), S18–S26.

Wallerstein, N. (1992) 'Powerlessness, empowerment and health: implications for health promotion programs', *American Journal of Health Promotion*, 6(3), 197–205.

Walsh, R.M. (1977) *Doctors Wanted: No Women Need Apply*, New Haven, CT: Yale University Press.

Wang, C., Burris, M.A. and Ping, Z.Y. (1996) 'Chinese village women as visual anthropologists: a participatory approach to reaching policymakers', *Social Science and Medicine*, 42(10), 1391–1400.

Watkins, K. (2001) *Oxfam Comments on the Human Development Report*, London: Oxfam.

Watts, R.J. and Serrano-Garcia, I. (eds) (2003) Special issue section: the psychology of liberation: responses to oppression, *American Journal of Community Psychology*, 31(1/2), 73–203.

Weinreb, B. and Hibbert, C. (1993) *The London Encyclopaedia*, London: Macmillan.

Wetherell, M. (1998) 'Positioning and interpretative repertoires: conversation analysis and post-structuralism in dialogue', *Discourse and Society*, 9(3), 387–413.

Weisz, J.R., Suwanlert, S., Chaiyasit, W. and Walter, B.R. (1987) 'Over and under controlled referral problems among children and adolescents from Thailand and the United States: the *wat* and *wai* of cultural differences', *Journal of Consulting and Clinical Psychology*, 55, 719–726.

White, J. and Martinez, M.C. (eds) (1997) *The Lesbian Health Book*, Seattle, WA: Seal Press.

Wilkinson, R.G. (1996) *Unhealthy Societies: The Afflictions of Inequality*, London: Routledge.

Wilkinson, S. (1988) 'The role of reflexivity in feminist psychology', *Women's Studies International Forum*, 11, 493–502.

Wilkinson, S. (1990) 'Women's organisations in psychology: institutional constraints on disciplinary change', *Australian Psychologist*, 25, 256–269.

Wilkinson, S. (1996) *Feminist Social Psychologies: International Perspectives*, Buckingham: Open University Press.

Wilkinson, S. (2000) 'Women with breast cancer talking causes: comparing content, biographical and discursive analyses', *Feminism & Psychology*, 10, 431–460.

Wilkinson, S. and Kitzinger, C. (1993) 'Whose breast is it anyway?', *Women's Studies International Forum*, 16, 229–238.

Wilkinson, S. and Kitzinger, C. (2000) 'Thinking differently about "thinking positive": a discursive approach to cancer patients' talk', *Social Science and Medicine*, 50, 797–811.

Williams, B. and Brydon-Miller, M. (2004) 'Changing Directions: participatory action research, agency, and representation', in S. G. Brown and S. Dobrin (eds), *Ethnography Unbound: From Theory Shock to Critical Praxis*, Albany, NY: State University of New York Press.

Willig, C. (1998) 'Constructions of sexual activity and their implications for sexual practice: lessons for sex education', *Journal of Health Psychology*, 3(3), 383–392.

Willig, C. (ed.) (1999) *Applied Discourse Analysis: Social and Psychological Interventions*, Buckingham: Open University Press.

Willig, C. (2001) *Introducing Qualitative Research in Psychology: Adventures in Theory and Method*, Buckingham: Open University Press.

Wilson, R.A. (1966) *Feminine Forever*, New York, NY: David McKay.

Wilton, T. (1997) *Good for You: A Handbook of Lesbian Health and Wellbeing*, London: Cassell.

Wilton, T. (2000) *Sexualities in Health and Social Care*, Buckingham: Open University Press.

World Development Report 2000/2001 (2001) *Attacking Poverty*, New York, NY: Oxford University Press.

World Health Organization (1995) *The World Health Report 1995: Bridging the Gaps*, Geneva: WHO.

World Health Organization (2002) *The World Health Report 2002: Reducing Risks, Promoting Health Life*, Geneva: WHO.

World Bank (2002) http://www.worldbank.org/poverty/health/data/index.htm.

Yadlon, S. (1997) 'Skinny women & good mothers', *Feminist Studies*, 23, 645–677.

Yardley, L. (1997) *Material Discourses of Health and Illness*, London: Routledge.

Yardley, L. (2000) 'Dilemmas in qualitative health research', *Psychology and Health*, 15, 215–228.

Yaskowich, Y. and Stam, H.J. (2003) 'Cancer narratives and the cancer support group', *Journal of Health Psychology*, 8, 203–220.

Yeich, S. (1996) 'Grassroots organizing with homeless people: a participatory research approach', *Journal of Social Issues*, 52(1), 111–121.

Index